Microsoft® Excel® 2000 MOUS Cheat Sheet

by Rick Winter

A Division of Macmillan Computer Publishing
201 W. 103rd Street, Indianapolis, Indiana 46290 USA

Trademarks

All terms mentioned in this book that are known to be trademarks or service marks have been appropriately capitalized. Que Corporation cannot attest to the accuracy of this information. Use of a term in this book should not be regarded as affecting the validity of any trademark or service mark.

Microsoft is a registered trademark of Microsoft Corporation.

Excel is a registered trademark of Microsoft Corporation.

"Microsoft and the Microsoft Office User Specialist Logo are registered trademarks of Microsoft Corporation in the United States and other countries. Que is an independent entity from Microsoft Corporation, and not affiliated with Microsoft Corporation in any manner. This book and CD may be used in assisting students to prepare for a Microsoft Office User Specialist Exam. Neither Microsoft Corporation, its designated review company, nor Que warrants that use of this book and CD will ensure passing the relevant Exam.

"Use of the Microsoft Office User Specialist Approved Courseware Logo on this product signifies that it has been independently reviewed and approved in complying with the following standards:

> 'Acceptable coverage of all content related to the Microsoft Office Exams entitled, "Excel 2000 Core and Excel 2000 Expert;" and sufficient performance-based exercises that relate closely to all required content, based on sampling of text.'"

Warning and Disclaimer

Every effort has been made to make this book as complete and as accurate as possible, but no warranty or fitness is implied. The information provided is on an "as is" basis. The author and the publisher shall have neither liability nor responsibility to any person or entity with respect to any loss or damages arising from the information contained in this book or from the use of the CD or programs accompanying it.

Executive Editor

Angela Wethington

Acquisitions Editor

Tracy Williams

Development Editors

Susan Hobbs
Lisa McGowan

Managing Editor

Lisa Wilson

Project Editor

Tonya R. Simpson

Copy Editor

Kelly Talbot

Indexer

Amy Bowling

Proofreader

Benjamin Berg

Technical Editor

Connie Myers

Media Developer

Andrea Duvall

Interior Design

Barb Kordesh

Cover Design

Tim Amrhein

Copy Writer

Eric Borgert

Layout Technicians

Brandon Allen
Tim Osborn
Staci Somers

Introduction

There are two levels of competency tested for Excel 2000—Proficient and Expert.

Some of the activities covered by the Excel 2000 exam are common to other programs such as PowerPoint or Word. You will need to know how to run the Spell Checker, for example. You can also be called on to locate and replace text. By reading the chapters and completing the practice exercises in this book, you can make sure that you understand these basic skills. Knowing how to perform basic skills quickly can give you extra time to use with more time-consuming procedures.

There are a few new features in Excel 2000. If you are familiar with previous versions, this exam should not present any major difficulty. Make sure you understand each activity in the Objectives list—it's better to be overly prepared than to be overly confident.

How This Book Is Different

Unlike most Excel books on the market, this book is strictly exam-focused. You will find that no tasks on the test will require you to use Visual Basic for Applications. Therefore, VBA is not covered in this book.

Examine the Cheat Sheet to see if there are any skills that you have not used before or have used infrequently. Go through the Practice Lab until you can quickly do what's asked of you without relying on the book or the Help file. You will have little time to look up information during the test.

Appendix C, "Objectives Cheat Sheet," outlines all the objectives. You will find alternative ways to perform the tasks. The only activities covered in this book are those required to pass the MOUS exam. You won't have to wade through material that, although good to know, is unrelated to the certification test.

How to Use This Book

Each chapter in this book covers several related activities, such as operations that focus on text. There is an Objectives Index in the back of the book that lists the official objectives determined by the test distributor and the page number in this book where you will find the discussion of each objective.

At the end of each chapter is a Cheat Sheet with a list of different ways to perform the action. Use this Cheat Sheet to review each chapter, both as you are progressing through the book and also as a recap in the last few hours before the exam.

There is also a Practice Lab at the end of each chapter in which you can practice the objectives learned. The tasks are in the same form as the real exam. To begin each Practice Lab, copy the designated practice file from the CD. Then complete the tasks listed. When you have finished the last task of the Practice Lab, download and open the designated solution file to check your work. You'll know immediately if you need to review the objectives in that chapter.

The appendixes contain some thoughts and information about exam preparation. This exam is a little different than others you might have taken in that it is a hands-on test of your application savvy.

What's New in Office 2000?

Office 2000 has some characteristics that differ from previous versions. You will need to be familiar with them so you are not thrown for a loss when under pressure.

Personalized Menus

The menus and toolbars in Office 2000 will show the most recently used items. They will, in effect, customize themselves as you work. When Excel is first opened, you will see only the basic menu items and buttons. As you continue to work with the program, the commands you use most often will start to appear and others might go away.

This can be disconcerting. At the bottom of the short version of the built-in menu is an arrow that will expand the menu to show all the commands. You can also double-click the menu or wait for a few seconds for it to expand. Toolbars also have an arrow at the far right that will display more buttons.

The items shown on the short version of the built-in menu will change with your use.

Document Icons on the Taskbar

One change shouldn't cause much of a problem in the examination. If you open two files at the same time, you could see two separate icons on the taskbar. To see both files at the same time, click the Window menu and select Arrange All. The Tile Windows command found by right-clicking the taskbar will not arrange the two files. This command works only with windows from separate programs, such as an instance of Excel and an instance of PowerPoint.

Toolbar Addition

There is another button on the Formatting toolbar for Common Tasks, such as New Slide, Slide Layout, and Apply

Contents at a Glance

Contents

Chapter 3   Formatting Worksheets   79

Chapter 5   Working with Worksheets and Workbooks   141

Chapter 6 Working with Formulas and Functions 169

Chapter 16   Auditing a Worksheet   **339**

Chapter 17   Displaying and Formatting Data   **353**

Dedication

To my sister, Patty, who has been my business partner for over 11 years. Thank you for your support, hard work, and caring about my family and me. I hope you find your dreams.

Acknowledgments

I would like to thank my agent, Chris Van Buren, and Waterside Productions for being a great go-between between Que and me and for the valuable conference you sponsor each year.

The team at Que for this book has been exceptional. Lisa McGowan and Susan Hobbs, the development editors, were fast, efficient, and extremely helpful at getting my questions answered and providing useful feedback when I needed it. Vicki Harding, the team coordinator, was good at coordinating my submissions and making sure they got to where they were supposed to go. Connie Myers, the technical editor, has been great at catching errors that I missed and providing good suggestions. Jill Hayden, series developer; Jim Minatel, associate publisher; Joe Habraken, author for the *Microsoft Access 2000 MOUS Cheat Sheet*; and Doug Klippert, author for the *Microsoft PowerPoint 2000 MOUS Cheat Sheet*, were helpful in bouncing ideas off and creating guidelines for this series.

I also appreciate the hard work of the editing team headed by Tonya Simpson, production editor, and Kelly Talbot, copy editor. Thanks to the production team for the attention to details and many changes you had to endure at the last minute.

Thanks to John Pierce, publisher, and everyone else at Que for the opportunity to work with you over the last 10 years (and for the great parties).

Of course, I would like to thank my wife, Karen, and children, Danny and Jimmy, for letting me spend time with this book and not as much time as I should with them.

I appreciate everyone's willingness to give up time with family, miss weekends, and work long nights to help get this book, *Microsoft Excel 2000 MOUS Cheat Sheet*

Excel Proficient/Core Objectives

The first step in using any program is becoming familiar with the basic operation of the program: how to start, look around, get help, and exit.

This part covers basic skills, including the following topics:

- Working with Cells
- Working with Files
- Formatting Worksheets
- Page Setup and Printing
- Working with Worksheets and Workbooks
- Working with Formulas and Functions
- Using Charts and Objects

Working with Cells

Following is a list of MOUS objectives:

- Enter Text, Dates, and Numbers
- Go to a Specific Cell
- Edit Cell Content
- Use Undo and Redo
- Clear Cell Content
- Insert and Delete Selected Cells
- Cut, Copy, Paste, Paste Special and Move Selected Cells, and Use the Office Clipboard
- Clear Cell Formats
- Use Find and Replace
- Work with Series (AutoFill)
- Create Hyperlinks

Enter Text, Dates, and Numbers

The most common task you will perform is entering data in your worksheet. When you enter data, the characters display simultaneously in the Formula bar and cell. The characters do not actually go into the cell until you press Enter.

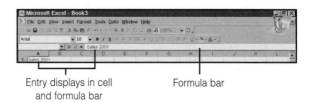

Entry displays in cell   Formula bar
and formula bar

Use the following steps to enter data in a cell:

1. Click in the cell in which you want to enter data.

2. Type the data (see the notes that follow) and press Enter or Tab.

Following are some notes that are specific to each type of data you type in the cell.

Text

This can be any combination of numbers, spaces, and non-numeric characters. If the entered text exceeds the column width, the data either overlaps the boundary into the next column or is hidden. The column width can be increased by dragging the right side of the column header with the double-headed pointer. Or you can make the column width fit the contents by double-clicking the boundary on the right side of the column.

When you enter text that matches an existing entry in a column, AutoComplete fills in the remaining characters for you. For example, if *England* is in cell D5 and you type an *E* in cell D6, Excel displays *England* and you can press Enter to accept the entry. For this to work, you must click Tools and select Options. On the Edit tab, select the Enable AutoComplete for cell values check box. Excel uses the number of characters to make the entry unique. If you have both *England* and *Ethiopia* in the column, you must type the first two characters to display the word.

	A	B	C
1	Sales 2001		
2			
3	Location	Salesperson	Amount (000)
4	England	Martinez	25
5	Ethiopia	Mitra	35
6	US	Wu	10
7	US	Bhimani	200
8	England		

Dates

You can enter dates in different formats, including the following:

11/1/01	M/d/yy
11/1/2001	M/d/yyyy
1-Nov-01	d-mmm-yy
01-Nov-2001	dd-mmm-yyyy

If no other formats are applied to the cell, the format displays as you entered it, with the exception of the year. The year is displayed in the settings you have for Short Date in your control panel (the default is a two-digit year). You can change your control panel settings by choosing the Windows Start button and clicking on Settings, and then Control Panel. Double-click on the Regional Settings icon, click the Date tab, and type m/d/yyyy (or another setting) in the Short date style text box.

You can also change the display by formatting the cell with the desired date format: Choose Format, click Cells, select the Number tab, and in the Category list choose Date and select a format in the Type column.

The way you enter dates depends on your choices in Regional Settings, and varies depending on the country. Settings in this book assume those that are common in the United States.

If you leave off the year, the current year is assumed. When you do not type the century, years 0–29 become 2000–2029, and years 30–99 become 1930–1999. For example, if you type 10/16/20, Excel interprets this date as 10/16/2020. However, when you type 10/16/30, Excel interprets it as 10/16/1930.

To enter today's date, the shortcut is Ctrl+; (semicolon).

Time

Based on a 12-hour clock, you can enter the time by typing a space followed by am or pm (or a or p). Excel uses the 24-hour clock as the default. If p.m. is not specified, a.m. is the default.

To enter the current time, press Ctrl+: (colon).

Numbers

In Excel, you can change the appearance of a number by using number formats. This does not change the number itself, just the appearance. For example, 1234 can be displayed as 1234.00.

You can also enter fractions in Excel. To avoid entering fractions that might be interpreted as dates, precede the fraction with a 0. Otherwise, Excel converts these to dates. For example, Excel converts 1/12 to 12-Jan. The correct way to enter this is to type 0 1/12.

Go to a Specific Cell

You identify a cell by its column letter and row number. The active cell is indicated by a dark outline, and the column letter and row number in the headers are raised.

You can move around the worksheet using the scrollbars and the arrows on the keyboard. However, if you have long distances to move, you can quickly go to a cell by using one of the following methods:

1. Click in the Name Box, which is located at the top left, above the worksheet.

2. Type the cell reference (for example, AB2000) or range name (see Objective 80, "Add and Delete a Named Range"). If you want to move to a different sheet, type the sheet reference followed by an exclamation mark and the cell reference (for example, Sheet2!C3).

3. Press Enter.

Type cell reference in the name box ——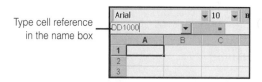

If you have named ranges in your workbook, you can click the pull-down arrow on the Name Box and choose a range. Move to the range, and it is selected at the same time.

1. Press either F5 or Ctrl+G, or click the Edit menu and choose Go To. The Go To dialog box displays.

2. Type the cell reference or range name in the Reference text box. If you've gone to other locations, they appear in the Go To list. You can click on one of these locations or on a range name in this list.

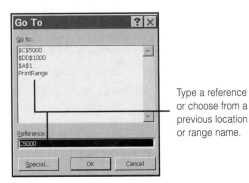

Type a reference or choose from a previous location or range name.

3. Press Enter or choose OK.

From the Go To dialog box, you can choose Special and then select cells that have numbers (click on Constants and check only Numbers under the Formulas option button). You can select all cells that have formulas by clicking on Formulas and then Numbers.

Following are the keyboard shortcuts for going to various cells:

Go To	Keyboard shortcut
A1	Ctrl+Home
Last cell on worksheet	Ctrl+End
First column of current row	Home
Last active cell on next sheet	Ctrl+Page Down
Last active cell on previous sheet	Ctrl+Page Up
Border of a range (edge with blank/non-blank cell)	End, Arrow

Edit Cell Content

If you make an error in a cell, you can press Delete to remove the entire entry. You can also use the following steps to change the contents of the cell:

1. Move to the cell to be edited.

2. Do one of the following:

- Click in the Formula bar with the I-beam mouse pointer to place the insertion point.

- Double-click in the cell to place the insertion point within the cell.

- Press F2.

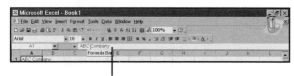

Click the I-Beam mouse pointer in
the Formula Bar to position the
insertion point for editing

3. Do one or more of the following:

- Press Backspace to delete characters before the insertion point.

- Press Delete to delete characters after the insertion point.

- Press Home to go to the beginning of the line.

- Press End to go to the end of the line.

- Press Ctrl+Right to move a word to the right.

- Press Ctrl+Left to move a word to the left.

- Double-click on a word to select it.

- Drag the mouse pointer across text to select it.

- Type characters to replace any selected text and insert the new characters.

4. Do one of the following:

- Press Enter or Tab to complete the correction.

- Press Esc to cancel the changes you made.

If the entire cell contents need to be replaced, you can also move to the cell and start typing. When you press Enter or Tab, the new entry replaces the old.

Use Undo and Redo

The Undo feature enables you to recover from most mistakes. The Redo feature reverses the action of the Undo command. In addition to recovering from mistakes, you can use Undo and Redo to test and then remove inputs in a worksheet.

Both  Undo and  Redo on the Standard toolbar have two parts, the button and an arrow to the right of the button. The button reverses the last command or deletes the last entry typed. To reverse several actions at once, click the arrow next to the Undo or Redo button and select the actions from the list.

You cannot Undo or Redo some actions, such as those dealing with files (save, open, close); printing or sending a document; running or recording a macro; and window tasks such as maximizing, minimizing, and arranging.

Undo

Use one of the following actions to undo the last action you performed:

- Click  Undo on the Standard toolbar.
- Press Ctrl+Z.

- Click the Edit menu and choose Undo. The Undo item on the Edit menu shows the name of the last completed action that can be undone. The command name changes to Can't Undo if the last action cannot be reversed.

- Click the arrow next to the Undo button and choose the first (or multiple) actions to undo.

Redo

If you want to change your mind and reverse your undo, you can click ⟲ Redo on the Standard toolbar. Sometimes the keyboard shortcut (Ctrl+Y) or the Edit, Redo command enables you to cancel your undo.

To undo while you are still typing an entry, press Backspace to remove each character or Esc to remove the whole entry.

The menu says Edit, Redo when your last command was an Undo. However, if the last thing you did was something besides Undo, the shortcut (Ctrl+Y) and menu item say Repeat. If you format text (bold, underline, font, and so on), the shortcut and menu item perform the command again. If Excel cannot do the command again, the menu item is dimmed and says Can't Repeat.

To cancel an Undo immediately, take one of the following actions:

- Click ⟲ Redo on the Standard toolbar.

- Press Ctrl+Y.

- Click the Edit menu and choose Redo. The Redo item on the Edit menu shows the name of the last completed action that can be redone.

- Click the arrow next to the Redo button and choose the actions to redo from the list. The selected action and all actions above it are reversed.

Clear Cell Content

During editing, you might occasionally want to go back and remove contents that you have entered in a cell. Use the following steps to clear the contents of a cell:

1. Click on the cell or select the range you want to clear.

2. Press Delete or choose the Edit menu, click Clear, and choose Contents.

If you have any text or number formatting (font, bold, currency) in the range, the formatting remains after you clear the cell contents. When you type your next entry, that entry is formatted. If you also want to remove formatting when you delete the contents, click the Edit menu, choose Clear, and then click All (See Objective 8, "Clear Cell Formats"). This also removes any comments you have attached to the cell.

Insert and Delete Selected Cells

If you've created a worksheet and want to add cells, you can select a range of existing cells where the new cells are to be added. Then, from the Insert menu, click Cells. The cells can be shifted to the right or down. To delete the contents of a cell and leave it blank, you just press Delete. You can also select the range to be deleted, choose Edit, Delete, and move the cells up or to the left.

Insert

Use the following steps to insert a cell or cells and move the contents of other cells:

1. Move to the cell you want or select the range of cells below or to the right of where you want to add cells.

2. Click the Insert menu and choose Cells. The Insert dialog box displays.

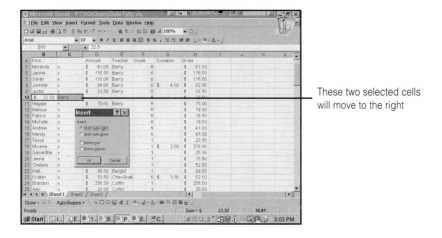

These two selected cells will move to the right

3. Do one of the following:

- If you want to move all the cells that follow the selected cells to the right, choose Shift cells right.

- If you want to move all cells that follow the selected cells down, choose Shift cells down.

- If you want to add the same number of rows as there are selected rows in your range, choose Entire row.

- If you want to add the same number of columns as there are columns in your selected range, choose Entire column.

4. Press Enter or choose OK.

Delete

Use the following steps to delete a cell or cells and move the contents of other cells:

1. Move to the cell you want, or select the range of cells below or to the right of which you want to remove cells.

2. Click the Edit menu and choose Delete. The Delete dialog box displays.

3. Do one of the following:

- To delete only the selected cells and move cells in the same rows, choose Shift cells left.

- To delete only the selected cells and move cells in the same columns, choose Shift cells up.

- If you want to remove the same number of rows as there are rows in your selected range, choose Entire row.

- If you want to remove the same number of columns as there are columns in your selected range, choose Entire column.

4. Press Enter or choose OK.

See also Objective 40, "Insert and Delete Rows and Columns."

Cut, Copy, Paste, Paste Special and Move Selected Cells, Use the Office Clipboard

There are numerous ways to copy and move items in a worksheet. You can use cut, copy, and paste; drag and drop; the new Office Clipboard; or paste special.

Cut, Copy, and Paste and the Office Clipboard

When you copy or cut a selection, object, or graphic, it goes into the Windows Clipboard. You can then take what is in the Clipboard and place it in a new location with the Paste command.

The Windows Clipboard stores only one item at a time. However, the new Office Clipboard lets you store up to 12 items at one time. Then you can paste any one of the 12 items into a new location as follows:

1. Select the range or object you want to place in the Clipboard. You can be in a different application, such as Word.

2. Do one or more of the following:

   To cut an item

   • Click [✄] Cut on the Standard toolbar.

   • Press Ctrl+X.

   • Click the Edit menu and choose Cut.

To copy an item

- Click 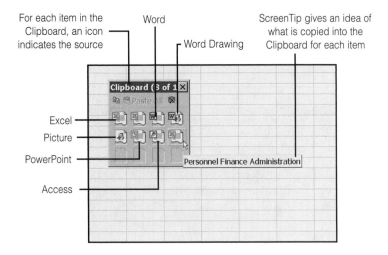 Copy on the Standard or Clipboard toolbar.

- Press Ctrl+C.

- Click the Edit menu and choose Copy.

When you cut or copy an item in Excel, a marquee (blinking dashes) appears around the selection.

3. Move to the location at which you want to place the copy.

4. Do one of the following:

- Click Paste on the Standard toolbar.

- Press Ctrl+V.

- Click the Edit menu and choose Paste.

- If it doesn't display, right-click on a toolbar and choose Clipboard to display the Clipboard toolbar.

- If the item was copied in Excel, press Enter to paste.

For each item in the Clipboard, an icon indicates the source

Word

Word Drawing

ScreenTip gives an idea of what is copied into the Clipboard for each item

Clipboard (3 of 1

Excel

Picture

PowerPoint

Access

Personnel Finance Administration

- Click one of the twelve buttons on the Clipboard toolbar to paste that item.

- Click 🖾 Clear Clipboard on the Clipboard toolbar to remove all items from the Office Clipboard.

In Excel, the selected Copy/Cut and Paste ranges must be the same size. Alternatively, you can select a range to Copy/Cut and then choose one cell to paste the range. Another option is to select one cell to Copy/Cut and then choose a range to paste multiple copies of the cell.

If a range in the Clipboard has a formula with cell references, the formula's cell references adjust to the new location (see Objective 53, "Use References Absolute and Relative").

In other applications, such as Word, you can also click 🖾 Paste All on the Clipboard toolbar to place all items from the Clipboard into the document.

An alternative to using cut, copy, and paste is to use drag and drop. Follow these steps:

1. Select the range you want to copy.

2. Move the mouse pointer to the black border of the range. The pointer becomes a left-facing white arrow.

3. Do one of the following:

   - Drag the border to the new location to move the selection. The new location is indicated by a ScreenTip before you release the mouse button.

   - Hold down Ctrl and drag the border to the new location to copy it. The white arrow mouse pointer also displays a plus to indicate that the item is copied.

Move and Copy Using Drag and Drop

New location indicated by ScreenTip

Plus indicates a copy (Ctrl is held down)

The location you drag to in step 3 can be in a different application's document or even on the Windows Desktop.

Paste Special

The default when you copy an Excel range to another range is that the contents, cell formatting, and comments are all pasted at once. If you want to control what you paste as well as have other choices, you can use paste special.

Follow these steps to use paste special:

1. Copy an item in the Clipboard using the  Copy button or one of the other copy methods.

2. Click the Edit menu and choose Paste Special. The Paste Special dialog box opens.

3. Choose one of the following options:

Option	To Do
Paste Section	
All	This is the same as Edit, Paste; it pastes all content and formatting.
Formulas	Pastes text and numbers as they were entered in the cell. If the entry is a formula, the cell references adjust relative to the new location.

Option	To Do
	Paste Section
Values	If the entry is a formula, this converts it to a number or characters.
Formats	Pastes just the formatting of the cells.
Comments	Pastes just the cell comments (see Objective 110, "Create, Edit, and Remove a Comment").
Validation	Pastes validation rules (see Objective 101, "Use Data Validation").
All except borders	Pastes all characters and formatting except borders.
Column widths	Converts the column widths of the new range to the same size of those in the Clipboard.
	Operation Section
None	Pastes numbers directly in the cell.
Add	Adds numbers from the Clipboard and the pasted range together.
Subtract	Subtracts numbers on the Clipboard from those in the pasted range.
Multiply	Multiplies the numbers from the Clipboard times those in the pasted range.
Divide	Divides the numbers from the pasted range by those in the Clipboard. If there are no numbers in the range to paste, it enters 0.

continues

Option	To Do

Unlabeled Section

Skip blanks — If there is a blank in the copied range, this does not place formatting in the pasted range.

Transpose — Changes rows to columns and columns to rows.

Paste Link — Creates a formula that refers to the original copied cells so that when you place a value in the original cell, the value appears in the pasted cell (see Objective 49, "Link Worksheets and Consolidate Data Using 3D References").

If the original copy was something other than an Excel range, you are offered other options that enable you to choose the formatting option (sometimes text or a picture) and whether you want the pasted information to be entered as an icon, as a copy of the item in the Clipboard, or as a link to the location in the other document.

Clear Cell Formats

You can remove simple formatting by choosing 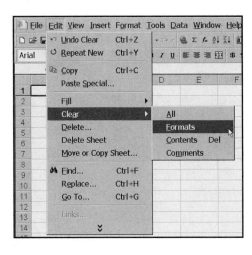 Undo on the Standard toolbar or by clicking the appropriate button on the Formatting toolbar. For example, to unbold a bolded entry, select the cell and click the **B** Bold button.

However, if multiple formats (text or number) are applied to the cell, use the following steps:

1. Select the cells from which you want to remove formatting.

2. Click the Edit menu, choose Clear, and click Formats.

You can drag to select cells. If you want to select multiple ranges, hold down Ctrl and drag on each range.

Bold, italic, non-default fonts, and number formats such as currency, comma, and percent are removed from the selected cells. To clear the cell contents, see Objective 5, "Clear Cell Content."

Use Find and Replace

If you have a large worksheet and know what text you want to locate but not the actual location, use Find to move to that location. Similarly, if you made the same mistake throughout your worksheet and need to edit the text and replace it with something else, use Replace. For example, suppose you typed Berry for a name when it should have been Barry.

Find

Use the following steps to look for data:

1. You can move to the beginning of the worksheet by pressing Ctrl+Home.

2. Press Ctrl+F or click the Edit menu and choose Find. The Find dialog box opens.

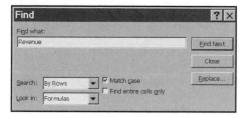

3. Type the text you want to look for in the Find what text box.

4. If you want additional options to help your search, do any of the following:

    • By default, the capitalization of your word or phrase doesn't matter. To find the same case, check Match case.

- By default, Excel will find the text anywhere within a cell. If you want the complete contents to match what is in the Find what text box, check Find entire cells only.

- If you want to change the direction of the search to down or across the worksheet, choose By Rows or By Columns in the Search drop-down box.

- If you want to limit your search based on the type of contents, make a choice in the Look in drop-down box. Choose Formulas to find both text and formulas. Choose Values to skip formulas. Choose Comments to find the text within a cell's comments.

5. Click Find Next to go to the next match on the worksheet. Repeat this step as many times as you want.

6. When you are finished, choose Close.

Replace

Finding data and replacing it with other characters requires almost the same steps:

1. Do one of the following:

- Press Ctrl+H.

- Click the Edit menu and choose Replace.

- Click Replace on the Find dialog box.

The Replace dialog box opens.

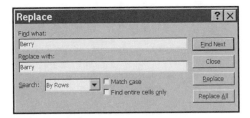

2. Type the text for which you want to search in the Find what text box.

3. Type the text you want to substitute in the Replace with text box.

4. If you want additional options to help your search, do any of the following:

- By default, the capitalization of your word or phrase doesn't matter. To find the same case, check Match case.

- By default, Excel will find the text anywhere within a cell. If you want the complete contents to match what is in the Find what text box, check Find entire cells only.

- If you want to change the direction of the search to down or across the worksheet, choose By Rows or By Columns in the Search drop-down box.

5. To move to the first location, choose Find Next. Repeat this step until you find the text you want to change.

6. Choose Replace each time you want to change the text. Or, if you want to change the entire worksheet, choose Replace All.

7. When you are finished, choose Close.

Work with Series (AutoFill)

AutoFill enables you to create a series of entries, such as times, dates, months, numbers, and your own custom-defined choices. To use AutoFill, drag the fill handle at the bottom-right of the cell. You can also use the fill handle to copy text, numbers, and formulas.

To use the fill handle, take the following actions:

Use the Fill Handle

1. Select the starting cell. If you want to create a pattern, select two or more cells.

2. Move the mouse pointer to the bottom-right corner of the last cell to the fill handle. The mouse pointer changes to a black plus sign.

3. Drag the fill handle over the range you want to fill. Dragging down or to the right fills in increasing order. Dragging up or to the left fills in decreasing order. As you drag, a ScreenTip shows the values that will appear in the cells.

To create the series in columns B and D, the first two cells were selected before the fill handle was used

ScreenTip

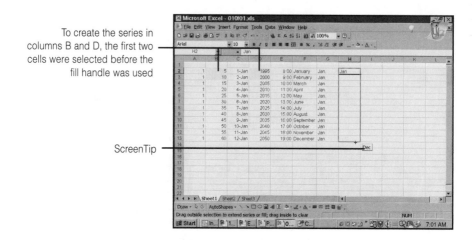

In the preceding figure, column A shows all ones, whereas column B is incremented by fives. For a number, the default when you drag the fill handle is that the number copies instead of incrementing. To change this you can select two cells first and then drag the fill handle. Then the difference between the two cells is added to each additional cell. If you select three or more cells, Excel creates an equation (regression) to use to change the values.

Another option with numbers is to hold down Ctrl when you drag, which causes the numbers in the series to increment by one for each cell.

For dates and times (columns C and E), AutoFill increments the values by one day or one hour. If you hold down Ctrl while dragging the fill handle, the value is copied instead of incremented.

For items in Excel's custom lists, AutoFill repeats all the items in the list. By default, the custom lists include the days of the week and months spelled out and abbreviated.

Create Custom Series

You can use the following steps to create your own custom series to use with AutoFill:

1. Click the <u>T</u>ools menu and choose <u>O</u>ptions. The Options dialog box opens.

2. Click the Custom Lists tab.

3. Highlight NEW LIST and click the Add button.

4. Type the entries for the new list, pressing Enter between each entry.

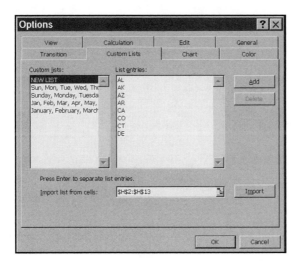

5. Click the Add button again.

To remove the list, move to it in the Custom lists column and click the Delete button. To create a list from items already in the worksheet, select the range with the Import list from cells range selector and choose Import.

To use a list, type an entry from any part of the list in a cell. Then drag the fill handle to continue the list from that point. When the end of the list is reached, the entries start again from the beginning.

You can also use the Series dialog box to fill a range and use several options:

Fill Using Series

1. Type the first value in the first cell, or type values in the first few cells.

2. Select the range you want to fill.

3. Click the Edit command, choose Fill, and click Series. The Series dialog box opens.

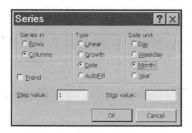

4. Fill out the dialog box with any of the following options:

Option	To do
Series in	If a rectangular range is selected, choose Rows to fill across or Columns to fill down (you can't do both).
Trend	Check this box to create a best line fit if Linear is selected or a geometric (increasing) fit if Growth is selected. Step value is ignored.
Type	If you choose AutoFill, most of the dialog box becomes grayed out and the dialog box acts as if you were dragging the fill handle. See also Trend and Date unit.
Date unit	If you check Date under the Type options, the Date unit options become available. Choose whether you want your dates separated by Day, Weekday (skip weekends), Month, or Year.
Step value	Type the increment you want to change each item.
Stop value	Type the last value you want in the series.

5. Choose OK. The selected cells fill with the series.

Create Hyperlinks

Hyperlinks enable you to go to a Web site, a different location on the same workbook, to a different workbook, to a different application, or to a new email.

The easiest way to create a hyperlink is to type it in a cell. For example, type www.mcp.com in a cell, and it is automatically formatted as a hyperlink. If you want to type someone's email address, type mailto: and their address, for example mailto:msot@egroups.com.

You can also use the Hyperlink dialog box:

1. Move to the cell in which you want the hyperlink.

2. Do one of the following:

   • Click 🖳 Insert Hyperlink on the Standard toolbar.

   • Press Ctrl+K.

   • Click the Insert command and choose Hyperlink.

   The Insert Hyperlink dialog box displays.

3. If you want to, you can type in the text that you want to appear in the cell (instead of the address).

4. If you want, click on ScreenTip and type the text you want to appear when you hover over the hyperlink with the mouse pointer.

5. In the Type the file or Web page name text box, type the link. You can also use one of the following options.

6. Click OK.

Insert Hyperlinks

31

The hyperlink appears in your worksheet as blue underlined text. To go to the linked location, click on the hyperlink (the mouse pointer changes to a hand). After you've gone to the location, the hyperlink changes to violet.

There are other options you can use to enter hyperlinks in the Insert Hyperlink dialog box:

- Choose the Bookmark command button to look for a location in this document. Click on the sheet name and type a cell reference or click on a defined name. This option is similar to the Place in this document option.

- Choose the File command button and navigate to the file you want to launch.

- Choose [Recent Files] Recent Files and pick from among the files you've recently opened.

- Choose [Browsed Pages] Browsed Pages and pick from among the pages you've recently looked at on the Web.

- Choose [Inserted Links] Inserted Links and pick from among the pages you've recently added to your file or typed in the Address box of your browser.

- Choose Existing File or Web Page. A dialog box appears.

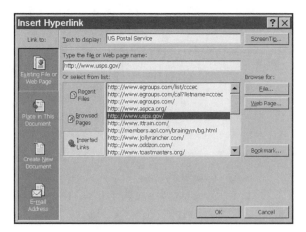

Do one of the following:

- Type the Web address in the Type the file or Web page name text box.

- Click on the file in the Or select from list box.

• Choose Place in This Document. A dialog box appears.

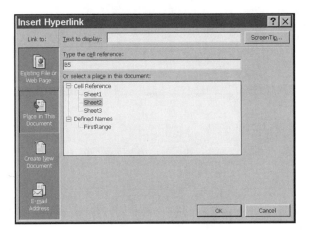

Do one of the following:

- You might have to expand the Cell Reference or Defined Names lines by clicking on the plus to the left of these entries.

- Click on a sheet name and type the cell reference in the Type the cell reference text box.

- If you have range names, click on a range name in the Defined Names area.

• Choose Create New Document. A dialog box appears.

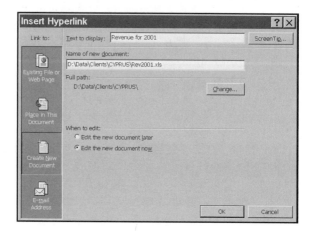

Do one of the following:

- Type the filename in the Name of new document text box.

- If you want to change the location and document type, choose the Change button and navigate to the location, and then choose a document type in the Save as type pull-down list.

- Choose whether you want to Edit the new document now or Edit the new document later.

- Choose E-mail Address. A dialog box appears.

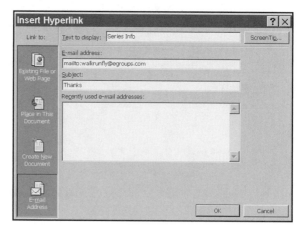

Do the following:

1. Type the email address. Notice that mailto: is entered in the box as soon as you start typing. Or choose from a list of Recently used email addresses.

2. Type the default text you want to appear in the email's Subject line.

Edit Hyperlinks

To edit the hyperlink, right-click on the link, click Hyperlink, and choose Edit Hyperlink, and then fill in the Edit Hyperlink dialog box as shown previously. You can also move to the cell using the arrows (not the mouse), and click on the Insert Hyperlink button to open the Edit Hyperlink dialog box.

To get rid of the link, right-click on the cell and choose Hyperlink, Remove Hyperlink.

Now that you know how to work with cells, it is time to prac-

TAKE THE TEST

tice what you've learned.

Objectives covered: 1, "Enter Text, Dates, and Numbers"; 10, Work with Series (AutoFill)"; 11, "Create Hyperlinks."

1. Create a new workbook and type the following text in cells A1–D5:

	A	**B**	**C**	**D**
1	Billy Bob's Car Sales			
2	Web site:			
3	For comments send email to:			
4				
5	Day	Sales	Units	Rating

2. For cells A6–A16 type 3/10/02 in A6 and then use AutoFill to increment until you reach 3/20/02 in A16.

3. Type the following information : in the indicated cells:

	B	**C**	**D**
5	Sales	Units	Rating
6	35,235	2	Good
7	50,123		Good

	B	C	D
8	10,345	3	OK
9	23,895	1	OK
10	34,298	2	Good
11	35,324	4	Good
12	12,345	2	OK
13	39,567	4	
14	40,098	4	
15	32,394	3	
16		3	

4. Type the hyperlinks www.BillyBobBoy.com in D2 and mailto:BillyBob@as.com in D3.

5. Create hyperlinks in cells A2 and A3 that will enable the user to click on these cells and be taken to the sites mentioned in cells D2 and D3 (www.BillyBobBoy.com and mailto:BillyBob@as.com).

6. Clear the contents and formats of D2 and D3.

7. Select range A5:D5 and click on the Bold, Italic, and Underline buttons on the Formatting toolbar.

Open solution file 0101S from the CD-ROM to check your work.

Task 2

Objectives covered: 1, :"Enter Text, Dates, and Numbers"; 5, "Clear Cell Content"; 7, "Cut, Copy, Paste, Paste Special and Move Selected Cells, Use the Office Clipboard" (drag to move); 8, "Clear Cell Formats"; 9, "Use Find and Replace."

Continue with the preceding workbook or open practice file 0102P from the enclosed CD-ROM and perform the following actions:

1. Insert a cell (by shifting cells down) in A2.

2. Input the current date in A2.

3. Use the fill handle and drag the range B6:D10 down so

the Sales, Units, and Ratings are in line with Day in column A.

4. Clear the contents for B9 (10,345) and type `9345` (notice that the comma is entered automatically).

5. Find and replace all OKs with `Poor`.

6. Use clear formats to remove all formatting in row 6.

Open solution file 0102S on the CD-ROM to check your work : (the date in A2 will be different than your date).

Task 3

Objectives covered: 2, "Go to a Specific Cell"; 6, "Insert and Delete Selected Cells"; 7, "Cut, Copy, Paste, Paste Special and Move Selected Cells, Use the Office Clipboard" (copy); 10, "Work with Series (AutoFill)"; 11, "Create Hyperlinks" (edit).

Continue with the preceding workbook or open practice file 0103P from the enclosed CD-ROM and perform the following actions:

1. Delete cell C8 so that all values move up.

2. Copy Good from D7 into cells D14–D17.

3. Select cells B7:B16 and, using AutoFill, predict what the sales will be for 3/20/02.

4. Go to A1 and edit the text to say `Billy Bob's Auto Sales`.

5. Edit the text in A3 to say `Home Page` and A4 to say `Click here to send a comment to Billy Bob`.

6. Using Go to, move to C17 and enter `3`.

Open solution file 0103S on the CD-ROM to check your work.

Task 4

Objectives covered: 4, "Use Undo and Redo"; 7, "Cut, Copy, Paste, Paste Special and Move Selected Cells, Use the Office Clipboard" (Office Clipboard, copy, paste special).

Continue with the preceding workbook or open practice file

0104P on the enclosed CD-ROM and perform the following actions:

1. Go to A18 and type Total.

2. Go to B18 and double-click on the ∑ AutoSum button.

3. Copy the formula from B18 to C18.

4. Cut the Range from A6:D18 and paste in B5.

5. Display the Office Clipboard, clear the Clipboard, and then copy the following into the Office Clipboard: A1:A2, A6:C6, and A18:C18.

6. Click on Sheet2 (click the tab on the bottom of the workbook) and type Summary in A1 and paste the items from the Office Clipboard in A2, A3, and A4, respectively.

7. Click back on Sheet1 and copy A18:C18 to F1. Notice the #REF! In cells G1 and H1. Click Undo and paste the values in the cells instead.

Open solution file 0104S on the CD-ROM to check your work.

Cheat Sheet

Use Undo and Redo

Undo reverses editing and formatting actions.

Edit, Undo (Ctrl+Z)

Redo reverses your Undo command.

Edit, Redo (Ctrl+Y)

Clear Cell Content

The contents of a cell can be a formula, a number, text, or a combination of all three.

To remove the contents of a cell, select the range you want to clear and press Delete, or choose Edit, Clear, Contents.

Enter Text, Dates, and Numbers

Type text, dates, and numbers in the cell and press Enter or Tab.

Edit Cell Content

Click in the Formula bar or double-click in the cell to position the insertion point for editing.

Press Backspace or Delete to remove characters before or after the insertion point.

Type additional text to insert at the insertion point.

To enter your changes, press Enter or Tab.

To cancel your changes, press Esc.

To add data to the end of a cell, press F2.

Go to a Specific Cell

To move to a cell, type the address in the Name Box or press F5. A Go To dialog box will appear. Type the cell or named range you want to go to in the Reference text box and click OK.

You can also move around the worksheet by pressing Ctrl+Home (to go to A1), Ctrl+End (to go to the last cell), and Home (to go to column A in the current row).

Insert and Delete Selected Cells

To insert cells, select the range of cells at which you want to insert. Then choose Insert, Cells and, on the Insert dialog box, choose to shift the cells or to insert entire rows or columns.

To delete cells, select the cells or range you want to delete. Then choose Edit, Delete, and the cells are removed.

Cut, Copy, Paste, Paste Special, and Move Selected Cells

You can copy or move data using cut, copy, and paste, or by dragging the range.

To copy or move, select the range, and then click the Copy or Cut icon, click on the new location, and click the Paste icon.

Alternatively, you can press Ctrl+C to copy, Ctrl+X to cut, and Ctrl+V to paste, or you can use these items on the Edit menu.

Another way to move a range is to drag the outline that surrounds the range with the white arrow mouse pointer. To copy, hold down Ctrl as you drag.

If you want to convert formulas to values, select the range with formulas and choose Ctrl+C. Then move to where you want the values and choose Edit, Paste Special, and then choose Values on the dialog box.

To rearrange a horizontal range of cells (rows) as a vertical range of cells (columns), or vice versa, copy the first area, position the cell pointer in a new location, choose Edit, Paste Special, and choose Transpose on the dialog box.

Continued

Use Find and Replace

Find enables you to go to an area on your worksheet based on content, not location.

Press Ctrl+F or choose Edit, Find and then type the entry in the Find What text box and choose Find Next to go to each occurrence.

To cancel a Find command, press Esc.

Replace enables you to find and replace text or numbers and replace multiple occurrences of those characters.

Press Ctrl+H or choose Edit, Replace and then type the entry in the Find What text box and the new entry in the Replace with text box. Choose Replace each time you want the new text to occur, or choose Replace All to change all occurrences.

Clear Cell Formats

You can remove text highlighting and number formats from existing entries.

Select the range and choose Edit, Clear, Formats.

Work with Series (AutoFill)

AutoFill enables you to fill a range with a series of numbers, dates, or text.

Select the range to start with and drag the fill handle in the bottom-right corner of the last cell.

If the selected cell contains a number, AutoFill copies the number. Holding down Ctrl while dragging increments the series by one.

If you want to create a number series with an increment of a specified amount, type the starting value in a cell. Select the next cell in the range and enter the next item in the series. Select the cells that contain the values, and drag the fill handle over the range you want to fill.

Months and days of the week can also be incremented with the fill handle.

Create Hyperlinks

Insert a link to a Web page or a different file by using a hyperlink.

Move to the cell and type the link or click the Insert Hyperlink button and fill in the dialog box.

Click on the hyperlink to move to the location.

To edit the hyperlink, right-click on the link and choose Hyperlink.

Working with Files

Following is a list of MOUS objectives:

- Use Save
- Use Save As (Different Name, Location, Format)
- Locate and Open an Existing Workbook
- Create a Folder
- Use Templates to Create a New Workbook
- Send a Workbook via Email
- Save a Worksheet/Workbook as a Web Page
- Use the Office Assistant

Use Save

The process of saving a file takes the file in memory on your screen and stores it on a disk. The disk could be a hard disk in your computer, a network drive somewhere else, a floppy, or any other removable disk. If you are ever going to use your file again, you must save it. If the document is long and there is a chance of making a mistake or having computer problems, you must save it so you won't lose your work.

Save a File for the First Time

To save a file for the first time, follow these steps:

1. Do one of the following:

   • Click 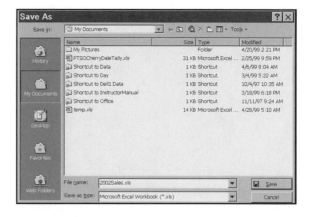 Save on the Standard toolbar.

   • Press Ctrl+S or F12.

   • Click the File menu and choose Save.

   The Save As dialog box opens.

2. If necessary, click the Save In drop-down arrow and
choose the drive and folder where you want to save the
file. Double-click each folder to select the location where
the document should be saved.

3. Type the File Name.

The filename can contain letters, numbers, spaces, and
many characters.

Filenames cannot include any of the following: forward
slash (/), backslash (\), greater-than sign (>), less-than
sign (<), asterisk (*), question mark (?), quotation mark
("), pipe symbol (¦), colon (:), or semicolon (;).

4. Press Enter or click Save.

The other options on the Save As dialog box are discussed in
Objective 13, "Use Save As (Different Name, Location, and
Format)."

**Save an
Existing
Workbook**

After you've saved a workbook, you should save it again with
each major update or before you perform major tasks.

To save the workbook again, do one of the following:

• Click 🖫 Save on the Standard toolbar.

• Press Ctrl+S or Shift+F12.

• Click the File menu and choose Save.

The changes you've made onscreen overwrite the document on
disk. The active file will be saved with its current location, file
format, and filename.

47

13

Use Save As (Different Name, Location, and Format)

Open Save As Dialog Box

The first time you save a file, the Save As dialog box displays. When you click the Save button or press Ctrl+S again, the dialog box does not open again, and Excel assumes you want to save with the original options. However, if you want to open the dialog box again to save a copy with a different name, file type, or location, use Save As.

To open the Save As dialog box, follow these steps:

1. Do one of the following:

   • Press F12.

   • Click the File menu and choose Save As.

   The Save As dialog box opens.

2. If necessary, type a new name for the workbook in the File name text box.

The File name text box has a pull-down arrow that enables you to use one of the recently used file names.

3. If necessary, choose a new drive or folder from the Save in drop-down list and double-click each folder until you get to your folder.

4. If you want to save the file in a different file format for use in another program or as another type of text, choose the desired file format from the Save as type drop-down list (see Objective 69, "Export to Other Applications," and Objective 18, "Save a Worksheet/Workbook as a Web Page").

5. Do any of the options listed in the following table.

6. Choose Save.

**Save As
Dialog Box**

The additional options on the Save As dialog box let you navigate to a different location, display the list differently, or set some options. The options include the following:

Icon	Name	Description
	Places bar	The bar located on the left side of the Save As dialog box. It contains shortcuts to History, My Documents, Desktop, Favorites, and Web Folders. (See Objective 14, "Locate and Open an Existing Workbook," or Objective 18, "Save a Worksheet/ Workbook as a Web Page.")
	Back	Click to go back to the previous folder or drive. A ScreenTip shows the name of the folder. You can also press Alt+1.
	Up one level	Move to the higher level in the hierarchy (either a folder or a drive). You can also press Alt+2.
	Search the Web	Click to open a search page and search for words and phrases. You can also press Alt+3.

Icon	Name	Description
[×]	Delete	Remove the selected file or folder. You can also press Delete.
[🗂]	Create New Folder	Click and type a new folder name that will appear in the Save in location. You can also press Alt+5.
[⊞]	Views	Click the arrow next to the Views button to choose the way the list appears (see the next five choices).
	List	Displays file folder icons and names for each file and folder.
	Details	Shows the folder icon and name, file size, file type, and date last modified in a column format. Click any of these column headers to toggle between ascending and descending sort.
	Properties	Shows file properties such as author, date created, DOS name, subjects, and more. To change properties, choose File, Properties.

continues

51

Continued

Icon	Name	Description
	Preview	Displays a portion of the file in the right side of the window. Preview will not be available unless the file is in a version of Excel that supports previews and the Save Preview Picture check box was checked on the Summary tab in the Properties dialog box when the file was saved.
	Arrange Icons	Click this to open a menu that enables you to sort files by Name, by Size, by Type, or by Date.
	Tools menu	Click this down arrow to get a menu that enables you to print, delete, rename, or display all the properties of, or add to the Favorites folder the selected file or folder. You can also set Web options for the file. Finally, you can save the file with other options (see below).

From the Tools menu on the Save As dialog box, you can save the file with a password, create a backup of the file, and suggest that the user open the document as a read-only file so he won't mess up the document.

File Save Options

To set the file options, do the following:

1. Click the File menu and choose Save As or one of the other methods mentioned above.

2. In the Save As dialog box, click the Tools menu and choose General Options.

   The Save Options dialog box opens.

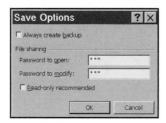

3. If you want to save a backup copy of the workbook each time you save, choose Always create backup.

4. If you want to require users to enter a password when the file is opened, type a password in the Password to open box. You will be prompted to verify the password after you choose OK. If the user does not have the password, she cannot open the file.

5. If you enter a Password to modify, the user can save changes to the file only if he knows the password. If he doesn't know the password, he can still open the workbook but cannot save the changes with the same filename (the file is read-only).

6. If you want the user to get a prompt suggesting that she opens the file as a read-only, choose Read-only Recommended.

7. Choose OK.

8. If prompted by Confirm Password dialog boxes, type the password you entered in steps 4 and 5 and choose OK.

To save all the workbooks you have open as one unit, see Objective 73, "Using a Workspace."

Locate and Open an Existing Workbook

After you've saved a workbook and want to use it again, you must find and open the file.

To open a file, follow these steps:

1. Do one of the following:

   - Click  Open on the Standard toolbar.

   - Press Ctrl+O.

   - Click the File menu and choose Open.

   The Open dialog box displays.

Open a Workbook

2. If you want to change the location of the file, do one or more of the following:

- Click the Look in drop-down arrow and choose a different drive or folder.

- Double-click a folder to see the contents.

- Click  History in the Places bar to display a list of recent files you've saved.

- Click  My Documents or  Favorites in the Places bar to display the contents of that folder.

- Click  Desktop in the Places bar to display the list of folders and files on your Windows desktop.

- Click  Web Folders in the Places bar to display a list of folders you've created on the Web.

- Click the  Back button or press Alt+1 to return to the last location you were viewing.

- Click the  Up One Level button or press Alt+2 to look at the contents of the folder or drive that is the parent of the current folder.

- Click the  Search the Web button or press Alt+3 to launch a search page in your Internet browser.

3. If necessary, click the Files of type drop-down arrow and choose a different file type (including current and previous versions of Excel, other spreadsheet programs, text, Web, and database files).

4. Click the file's icon in the list or type the File Name (you can also double-click on an icon to open a file and skip step 5).

5. Do one of the following:

- Press Enter to open the file.

- Click the Open button.

- Click the drop-down arrow on the Open button and choose Open Read-Only to open a copy of the file that you cannot save with the same name.

- Click the drop-down arrow on the Open button and choose Open as Copy to open a copy of the file that you cannot save with the same name.

For other options on the Open dialog box, see Objective 13, "Use Save As (Different Name, Location, and Format)."

Find File

If you forgot where you put your file, you can use the Find file feature. Do the following:

1. Click 📂 Open on the Standard toolbar or another option mentioned previously.

2. On the Open dialog box, choose the Tools button and choose Find.

The Find dialog box opens.

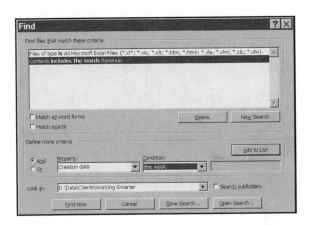

3. In the Property drop-down box, choose one of the options such as Author, Contents, Creation date, or other.

4. In the Condition drop-down box, choose one of the options such as includes words, includes phrase, yesterday, or other. The Condition drop-down choices depend on your choice in the Property drop-down box.

5. If requested, type in the Value text box.

6. Click the Add to List button.

7. If desired, click the And (all properties must be met) or the Or (any properties can be met) option and repeat steps 3—6.

8. If desired, click the Look in drop-down arrow and change the location of where to look.

9. If you want to search subfolders of the selected folders, check the Search subfolders box.

10. If you want to conduct a search based on different word forms (am, is, are) for the same word, check Match all word forms, or if you want to match the word exactly, choose Match exactly.

11. To save search criteria, choose Save Search and type a name. If you want to use these criteria later, choose Open Search and double-click the name.

12. When you're ready to look for the file, click Find Now.

After the search, the results will appear in the list in the Open dialog box.

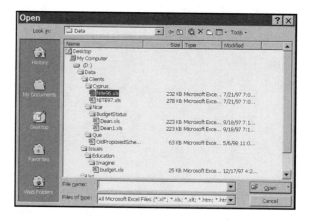

13. To open the file, double-click the icon.

Create a Folder

If you don't have a location you want to save a file to, you can create one at the same time you are saving the file.

To create a folder, follow these steps:

1. Do one of the following:

   • Press F12.

   • Click the File menu and choose Save As.

   The Save As dialog box opens.

2. If necessary, choose a new drive or folder from the Save in drop-down, and double-click each folder in the list until you get to your folder.

3. Click the 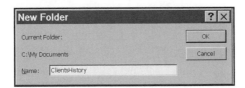 Create New Folder button or press Alt+5.

   The New Folder dialog box appears.

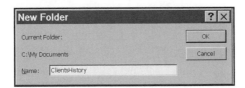

4. Type the folder name and choose OK.

Continue saving the document by adding the filename and choosing OK. You can also create a folder by using File, Open and selecting Create New Folder from the Open dialog box.

16

Use Templates to Create a New Workbook

There are documents that ship with Office 2000 that you can use as a source for new workbooks. These documents are called templates. You can use the templates that come with Excel or use those that you or another user create. Templates can contain text, formatting, formulas, and macros that speed up the creation of a file. When you use a template, a new document is created and the original template is not changed.

To create a new workbook based on a template, follow these steps:

1. Click the File menu and choose New.

   The New dialog box opens.

2. Click one of the tabs in the dialog box. Spreadsheet Solutions contains templates that ship with Excel.

3. Double-click one of the template files.

4. If prompted, you might need to insert the Office 2000 CD-ROM if the template was not installed on your computer.

5. If you want to use the automation provided with the file, choose Enable Macros if prompted. If you aren't confident of the source of the file, choose Disable Macros to avoid the possibility of a macro virus.

The template opens with a generic name based on the name of the template. You can edit this workbook like any other. Additionally, there might be buttons on the workbook, toolbar buttons, and menu choices that will help you create the workbook. When finished inputting data, save this like any other workbook (see Objective 12, "Use Save").

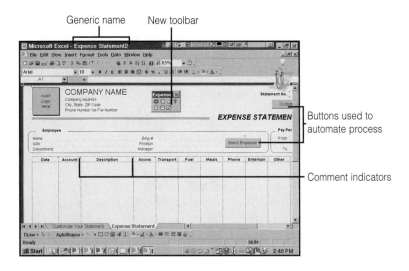

The preceding figure shows a new Expense workbook based on the Expense Statement template. To use this template, you can do any of the following:

If you want to see an example of a completed statement, click on the ⊞ Display Example/Remove Example button on the small Expenses toolbar. Click this button again to get rid of the example.

There are small red triangles throughout the screen. Move the mouse pointer to each one to get a ScreenTip explaining the item.

If you don't see the red triangles, click the ⊞ Hide Comments/Display Comments button on the Expense toolbar.

Click the Customize button on the right of the screen to display the Customize Your Expense Statement worksheet. Enter the data in the worksheet and click on the Expenses Statement tab to return to the statement.

Click the Select Employee button and choose from a list of employees.

⊞ The Assign a Number button enables you to assign a unique statement number. If you want to edit the template, you can make formatting changes and save them.

Templates that Come with Excel 2000

Microsoft Excel has the following automated templates that ship with Office 2000:

Expense Statement

Invoice

Purchase Order

Village Software (order form for more templates)

You can also go to Microsoft's Web site (click Help and choose Office on the Web) and look for additional templates.

Send a Workbook via Email

If you want to mail your workbook, you can use Outlook's email feature from within Excel.

To email your workbook, do the following:

1. Click the <u>F</u>ile menu and choose Sen<u>d</u> To.

2. Do one of the following:

   - To send the workbook as an attachment where users of most mail programs can open the workbook with Excel, choose M<u>a</u>il Recipient (as Attachment). Outlook opens with the workbook displayed as an icon.

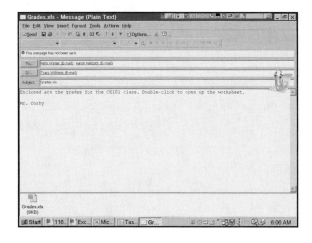

*If the work-
book contains
more than one
sheet, you will
be prompted to
send the
entire work-
book as an
attachment or
send the cur-
rent work-
sheet as the
message body.
Even when
you choose to
send the
worksheet, you
still see all
sheets.
However,
when you click
the Send this
Sheet button,
the user only
sees the active
sheet.*

- To send the active worksheet as the contents of the email message, choose Mail Recipient. If the recipient has Outlook, they can see the contents of the active worksheet without opening Excel. The toolbars and menus for Excel remain with the addition of Outlook's toolbar buttons and the email addressing and subject text boxes.

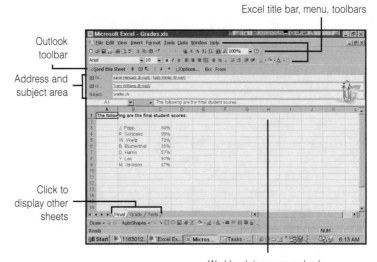

Excel title bar, menu, toolbars

Outlook toolbar

Address and subject area

Click to display other sheets

Workbook is message body

3. If prompted for a profile, select one and choose OK.

4. In the To and Cc text boxes, type in the email address or click the To button and choose the address(es).

5. If desired, edit the Subject text box.

6. If you choose the attachment option, type a message in the message area. If you choose Mail Recipient, edit the workbook as desired.

7. Choose any additional email options such as an additional attachment, a priority level, and delivery options.

8. Choose the Send or Send this Sheet button.

If you choose M<u>a</u>il Recipient (as Attachment), when the user opens the email message, the attachment looks like the preceding figure. If you choose <u>M</u>ail Recipient, the user's email message shows the active worksheet as a picture (see the following figure).

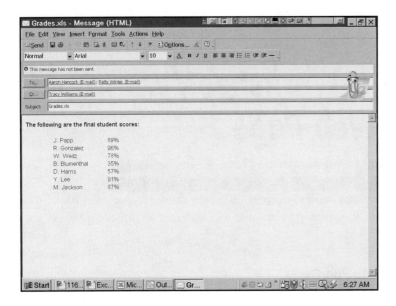

18

Save a Worksheet/Workbook as a Web Page

You can publish a worksheet or workbook to the Web. If you publish a worksheet to the Web, you have the option of making it interactive; you can edit and input text and values, increase the column width, sort, add a formula, and save this worksheet as a new workbook.

Workbook Web Page

When you save an entire workbook as a Web page, it cannot be interactive. However, you can view all contents, including multiple sheets.

To save a workbook as a Web page, do the following:

1. With the workbook open, click File and choose Save as Web Page.

   The Save As dialog box opens with the File type listed as Web Page and additional Web options available.

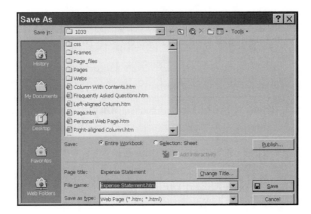

2. Under Save, choose the Entire Workbook option button.

3. Type in a File Name.

4. If desired, click the Change Title command button and type the page title that will appear in the title bar of your browser.

5. Choose a location by doing one of the following:

   - Click the Save in drop-down arrow and choose a location such as a drive, folder, Web folder, or FTP location.

   - Click the [icon] Web Folders icon and double-click the specific Web folder you want to publish to and then navigate to a subfolder if necessary.

6. Choose Save.

Worksheet buttons —

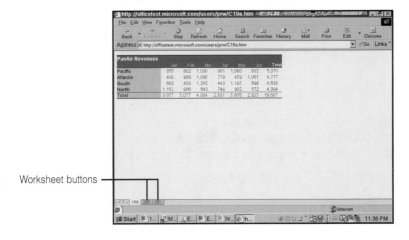

67

When you open the file in a Web browser, you see each worksheet name displayed as a button on the bottom of the screen.

See Objective 39, "Use Web Page Preview," to see how the document will look in a browser.

Add Interactivity

If you want to have the capability to modify files on the Web, do steps 1—5 above, and then the following:

1. On the Save As dialog box in the Save area, select the Selection: (or Republish: if it has already been published once) Sheet option.

2. Check <u>A</u>dd interactivity.

3. Select the <u>P</u>ublish command button.

    The Publish as Web Page dialog box displays.

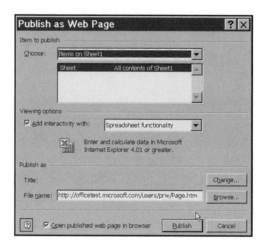

PivotTable Functionality enables you to use this feature (see Objective 108, "Create Interactive PivotTables for the Web").

4. In the <u>C</u>hoose drop-down box, select the worksheet or item you want to publish.

5. <u>A</u>dd interactivity with is already checked. Spreadsheet functionality is the default and enables you to edit the worksheet.

6. If you want to see the Web page, check the <u>O</u>pen published web page in browser check box.

7. Choose the <u>P</u>ublish button.

If you checked <u>O</u>pen published web page in browser in step 6, you will see your worksheet in the Web browser with a toolbar for Excel functions.

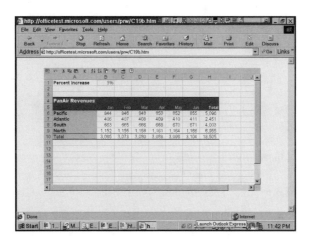

You can do common Excel procedures with the interactive worksheet including the following:

- Edit or input the value of a cell. In the preceding figure, you could change the percentage increase value in B1 to affect the numbers in the rest of the example.

- Increase and decrease column widths and row heights (see Objective 27, "Modify Size of Rows and Columns").

- ⟳ Undo your latest change (see Objective 4, "Use Undo and Redo").

- ✂ Cut, ▣ Copy, and ▣ Paste data from one part of the worksheet to another (see Objective 7, "Cut, Copy, Paste, Paste Special and Move Selected Cells, Use the Office Clipboard").

- Create a total in a cell by clicking on the Σ AutoSum button (see Objective 54, "Use AutoSum").

- Sort a range of cells by values in a column by clicking ⬇ or ⬆ (Objective 94, "Perform Single and Multi-Level Sorts").

- Turn on  AutoFilter and then choose which rows of data you want to see by choosing items on the drop-down arrow in the first row of values (see Objective 98, "Apply Data Filters").

- Save a copy of the latest values to an Excel workbook (see Objective 12, "Use Save").

- Change the Formatting of a selected range by clicking the Property Toolbox button and selecting a font, format, and alignment options (see Chapter 3, "Formatting Worksheets").

The Show/Hide section of the Property Toolbox also enables you to choose which items you want to see onscreen, such as the toolbar, headers, and gridlines.

The default is for the worksheet to recalculate with every change. You can change this to manual recalculation in the Calculations section of the Property Toolbox.

If your worksheet is large, you can find text though the Find section of the Property Toolbox.

Use the Office Assistant

The Office Assistant enables you to type a question and then finds possible answers to the question.

To use the Office Assistant, follow these steps:

1. If the Office Assistant is not displayed, do one of the following:

- Click  Microsoft Excel Help on the Standard toolbar.

- Click the <u>H</u>elp menu and choose Microsoft Excel Help.

- Press F1.

The Assistant displays.

For F1 to display the Office Assistant, this option must be turned on. Right-click the Assistant, choose Options, and check Respond to F1 key.

2. Type a question and press Enter.

The Assistant interprets your question and gives you some possible choices in Help.

3. Click one of the choices to display the Help page.

The Microsoft Excel Help window opens, displaying the answer to your question.

The choice selected
on the Assistant Help toolbar

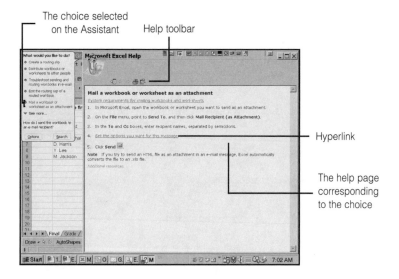

Hyperlink

The help page
corresponding
to the choice

4. While in Help, you can do the following:

- Click a hyperlink (blue underline) to display the Help page.

- Click a definition (blue only) to display an explanation of the term.

- Click the 🖨 Print button to display the Help page.

- Click the 🔲 Show button to display three tabs: Contents views the Help table of contents. Answer Wizard enables you to ask another question just like you did for the Assistant. The Index searches for specific keywords, phrases, or words. Click the 🔲 Hide button to hide these tabs.

5. When finished with the Help window, click the Close (×) button.

To change the Office Assistant character, do the following:

1. Click the Office Assistant and choose Options.

2. Click the Gallery tab.

3. Choose Next or Back to see other Assistants.

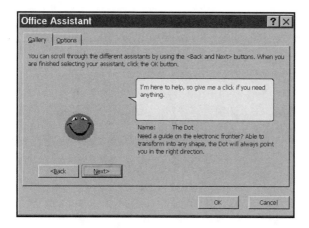

4. If desired, choose the Options tab and select how you want the Assistant and tips displayed.

5. Choose OK.

If the Assistant character is not loaded on your computer, you will be prompted to load the CD-ROM.

If you don't want to see the Assistant, click the Help menu and choose Hide the Office Assistant. If you want to look on the Internet for help, choose Help, Office on the Web.

TAKE THE TEST

Task 1

Objectives covered: 12, "Use Save"; 13, "Use Save As (Different Name, Location, and Format)"; 14, "Locate and Open an Existing Workbook"; 15, "Create a Folder"; 19, "Use the Office Assistant."

1. Create a new workbook based on the Invoice template.

2. Save the workbook as a Microsoft Excel Workbook with a filename of Inv01. If prompted, choose to continue without updating.

3. For the company information, use the following: State Auto, 123 Fox Street, Denver, CO 80221, (303) 555-1234, fax (303) 555-1212. For customer information use the following: Minney Moore, 955 17th Street, Denver, CO, 80221, (303) 555-7777. The date is 5/22/99, the order number is 1, and the rep is RW. There are 35 Excel MOUS Cheat Sheets for $20 each. You can customize the invoice logo with a graphic file from your hard drive. To customize your invoice logo, click the Customize button located in the top-right corner. The Customize Your Invoice sheet will appear. Click the Select Logo button located in the lower-left corner and select a picture file from your hard drive to insert. Click the Insert button, and your customized logo appears.

4. Use the Office Assistant to look up the phrase "template problems." Select the Troubleshoot templates topic and view the topic's links to additional information.

5. Save the workbook again as INV02. If prompted, choose to continue without updating.

6. Create a new folder on your C drive as State and save the document INV02 in that folder.

7. Open solution file 0201s.xls from the CD to check your work.

Objectives covered: 13, > "Use Save As (Different Name, Location, and Format"; 14, "Locate and Open an Existing Workbook"; 17, "Send a Workbook via Email"; 18, "Save a Worksheet/Workbook as a Web Page."

Task 2

1. Close and reopen Excel.

2. Using File, Open, load INV01 from its original saved location.

3. Use the find feature to locate and open INV02 from the State folder.

4. Send INV01 as an attachment to a mail recipient.

5. Send INV02 as a message to a mail recipient.

6. Save the entire INV02 workbook as a Web page. Compare your work with solution file 0202s.htm.

7. Save the worksheet as an Interactive Web page. If prompted, choose to continue without updating.

   The worksheet automatically opens in your Web browser. Edit the price per book to be $19 and save from the Web browser to a new workbook. Compare your work with solution file 0202s.xls.

8. Save the workbook as a text file (you can verify that it is okay that text does not support multiple worksheets and that the worksheet is not compatible with txt). Compare your work with solution file 0202s.txt.

Cheat Sheet

Save Workbooks

Saving enables you to keep a copy of your workbook for later use or in case of catastrophes while you're working.

File, Save (Ctrl+S). The first time a file is saved, the Save As dialog box appears.

The Save As dialog box enables you to change the filename, location, display of filenames, and set file options.

To open the Save As dialog box, choose File, Save As (F12). Change the location in the Save in drop-down and type the name in the File name text box.

Click the arrow next to the Views icon to list, preview, and view file details and properties.

Open Workbooks

To work on an existing workbook, you must find and open it.

Choose File, Open (Ctrl+O) to display the Open dialog box.

In the Open dialog box, you can change the searched location by choosing a drive or folder from the Look in drop-down list. Alternatively, click one of the icons in the Places bar located on the left side of the dialog box.

Create a Folder

You can create an additional folder to store your workbooks and other documents.

From a file dialog box (choose File, Save As or Open), click the Create New Folder button or press Alt+5, type the new name of the folder in the Name box, and click OK.

Templates

A template is a preformatted document that can contain text, formulas, styles, and macros.

Choose File, New and choose one of the templates in the New dialog box.

When you save, you do not change the template, but you create a new workbook.

Publish to Web Pages

If you publish an entire workbook to a Web page, users can see multiple sheets, but items in the workbook will not be interactive.

If you publish a worksheet as a Web page, you can add interactivity and users will be able to analyze, calculate, enter, format, and sort data. Users will also be able to export the Web page back to Excel and save the file as a new workbook.

Choose File, Save as Web Page. If desired, choose Entire Workbook or Selection: Sheet, and then click the Publish button.

If you choose Selection: Sheet, check Add interactivity to allow users to change and analyze the data.

Attachments

You can send a workbook as an attachment to an email document or have the active sheet be the message displayed in Outlook.

Choose File, Send To and choose one of the Mail Recipient options.

Formatting Worksheets

Following is a list of MOUS objectives:

- Apply Font Styles (Typeface, Size, Color, and Styles)
- Modify Alignment of Cell Content
- Merge Cells
- Rotate Text and Change Indents
- Apply Number Formats (Currency, Percent, Dates, and Comma)
- Adjust the Decimal Place
- Apply Cell Borders and Shading
- Modify Size of Rows and Columns
- Use the Format Painter
- Apply AutoFormat
- Define, Apply, and Remove a Style

Apply Font Styles (Typeface, Size, Color, and Styles)

When you apply font characteristics that are different from the normal text, you can make the entry stand out. Changes in font styles are usually appropriate for labels of columns and rows, totals, and other entries that you want to draw attention to. You can format a cell, a range of cells, or some of the text within a cell.

You can change the shape of the text (typeface) as well as its size, color, weight (amount of bold), and effects. You can use the Formatting toolbar or the Format Cells dialog box.

Formatting Toolbar

To change the font style using the Formatting toolbar, follow these steps:

1. Do one of the following:

   - Move to or click on a single cell.

   - Drag the mouse across cells or hold down Shift and use the arrows to select a range of cells. If desired, hold down Ctrl and select another group of cells.

   - When the entry is text and not a number, drag the I-beam mouse pointer in the Formula Bar or double-click a cell and drag the I-beam across text within the cell to select some of the text in a cell.

2. Do one or more of the following:

   - Click **B** Bold or press Ctrl+B.

   - Click *I* Italic or press Ctrl+I.

- Click  Underline or press Ctrl+U.

- Click the down arrow in the Font box and choose a font from the list. The font list now shows what each font looks like rather than just showing the font name.

- Click the down arrow in the Font Size box and choose a size from the list or type a number in the box. The size is in points. There are 72 points to an inch.

- Click Fill Color to apply the most recently used color for the background of the range, or click the down arrow next to Fill Color and choose a color.

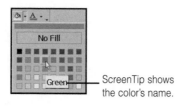

ScreenTip shows the color's name.

- Click Font Color to apply the most recently used color for the text of the range, or click the down arrow next to Font Color and choose a color.

Format Cells Dialog Box

You can do multiple formats at one time with the Format Cells dialog box. Do the following:

1. Do one of the following:

- Move to or click on a single cell.

- Drag the mouse across cells or hold down Shift and use the arrows to select a range of cells. If desired, hold down Ctrl and select another group of cells.

- Drag the I-beam mouse pointer in the Formula Bar or double-click on a cell and drag the I-beam across text within the cell to select some of the text in a cell.

2. Press Ctrl+1 or click the Format menu and choose Cells.

The Format Cells dialog box displays.

3. Click on the Font tab.

Preview shows what your formatting choices will look like

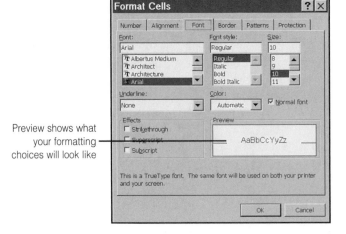

4. Do any of the following:

- Choose a Font (typeface) from the list.

- Choose a Font style indicating bold or italic from the list.

- Choose a Size for the text from the list.

- Choose an Underline from the drop-down list. Single or Double underlines the complete entry, whereas Single Accounting or Double Accounting underlines just the width of the cell.

- Click the Color drop-down arrow and choose the text color from the palette.

- To place a line through the selected text or numbers, check Strikethrough.

- To elevate the selected text above Normal text, check Superscript.

- To drop the selected text below Normal text, check Subscript.

5. If you want to return all settings to those for the Normal style, check Normal font. For information on styles, see Objective 30, "Define, Apply, and Remove a Style.

6. Choose OK.

Modify Alignment of Cell Content

Cell alignment is how text is centered or justified in the range. The default is left justified for text and right justified for numbers, dates, and times. Labels above columns are sometimes centered or right justified. You can use the Formatting toolbar for alignment or if you want more options, you can use the Alignment tab of the Format Cells dialog box. See Objective 22, "Merge Cells," and Objective 23, "Rotate Text and Change Indents."

Formatting Toolbar

The Formatting toolbar is the quickest way to align cells. Do the following:

1. Move to a cell or select a range of cells.

2. Do one of the following:

    • Click ▤ Align Left.

    • Click ▤ Center.

    • Click ▤ Align Right.

    • Click ▦ Merge and Center to combine all selected cells into one cell and center the contents across the range.

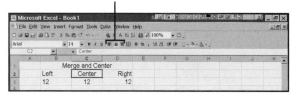

The Format Cells dialog box gives you more options than are on the Formatting toolbar such as the capability to wrap text within a cell and align text vertically as well as horizontally.

To align text with the Format Cells dialog box, do the following:

1. Move to a cell or select a range of cells.

2. Press Ctrl+1 or click the Format menu and choose Cells.

   The Format Cells dialog box displays.

3. Click on the Alignment tab.

Format Cells Dialog Box— Alignment Tab

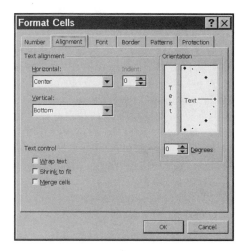

4. Do one or more of the following:

- Click the Horizontal drop-down and choose whether you want text left and numbers right (General) or the entry Left, Right, or Center. You can also center the entry across the selected range. Justify means that wrapped lines are lined up on both the left and right. Fill means that the contents of the cell repeat to fill to the width of the cell.

- Click the Vertical drop-down and choose whether you want text on the Top, Bottom, or Center of the cell. If you have multiple lines (wrapped text), the lines are spaced evenly if you choose Justify.

- Check Wrap text if you want to display multiple lines of text within a cell.

- Check Shrink to fit if you want the text to display smaller in order to fit in the column width. You can't use this option and Wrap Text at the same time.

The Merge cells option is discussed in Objective 22, "Merge Cells." Orientation and Indent are discussed in Objective 23, "Rotate Text and Change Indents."

5. Choose OK.

If you want to reset the formats to what is normally in the cell, choose Edit, Clear, Formats (see Objective 8, "Clear Cell Formats").

Merge Cells

If you want multiple cells to act as one cell, use merge cells. The gridlines around these cells are removed and the range looks like one large cell. Any horizontal or vertical formatting within the range is treated as if the range was one cell. For example, text is centered across the whole range if you use the ▤ Center button.

To merge cells, do the following:

1. Select a range of cells. If you select just a horizontal range, the text will be merged in the row into one cell. However, if you select multiple cells in rows and columns, the entire range will be merged into one cell.

2. Click the ▦ Merge and Center button on the Formatting toolbar.

The selected cells become one, and text is centered in the range.

3. If you want to horizontally justify text within the merged cell, do one of the following:

- Click ▤ Align Left.
- Click ▤ Align Right.

If the range included more than one row, the text can also be vertically centered in the cell. See the following section.

Format Toolbar

Format Cells Dialog Box— Alignment Tab

The Format Cells dialog box allows you to merge cells and align text vertically or horizontally. Do the following:

1. Select a range of cells.

2. Press Ctrl+1 or click the F<u>o</u>rmat menu and choose C<u>e</u>lls. The Format Cells dialog box displays.

3. Click on the Alignment tab.

4. Check <u>M</u>erge cells.

5. If desired, select an option in the Horizontal list box to change the text alignment across the width of the cell.

6. If desired, select an option in the Vertical list box to change the text alignment across the height of the cell.

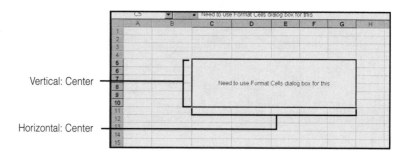

7. Choose OK.

If you want to unmerge the range, select it and return to the Alignment tab and uncheck <u>M</u>erge Cells or click the <u>E</u>dit menu and choose Cle<u>a</u>r, then <u>F</u>ormats (see Objective 8, "Clear Cell Formats").

Rotate Text and Change Indents

You can rotate text (place text in a cell at an angle). This is use-ful if you have long labels for the heading of a column but short entries. You can also indent text within a cell so it is still left aligned but is spaced in a few characters compared to nor-mal text. This is helpful if you have subcategories that you want to identify within a category.

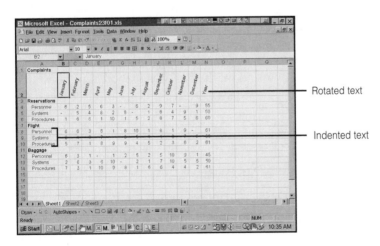

Rotated text

Indented text

To rotate text within a cell as shown in the preceding figure, do the following:

Rotate Text

1. Move to the cell or select the range.

2. Press Ctrl+1 or click the F**o**rmat menu and choose C**e**lls.

The Format Cells dialog box displays.

3. Click on the Alignment tab.

4. Do one of the following in the Orientation section of the dialog box:

   • Click on the first box to display text vertically with each letter below the other letters.

   • Drag the text line in the second box to keep text with letters next to each other but to change the angle.

   • Type an amount in the Degrees text box or use the up or down arrows to change the amount.

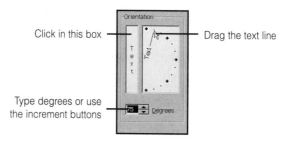

Click in this box ──── Orientation ──── Drag the text line

Type degrees or use the increment buttons

5. Choose OK.

Indent Text

To add space before the text within a cell as shown in the preceding figure, you can click the ▦ Decrease Indent or ▦ Increase Indent buttons on the Formatting toolbar one or more times or do the following:

1. Move to the cell or select the range.

2. Press Ctrl+1 or click the Format menu and choose Cells.

   The Format Cells dialog box displays.

3. Click on the Alignment tab.

4. Change Horizontal to Left (Indent).

5. Type the number of characters to Indent or use the up or down arrows.

6. Choose OK.

Apply Number Formats (Currency, Percent, Dates, and Comma)

Formats for numbers do not change the value of a number but they do change the way a number is displayed. A formatted number is often easier to read than an unformatted number. For example, 1234567 is hard to read without counting the digits, but with commas added to 1,234,567 it is easier to tell that the 1 is a million. You can type an entry with the format $25.00, or it is often easier to type numbers without formatting and then format after you've entered all the data.

You can format numbers through the toolbar, but you have more options when you use the Number tab of the Format Cells dialog box.

Select the cells you want to format and click one of the following buttons on the Formatting toolbar:

Formatting Toolbar

Toolbar	Button Name	Shortcut	Description Button
$	Currency Style	Ctrl+Shift+$	Adds a dollar sign, commas, and two decimal places. 25 becomes $25.00.
%	Percent Style	Ctrl+Shift+%	Multiplies the number by 100 and adds a percent sign. 1 becomes 100% and .5 becomes 50%.
,	Comma Style	Ctrl+Shift+!	Adds a comma for every three digits to the left of the decimal place (thousands, millions, and so on) and two decimal places. 1234 becomes 1,234.00.

For numbers after the decimal point, see Objective 25, "Adjust the Decimal Place."

Format Cells Dialog Box— Number Tab

The Format Cells dialog box gives you many more options than the options on the toolbar. Do the following:

1. Move to the cell or select the range.

2. Press Ctrl+1 or click the Format menu and choose Cells.

   The Format Cells dialog box displays.

3. Click on the Number tab.

4. Choose a Category. The right side of the dialog box changes depending on the choice:

- **General**—There are no additional choices, numbers have no commas, symbols, and they display the number of decimal places you entered.

- **Number**—Lets you choose Decimal places, check Use 1000 Separator (,) if you want a comma, and choose whether you want Negative Numbers in red or with parentheses.

The right side of the dialog box changes depending on the Category selected

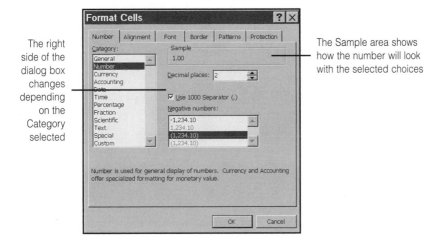

The Sample area shows how the number will look with the selected choices

- **Currency**—Gives you the same choices as Number and lets you choose a currency Symbol.

- **Accounting**—Also lets you choose a currency Symbol (the symbols are all lined up and the decimal places are lined up. In currency format, just the decimal places are lined up). You can also choose the number of decimal places.

93

- **Date**—Lets you choose examples that display the date in different formats. These formats display numbers (1–12) or the name of the month. You also choose the order and whether you have slashes or dashes separating month, day, and year. Some options also include the time as well as the date.

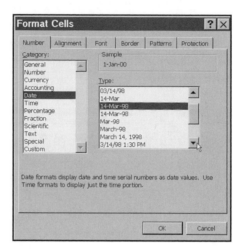

- **Time**—Choose from different time formats that give you the option of showing seconds, AM or PM, and a 12-hour or 24-hour clock. Time format also has date options.

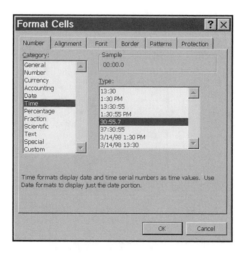

- **Percentage**—Like the Percent button on the formatting toolbar, this multiplies the number by 100 and adds a percent sign. This also gives you the option to identify how many decimal places you want.

- **Fraction**—Lets you choose a fraction format including how many digits are in the denominator and whether the display represents halves, eighths, quarters, sixteenths, tenths, or hundredths.

- **Scientific**—Displays in scientific format. 123 becomes 1.23E02. 1200 becomes 1.2E03. 0.01 becomes 1E-02. For every unit past the ones, a positive number is added. For the first significant units to the right of the decimal place, a negative number is added. You can also choose the number of decimal places.

- **Text**—Displays a number or formula as it is in the Formula Bar rather than evaluating a result. For example, =SUM(A1:A10) will display in the cell rather than the value.

- **Special**—Lets you choose Zip Code, Zip Code+4, Phone Number, or Social Security Number formats. If Social Security Number were applied to the entry with a value of 123456789, 123-45-6789 displays.

- **Custom**—Lets you be more specific when choosing the format in the Type list, or you can type your own characters, especially if one of the formats you want is not listed above. For example, you might want to spell out the entire month when working with dates.

The complete list of characters is in Help (see "Create a Custom Number Format"), but the following are some of the common characters:

For months, use the following: Type m for one digit (1–12). Type mm for two digits (01–12). Type mmm for three-letter abbreviations (Jan–Dec). Type mmmm for full months (January–December). For example, mmm d, yyyy will produce Jan 1, 2001.

For days, use the following: Type d for one digit (1–31). Type dd for two digits (01–31). Type ddd for a three-letter abbreviation (Sun–Sat). Type dddd to spell out the day of the week (Sunday–Saturday). For example, dddd, mm/dd/yy will produce Monday, 01/15/01.

Type 0 if a digit is required. If .5 is formatted as 0.00, it displays as 0.50.

Type # if a digit is optional. If .5 is formatted as #.00, it displays as .50.

If the data is time, type h for hours, mm for minutes (01–60), ss for seconds (01–60), AM/PM to display AM or PM. For example, type h:mm:ss AM/PM to display 5:06:15 PM.

For numbers where the first entry is a positive number, the second entry after a semicolon is a negative number. #,##0_);[Red](#,##0) will display negative numbers in parentheses and in red.

Underscore parenthesis _) leaves room for parentheses if the number is negative so all positive and negative numbers line up.

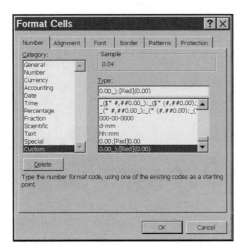

5. When finished, choose OK.

Adjust the Decimal Place

Decimal places are the digits to the right of the period on a number. Format a range of numbers using decimal places so all the numbers line up on the decimal place, making the numbers easier to read and compare.

To change the number of decimal places click  Increase Decimal or Decrease Decimal on the Formatting toolbar or do the following:

1. Move to the cell or select the range.

2. Press Ctrl+1 or click the Format menu and choose Cells.

   The Format Cells dialog box displays.

3. Click on the Number tab.

4. Choose a Category that supports decimal places (Number, Currency, Accounting, Percentage, or Scientific).

5. Type a number in Decimal Places or click the up or down arrows to increase or decrease the number in the text box.

6. Choose OK.

Apply Cell Borders and Shading

In addition to formatting text with bold, italic, and fonts, you can also draw attention to areas of your worksheet by adding cell borders and shading. Cell borders are lines around the edge or diagonally through the cell. Shading is the background color or pattern of the cell. You can use cell borders or shading to separate rows or columns or to make a range stand out. Like the other formatting options above, you have buttons on the Formatting toolbar and on the Format Cells dialog box.

To add borders and shading using the Formatting toolbar, do the following:

Formatting Toolbar

1. Move to the cell or select the range.

2. Do one or more of the following:

   • Click 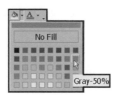 Fill Color to choose the most recently used color or click the down arrow next to Fill Color and choose one of the colors on the palette.

   No Fill

   Gray-50%

   • Click ▦ Borders to choose the most recently used border or click the arrow next to Borders and choose one of the borders on the palette.

99

Format Cells Dialog Box— Border and Patterns

The Format Cells dialog box gives you more options than the Formatting toolbar. Do the following:

1. Move to the cell or select the range.

2. Press Ctrl+1 or click the F**o**rmat menu and choose C**e**lls. The Format Cells dialog box displays.

3. If you want a border, click on the Border tab and do one or more of the following:

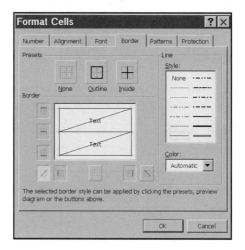

- Click on an option in the **S**tyle box to choose solid, dashed, thick, or double lines. Choose this and the color option before choosing what kind of borders you want within the range.

- Click on the **C**olor arrow and choose a color for the borders.

- Click **O**utline to place lines around the edge of the range.

- Click **I**nside to place lines on all internal lines of the range.

- Click one of the buttons in the Border area to add or remove a line on the top, inside horizontal, bottom, left, inside vertical, or right side of the range. You can also click on one of the two diagonal buttons to create diagonal lines through the range.

- If you want to remove all borders, click on the None button.

4. If you want the cell background filled in, click the Patterns tab on the Format Cells dialog box and do one or more of the following:

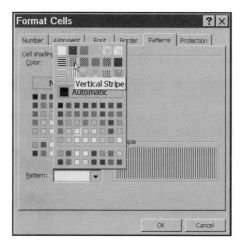

- Click on one of the boxes in the Color palette for the background.

- Click on the Pattern arrow and choose one of the hatched patterns at the top of the palette.

- Click on the Pattern arrow and choose one of the colors for the lines of the pattern in the bottom of the palette.

- If you want to clear any background color and pattern, click the No Color button.

5. Click OK.

If you want to remove borders and shading, select the range and choose Edit, Clear, Formats (see Objective 8, "Clear Cell Formats").

101

Modify Size of Rows and Columns

Generally, Excel will automatically make your row height and column width as tall or as wide as necessary to accommodate the size of text or amount of text within the cells. Row height is the vertical size of a row. Column width is the horizontal length of a column. However, if you need to fix the size of a row or column, you can use the mouse or the Format menu options. In addition to fitting the text, you might want to create more white space so the worksheet is not as cluttered.

Row Size

You can change your row height with the mouse or the Format menu.

Move your mouse pointer to the line between row headings and drag the double-headed arrow to manually size the row or double-click to automatically have the entry fit the tallest font.

ScreenTip shows how tall row will be

You can also do the following:

1. Select the rows you want to change by dragging the white cross in the row headings or selecting a range.

2. Click the Format menu and choose Row.

3. Do one of the following:

- If you want to fit the tallest entry, choose <u>A</u>utoFit.

- If you want to manually set how tall the row is,
  choose H<u>e</u>ight, and type a value in points (72 points
  to an inch) in the <u>R</u>ow height text box and click OK.

You can move your mouse pointer to the line between column
headings and drag the double-headed arrow to manually size
the column, or double-click to automatically have the entry fit
the widest entry.

Column Width

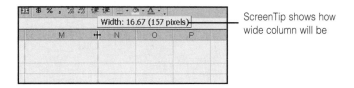

ScreenTip shows how
wide column will be

You can also do the following:

1. Select the columns you want to change by dragging the
white cross in the column headings or selecting a range.

2. Click the F<u>o</u>rmat menu and choose <u>C</u>olumn.

3. Do one of the following:

- If you want to fit the widest entry, choose <u>A</u>utoFit
  Selection.

- If you want to manually set how wide the column is,
  choose <u>W</u>idth, and type the number of characters you
  want (formatted with standard font) in the <u>C</u>olumn
  Width text box. Click OK.

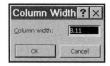

103

- If you want to change the width for all columns not set manually with one of the preceding methods, choose <u>S</u>tandard Width and type the number of characters you want (formatted with the standard font) in the <u>S</u>tandard column width text box. Click OK.

Use the Format Painter

After you format a cell the way you want, you can copy the format (without the contents) to other cells. The format you copy includes font styles, number formatting, and borders and shading.

To copy formats, do the following:

1. Format the cell or range the way you want.

2. Click on the cell that has the format you want.

3. Do one of the following:

- Click once on 🖌 Format Painter if you want to select only one cell or range.

- Click twice on 🖌 Format Painter if you want to select only multiple cells or ranges.

4. Select the cell or range to accept the new format. If you did the second option above, you can select multiple cells or ranges.

5. If you clicked twice in step 3, click once on 🖌 Format Painter to turn it off.

If you want to copy the column width or row height, click on the column or row header, and then click on the Format Painter button, then select the columns or rows to get the new size (see Objective 27, "Modify Size of Rows and Columns").

If you want to copy the formatting of the whole worksheet, click the Select All button above the row numbers and to the left of the column letters and select the worksheet. Then click the Format Painter button and click on the Select All button of another worksheet.

Apply AutoFormat

If you want to choose from several preset formatting options, you can use the AutoFormat feature. Each AutoFormat scheme contains formatting for numbers, text, borders, and shading.

To choose an AutoFormat option, do the following:

1. Position the cell pointer within the range to be formatted.

2. Click the F̲ormat menu and choose A̲utoFormat.

The AutoFormat dialog box displays.

3. If you want to choose only partial formats, click the O̲ptions button and check to apply any or all of the following: N̲umber, F̲ont, A̲lignment, B̲order, P̲atterns, and column and row W̲idth/Height.

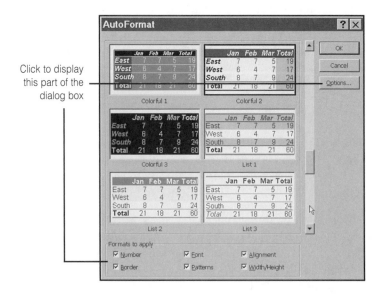

Click to display this part of the dialog box

4. Choose one of the styles in the main part of the dialog box (the last style, None, will remove formatting).

5. Choose OK.

30

Define, Apply, and Remove a Style

Like AutoFormat, styles contain a mixture of font, alignment, border, and pattern formatting. Unlike AutoFormat, styles also contain protection options and you can define and modify your own styles.

Apply a Style

To apply an existing style, do the following:

1. Move to the cell or select the range.

2. Click the Format menu and choose Style.

   The Style dialog box opens.

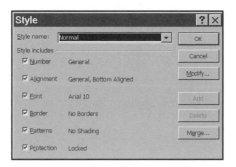

3. Click the Style name arrow and choose one of the styles.

4. The Style dialog box indicates the types of formatting that the style contains. Uncheck any of the options if you don't want to apply with that format.

5. Click OK.

You can also create a style to use later. One of the easier ways is to format a cell first with all the choices you want for the style.

To make a new style, do the following:

1. Format a cell with text, alignment, borders, shading, and other formats you want.

2. Click the Format menu and choose Style.

   The Style dialog box opens.

3. Click in the Style name box and type a new name.

Just below the Style name, the section changes to say Style Includes (By Example).

4. Uncheck any of the formatting options in the lower half of the dialog box that you don't want to include with the style.

5. If you want to change any of the options, click the Modify button to open the Format Cells dialog box and change any of the options as discussed in other sections. Click OK when you're finished.

   - For Number options, see Objective 24, "Apply Number Formats (Currency, Percent, Dates, and Comma)," and Objective 25, "Adjust the Decimal Place."

   - For Alignment options, see Objective 21, "Modify Alignment of Cell Content."

   - For Font options, see Objective 20, "Apply Font Styles (Typeface, Size, Color, and Styles)."

- For Border and Patterns options, see Objective 26, "Apply Cell Borders and Shading."

- For Protection options, see Objective 111, "Apply and Remove Worksheet and Workbook Protection."

6. To create the style, click the <u>A</u>dd button.

**Remove a
Style**

To delete a style you've added (or a predefined style), click the Delete button on the Style dialog box. Do the following:

1. Click the F<u>o</u>rmat menu and choose <u>S</u>tyle.

The Style dialog box opens.

2. Click the <u>S</u>tyle name arrow and choose one of the styles.

3. Click the <u>D</u>elete button.

4. Choose OK.

If you delete the Comma, Currency, or Percent styles, these toolbar buttons no longer work.

TAKE THE TEST

Objectives covered: 20, "Apply Font Styles (Typeface, Size, Color, and Styles)"; 23, "Rotate Text and Change Indents."

Task 1

Open practice file 0301P from the enclosed CD and perform the following actions:

1. Format cell A1 with 18-point Arial MT Black.

2. Bold cells A3, A5, A9, and A13.

3. Italicize A6:A8, A10:A12, and A14:A16.

4. Indent A6:A8, A10:A12, and A14:A16.

Check your work against the solution file 0301S.

Objectives covered: 23, "Rotate Text and Change Indents" (rotate text); 27, "Modify Size of Rows and Columns"; 22, "Merge Cells"; 21, "Modify Alignment of Cell Content."

Task 2

Open practice file 0302P from the enclosed CD and perform the following actions:

1. Rotate B4:N4 so the text has an orientation of 75 degrees.

2. Change the column width of columns B:N to five characters.

3. Center the title in A1 in the range A1:N1.

4. Change the column width of column A to automatically fit the widest entry.

5. Center the range B6:N16.

6. Set the row height of rows 5, 9, and 13 to 24 points.

7. Set the row height of row 2 to 6 points.

8. Set the row height of row 1 to 40 points and center the title vertically.

9. Right-align ranges A6:A8, A10:A12, and A14:A16.

Check your work against the solution file 0302S.

Task 3

Objectives covered: 26, "Apply Cell Borders and Shading"; 20, "Apply Font Styles"; 28, "Use the Format Painter."

Open practice file 0303P from the enclosed CD and perform the following actions:

1. Apply a thick box border around the ranges A5:N8, A9:N12, and A13:N16.

2. Apply blue font color to cells A1 and B4:N4.

3. Change the size of A1 to 12 points.

4. Copy the format of A1 to cells A3, A5, A9, and A13.

5. Add yellow fill color to cells A1:N1, A5:N5, A9:N9, and A13:N13.

6. Apply a pattern that is 50% gray and yellow to the ranges N4, N6:N8, N10:N12, and N14:N16.

Check your work against the solution file 0303S.

Task 4

Objectives covered: 29, "Apply AutoFormat," 24, "Apply Number Formats (Currency, Percent, Dates, and Comma)," 25, "Adjust the Decimal Place," 26, "Apply Cell Borders and Shading," 30, "Define, Apply, and Remove a Style."

Open practice file 0304P from the enclosed CD and perform the following actions:

1. Click in B5 and apply the List 3 AutoFormat to the range.

2. Apply the List 3 AutoFormat to the range surrounding B13.

3. Change the numeric format of B9:F9 and B17:F17 to currency and B5:F8 and B13:F16 to commas. Remove decimal places for all. If necessary, change column widths.

4. Change the numeric format of G6 to percent with one decimal place.

5. Add yellow Fill Color to cell G6.

6. Create a new style based on the formatting in G6 and call the style Yellow Percent. Include the Number and Patterns choices in the style.

7. Apply this Yellow Percent style to the ranges G5:G9 and G13:G17.

8. Type Submitted: in A20, today's date in B20, and format the date in the d-mmm-yyyy format (for example, 3-Jan-2001).

Check your work against the solution file 0304S.

Cheat Sheet

Format Text

Formatting text helps it stand out and organizes the document.

To format text, select a cell, a range, or a portion of text in the Formula Bar and do any of the following:

- **B** Click Bold (Ctrl+B).
- *I* Click Italic (Ctrl+I).
- U Click Underline (Ctrl+U).
- Choose from the Font list.
- Choose from the Font Size list.
- Format, Cells (Ctrl+1), Font tab and make choices.

Text Alignment

Alignment changes the placement of text within a cell:

- Click to Align Left.
- Click to Center.
- Click to Align Right.
- Click Merge and Center to center the text across the selection.
- Format, Cells (Ctrl+1), Alignment tab enables you to center Horizontally and Vertically in the cells, Wrap Text, Shrink to Fit text in the cell, Merge cells into a larger cell, and change the Orientation (rotation) of a text within a cell.
- To add spaces before text in a range of cells, choose Left (Indent) on the Horizontal drop-down of this Alignment tab of the Format Cells dialog box.

Format Numbers

Formatting numbers does not change the value, only the way they display:

- $ Click to add dollar sign and two decimals (Ctrl+Shift+$).
- % Click to multiply by 100 and add percent sign (Ctrl+Shift+%).
- , Click to add commas and two decimals (Ctrl+Shift+!).
- Increase Decimal adds more digits after the decimal point.
- Decrease Decimal removes digits after the decimal point.
- Format, Cells (Ctrl+1) Number tab enables you to format numbers and dates with options for decimal places, negative numbers, currency symbols, date and time digits or words, and custom options.

Borders add lines around a range and shading adds color or degrees of gray to the background of cells:

- Fill Color enables you to choose a color for the range.
- Borders enables you to choose which sides of the range will have lines.
- Format, Cells (Ctrl+1) Border tab enables you to choose the location and style of lines around or in cells.
- Format, Cells (Ctrl+1) Pattern tab enables you to choose the color and hatched pattern for the cell background.

You can increase or decrease the height of rows and the width of columns:

- Drag the double-headed black arrow on a row or column header line to change the size, or double-click to fit the entry.
- When you get the formatting you like, you can copy the formatting from one cell to a range.

Continued

- Select the cell to copy from, click Format Painter, and then select the range to copy the format to.

- AutoFormat enables you to choose from a set of formats at once to a range (Format, AutoFormat).

- Styles also add one or more formats to a range. You can define and modify the formats associated with a style (Format, Style).

Page Setup and Printing

Following is a list of MOUS objectives:

- Preview and Print Worksheets and Workbooks
- Print a Selection
- Set Print and Clear Print Area
- Set Page Margins and Centering
- Change Page Orientation and Scaling
- Set Up Headers and Footers
- Insert and Remove a Page Break
- Set Print Titles and Options (Gridlines, Print Quality, Row and Column Headings)
- Use Web Page Preview

Preview and Print Worksheets and Workbooks

After entering and editing data, printing is probably one of the most-used features of Excel or any application. You can preview your worksheet before you print it to see spacing on the page and where pages will break. After previewing, you can print the worksheet or workbook.

Print Preview

Print Preview enables you to save paper and adjust the way the worksheet will print before you print it. You can use Print Preview to see exactly how the document is laid out for printing, to determine the number of pages the document will be, and to change margins.

To see how a worksheet will look before you print it, follow these steps:

1. Do one of the following:

- Click 🔍 Print Preview.
- Choose the File menu and choose Print Preview.

The window changes to Print Preview.

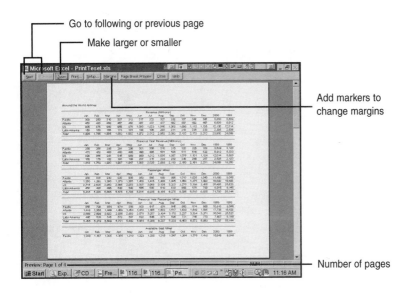

Go to following or previous page

Make larger or smaller

Add markers to change margins

Number of pages

2. While you are in Print Preview, you can do the following:

- See the number of pages on the bottom of the screen.

- Click <u>N</u>ext to move to the following page.

- Click <u>P</u>revious to move to the preceding page.

- Click <u>Z</u>oom or click the magnifying glass mouse pointer to make the screen larger at that part of the screen. Click the <u>Z</u>oom button again or the arrow mouse pointer to return the screen to whole page view.

- Click the <u>P</u>rint button to go to the Print dialog box and print the document.

- Click the <u>S</u>etup button to go to the Page Setup dialog box (see Objectives 33–36 and 38).

- Click <u>M</u>argins and drag the markers to change the margins or the column widths.

Drag to change the column width

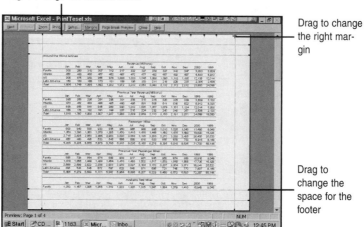

Drag to change the right margin

Drag to change the space for the footer

- Click Page Break Preview to see where the pages will break (see Objective 37, "Insert and Remove a Page Break").

3. When finished with the Print Preview window, click Close.

You can also click the Preview button on the Print dialog box to get to Print Preview.

Print Worksheet

When you are ready to print the active worksheet, follow these steps:

1. Do one of the following:

- Click the 🖨 Print button.
- Press Ctrl+P and click OK.
- Click File, choose Print, and click OK.

The active worksheet prints.

Print Workbook

The workbook includes all the sheets (worksheets and chart sheets) in the file.

To print the workbook, do the following:

1. Press Ctrl+P or click File and choose Print.

2. Click the Entire workbook option.

3. Do one of the following:

- Choose OK to print the workbook now.

- If you want to see a preview of how all the sheets will look, click Preview. Then click Print to return to the Print dialog box and click OK to print.

The other print options on the Print dialog box let you print a number of copies, print specific pages, and choose a printer:

Print Options

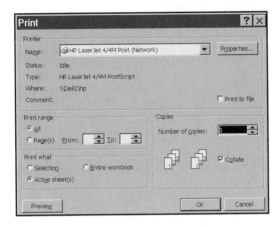

- Click the Name drop-down button to choose a different printer or fax.

- Choose Pages and then type the starting page in the From box and ending page in the To box. You can see these page numbers in Print Preview.

- Type or use the Number of copies increment button to print multiple copies.

- Check Collate to print and organize all pages in the set and then print the pages again if multiple copies are chosen.

When you're finished with these options, click OK.

Print a Selection

In the Print What section of the dialog box you can choose to print the range you have selected.

Do the following:

1. Select the range you want to print by

- Dragging the white cross mouse pointer across the range.

- Holding down the Shift button and using the keyboard keys to select the range.

2. Press Ctrl+P or click File and choose Print.

3. Click the Selection option.

4. Choose OK.

You can also print a selection by setting the print range (see Objective 33, "Set Print and Clear Print Area").

Set Print and Clear Print Area

Instead of using the procedure described in Objective 32 to print the selected area, you may want to set the range so you don't have to choose the range each time.

To set the print area, do the following:

1. Select a range.

2. Click the File menu and choose Prin_t_ Area, and then _S_et Print Area.

File, Print Area

Whenever you click the 🖨 Print button or click the _F_ile menu, choose _P_rint, and click OK the set range prints.

You can also set the print area through the Page Setup dialog box. Do the following:

1. Click _F_ile and choose Page Set_u_p.

2. Click the Sheet tab.

3. Type the range in the Print _a_rea text box or click the Collapse Dialog button to the right of the text box and select the range. Click the button again.

4. Click OK.

File, Page Setup

The Page Setup dialog box is discussed in more detail in Objectives 34–36 and 38.

After you choose either method for setting the print area, click 🖨 Print or choose any of the methods to print the worksheet (see Objective 31, "Preview and Print Worksheets and Workbooks").

Clear Print Area

Regardless of which of the two procedures you used above, you can clear the print area. To remove the print area, click File, choose Print Area, and click Clear Print Area.

Set Page Margins and Centering

Margins are the white space around the edge of the paper. You can set the margins and center the page through the Page Setup dialog box. You can also set margins through Print Preview (see Objective 31, "Preview and Print Worksheets and Workbooks").

To change the margins or center the page through the Page Setup dialog box, do the following:

1. Click <u>F</u>ile and choose Page Set<u>u</u>p.

2. Click the Margins tab.

3. Do any of the following:

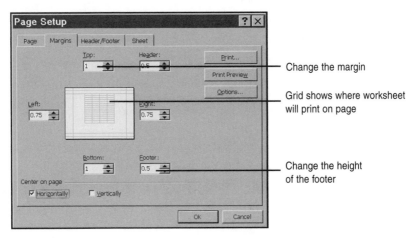

Change the margin

Grid shows where worksheet will print on page

Change the height of the footer

- To change the margins, type in the boxes or use the increment buttons in the Top, Left, Bottom, and Right boxes.

- To change the height of the Header or Footer, type in the box or use the increment buttons.

- To center the document, check Horizontally, Vertically, or both.

4. When finished with the settings, do one of the following:

- Click Print to go to the Print dialog box, and choose OK to print the worksheet with these settings.

- Click Print Preview to see what the document will look like on the page.

- Click OK to save these settings for later.

Change Page Orientation and Scaling

When you need to fit a worksheet on a page you might need to change the orientation—the direction the document prints on the page. To fit the document, you can also change the scaling—the amount the text is shrunk or enlarged.

To change the orientation or scaling, do the following:

1. Click File and choose Page Setup.

2. Click the Page tab.

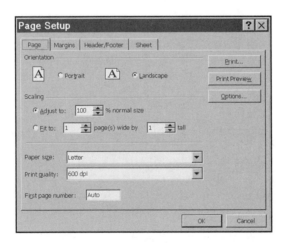

3. Choose to print the document across the long edge of the page (Landscape) or across the short edge of the page (Portrait).

4. If desired, to shrink the text on the document, do one of the following:

- To fit the document on one page click Fit to and leave 1 page(s) wide by 1 tall.

- If you want to size the document to fit on multiple pages, click Fit to and change the number of page(s) wide by and/or the number of pages tall.

- To reduce or enlarge the text, type a number in the Adjust to text box or use the increment buttons. The default, which is 100%, prints the text in the size shown on the worksheet.

5. You can set additional options on the dialog box:

- To change the Paper size, choose from the drop-down list.

- To change the Print quality (printer resolution) if your printer has this option, choose from the drop-down list.

- If you want to change the starting page number, type it in the First page number text box.

6. When finished with the settings, do one of the following:

- Click Print to go to the Print dialog box, and choose OK to print the worksheet with these settings.

- Click Print Preview to see what the document will look like on the page.

- Click OK to save these settings for later.

The Scaling option mentioned earlier changes how the text is magnified or shrunk on a printed page. If you want to change how the text is magnified onscreen, use the Zoom button on the Standard toolbar (see Objective 43, "Change the Zoom Setting").

Set Up Headers and Footers

Headers print at the top of each page, and footers print at the bottom of each page. They are more common in long documents and often contain page numbers and document information such as the filename, author, company, or the word "confidential." See Objective 34, "Set Page Margins and Centering," to change the height of the header or footer.

To add a header or footer, do the following:

1. Click File and choose Page Setup.

2. Click the Header/Footer tab.

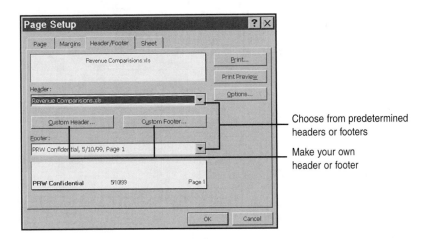

Choose from predetermined headers or footers

Make your own header or footer

3. Do one or more of the following:

- Click the He**a**der drop-down arrow and choose from a list of built-in headers.

- Click the **F**ooter drop-down arrow and choose from a list of built-in footers.

- Click the **C**ustom Header or Cu**s**tom Footer button. Type or use the buttons for the text you want in the **L**eft section, **C**enter section, or **R**ight section of the page. When you click a button, a code appears in the header or footer. For example, the page button enters the &[Page] code. Click OK when you're finished with the Header or Footer dialog box.

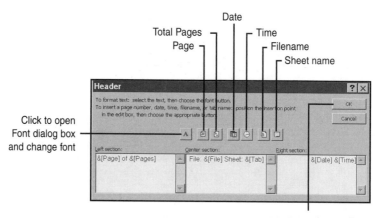

4. When finished with the settings, do one of the following:

- Click **P**rint to go to the Print dialog box, and choose OK to print the worksheet with these settings.

- Click Print Preview to see what the document will look like on the page.

- Click OK to save these settings for later.

To remove a header or footer, return to the Page Setup dialog box (**F**ile, Page Set**u**p, Header/Footer tab) and choose (none) from the He**a**der or **F**ooter drop-down list.

Insert and Remove a Page Break

If you have a worksheet that is multiple pages, the pages might start in awkward spots in the middle of a section. You can set your own page breaks to make each page easier to read. You can use Insert Page Break or Page Break Review to set page breaks.

To set a page break, do the following:

1. First, select Print Preview or Print the worksheet (see Objective 31, "Preview and Print Worksheets and Workbooks"). The automatic page breaks show as dotted lines on the worksheet.

Insert Page Break

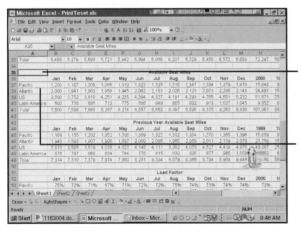

The page break would be more appropriate above row 35 between sections. Position cell pointer in A35 and choose Insert, Page Break.

After previewing, the page break shows in the middle of a section with small dashes

2. Move the cell pointer above or to the left of where the automatic page break is (or at any location where you want the page to break). If you position the cell pointer in the first column or row, you get only one page break. If not, you get both horizontal and vertical page breaks.

3. Click Insert and choose Page Break. Longer dashes show a set page break.

4. After you've set page breaks, click 🖨 Print or choose another method as described in Objective 31, "Preview and Print Worksheets and Workbooks."

To remove the page break, position the cell pointer below the set page break, click Insert, and choose Remove Page Break.

Page Break Preview

You can also set a page break with the Page Break Preview feature. This enables you to see page numbers as well as manually move page break lines.

To use Page Break Preview, do the following:

1. Click View and choose Page Break Preview. The view shrinks to show more of the worksheet and where the current page breaks and page numbers are.

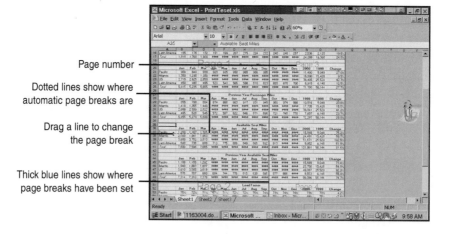

Page number

Dotted lines show where automatic page breaks are

Drag a line to change the page break

Thick blue lines show where page breaks have been set

2. Move the mouse pointer to one of the lines separating a page until you get a double-headed arrow. Drag to change where a page breaks.

3. After you've set page breaks, click 🖾 Print or choose another method as described in Objective 31, "Preview and Print Worksheets and Workbooks."

To return to normal view, choose <u>V</u>iew, <u>N</u>ormal.

Set Print Titles and Options (Gridlines, Print Quality, and Row and Column Headings)

Some of the other setup options enable you to work with larger worksheets, add or remove column and row lines (gridlines) on the worksheet, and determine the printing resolution.

To set additional setup options, do the following:

1. Click File and choose Page Setup.

2. Click the Sheet tab.

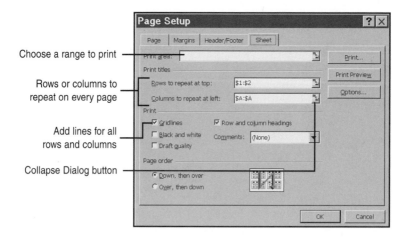

Choose a range to print

Rows or columns to repeat on every page

Add lines for all rows and columns

Collapse Dialog button

3. Do any of the following:

- To choose a range to print, type the range in the Print area text box, or click the Collapse Dialog button, select the range, and click the button again.

- To duplicate text in rows on every page, type a row reference (for example, 1:2) in Rows to repeat at top, or click the Collapse Dialog button, select one or more rows, and click the Collapse Dialog button again.

- To duplicate text in columns on every page, choose Columns to repeat at left or click the Collapse Dialog button, select one or more rows, and click the Collapse Dialog button again.

- To print lines for all columns and rows, check the Gridlines box. If you've added borders to the worksheet, you might want to clear this box.

- To display all colors as either black or white, check Black and white. If this check box is clear, colors will print as shades of gray on a black and white printer.

- To speed up printing and not print most lines and graphics, check Draft quality. With this box unchecked, the print quality will be better but printing will take longer.

- To add column letters and row numbers to the printout, check Row and column headings.

- To print notes you've added to the worksheet, click Comments and choose either to print them At end of sheet or As displayed on sheet (see Objective 110, "Create, Edit, and Remove a Comment").

- To change the order of how multiple pages will print, choose Down, then over or Over, then down.

4. When finished with the settings, do one of the following:

   - Click Print to go to the Print dialog box, and choose OK to print the worksheet with these settings.

   - Click Print Preview to see what the document will look like on the page.

   - Click OK to save these settings for later.

135

Use Web Page Preview

If you are going to convert your worksheet to a Web page (see Objective 18, "Save a Worksheet/Workbook as a Web Page"), you'll probably want to see how the worksheet will look before you go through the process.

To preview how a worksheet will look as a Web page, do the following:

1. Click on the <u>F</u>ile menu and choose We<u>b</u> Page Preview.

   Internet Explorer launches and displays a temporary copy of the worksheet in this Web browser.

Web browser —

Temporary location of file —

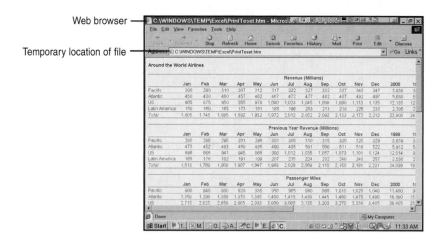

2. If you want to save this document as a Web file, choose <u>F</u>ile, click Save <u>A</u>s, and the Save Web Page dialog box opens. Choose a location in Save <u>i</u>n, type a File <u>n</u>ame, and click <u>S</u>ave.

3. When finished with the Web preview, click the close (×) window button or choose <u>F</u>ile, <u>C</u>lose.

TAKE THE TEST

Objectives covered: 31, "Preview and Print Worksheets and Workbooks, " 34, "Set Page Margins and Centering, " 35, "Change Page Orientation and Scaling," 39, "Use Web Page Preview. "

Open practice file 0401P from the enclosed CD and perform the following actions:

1. Choose the Summary sheet.

2. Do Print Preview and change the orientation to Portrait.

3. Center the printing horizontally and vertically on the page.

4. Change the scaling to 150%.

5. Print the worksheet.

6. Preview this worksheet as a Web page.

Check your work against the solution file 0401S. You will also have to check your printout and Internet browser view.

Objectives covered: 31, "Preview and Print Worksheets and Workbooks," 34, "Set Page Margins and Centering," 36, "Set Up Headers and Footers," 37, "Insert and Remove a Page Break."

Open practice file 0402P from the enclosed CD and perform the following actions:

1. Print the entire workbook and notice where the page breaks fall.

2. Choose the Details sheet.

3. Change the right and left margins so that all columns print across the width of a page.

4. Insert a page break so the page does not break in the middle of a section.

5. Add the word Confidential centered in the footer.

6. Choose a predefined header that shows the name of the sheet and page number.

7. Preview the worksheet to make sure it prints as landscape only on two pages.

Check your work against the solution file 0402S (preview the Detail sheet).

Task 3

Objectives covered: 31, "Preview and Print Worksheets and Workbooks," 32, "Print a Selection," 33, "Set Print and Clear Print Area," 35, "Change Page Orientation and Scaling," 36, "Set Up Headers and Footers," 38, "Set Print Titles and Options (Gridlines, Print Quality, and Row and Column Headings)."

Open practice file 0403P from the enclosed CD and perform the following actions:

1. Change the orientation to Portrait.

2. Add gridlines.

3. Display rows 1–3 on every printed page.

4. Add a footer showing your name in italics.

5. Include the row and column numbers and letters.

6. Preview the worksheet and print it if a printer is available.

7. Select the range A1 through F13 and print just this selection.

8. Set the print range to print only flights 1001–1015.

Check your work against the solution file 0403S.

Cheat Sheet

Preview and Print Worksheets and Workbooks

Click 🖨 Print to print the worksheet with the current settings.

Choose File, Print (Ctrl+P) to open the Print dialog box. Choose to print the current Selection, Active sheet(s), or the Entire Workbook and whether you want All pages or a range From and To a certain set of pages.

Click 🔍 Print Preview to see what the worksheet will look like on a printed page, or choose File, Print Preview.

Print a Selection

To print a specific range, select the range, and choose File, Print (Ctrl+P), and choose Selection.

Set Print and Clear Print Area

To set a range for printing each time, choose File, Print Area, Set Print Area. Then click 🖨 Print. To clear this range, choose File, Print Area, Clear Print Area.

Set Page Margins and Centering

The margin is the space on the edge of the paper where there is no printing.

To set the margins, choose File, Page Setup, click on the Margins tab, and type in the Left, Bottom, Right, Top text boxes. To center between the margins, check Horizontally and/or Vertically.

Change Page Orientation and Scaling

To fit the worksheet to a printed page, choose File, Page Setup, click on the Page tab, and choose Fit to 1 page(s) wide by 1 tall.

Continued

Set Up Headers and Footers

To add text to the top or bottom of every page, choose File, Page Setup, click on the Header/Footer tab, and choose a Header or Footer from the list. Or, choose Custom Header or Customer Footer and click on the buttons or type your own text.

Insert and Remove a Page Break

To force a page to break, move the insertion point to the first row and/or column and choose Insert, Page Break. To remove this break, choose Insert, Remove Page Break. You can also use View, Page Break Preview and drag the lines to set page breaks.

Set Print Titles and Options

To set rows or columns to print on every page of a multiple-page document, choose File, Page Setup, click on the Sheet tab, click on the Collapse Dialog button of Rows to repeat at top or Columns to repeat at left, select the row or columns, and click on the button again.

To print lines for the rows and columns, choose File, Page Setup, click on the Sheet tab, and check Gridlines.

To display the column letters and row numbers when you print, choose File, Page Setup, click on the Sheet tab, and check Row and column headings.

Use Web Page Preview

To see what the worksheet would look like if you saved it as a Web page, choose File, Web Page Preview.

Working with Worksheets and Workbooks

Following is a list of MOUS objectives:

- Insert and Delete Rows and Columns
- Hide and Unhide Rows and Columns
- Freeze and Unfreeze Rows and Columns
- Change the Zoom Setting
- Check Spelling
- Move Between Worksheets in a Workbook
- Rename a Worksheet
- Insert and Delete Worksheets
- Move and Copy Worksheets
- Link Worksheets and Consolidate Data Using 3D References

40

Insert and Delete Rows and Columns

Occasionally, you will want to insert or delete one or more rows or columns. Perhaps you have a new or discontinued product or expense item, so you need to work with rows. Instead of a six-month listing of sales, you are going to expand the worksheet to include 12 months. If you want to insert or delete just a cell or range, see Objective 6, "Insert and Delete Selected Cells."

Insert Rows

The rows you insert will appear above your selection. To insert a row or rows, do the following:

1. To insert a single row, click a row heading number below where you want to insert the new row. If you want to insert multiple rows, select the same number of rows immediately below where you want the new rows to be inserted.

2. Do one of the following:

   • Right-click the row heading and choose Insert.

   • Click the Insert menu and choose Rows.

If you have cells selected instead of rows, you can also right-click the selection, choose Insert, click the Entire row option, and choose OK.

Insert Columns

Inserting columns is almost identical to inserting rows. The columns you insert will appear to the left of your selection. To insert a column or columns, do the following:

1. To insert a single column, click a column heading number to the right of where you want to insert the new column. If you want to insert multiple columns, select the same number of columns immediately to the right of where you want the new columns to be inserted.

2. Do one of the following:

   • Right-click the column heading letter and choose Insert.

   • Click the Insert menu and choose Columns.

If you have cells selected instead of columns, you can also right-click the selection, choose Insert, click the Entire column option, and choose OK.

Delete Rows or Columns

Deleting rows or columns removes them from the worksheet and shifts cells to fill the space where they were. This is different from deleting the contents where the row or column would remain but the cells would be empty (see Objective 5, "Clear Cell Content"). To delete rows or columns, do the following:

1. Select the column heading letters or row heading numbers you want to delete.

2. Do one of the following:

   • Right-click the row or column heading letter and choose Delete.

   • Click the Edit menu and choose Delete.

If you have cells selected instead of rows or columns, you can also right-click the selection, choose Delete, click the Entire row or Entire column option, and choose OK.

143

41

Hide and Unhide Rows and Columns

Instead of deleting rows and columns, you might want to hide them. Hiding removes the information from view but does not delete the data from the workbook. You will see a gap in the row number or column letter sequence.

Hide Rows or Columns

To hide rows or columns, do the following:

1. Select the row heading numbers or column heading letters you want to hide.

2. Do one of the following:

    • Right-click the row or column heading and choose Hide.

    • Click the Format menu, choose Row or Column, and then choose Hide.

    • Press Ctrl+9 to hide rows or Ctrl+0 to hide columns.

Unhide Rows and Columns

The trick to unhiding rows or columns is to select the hidden rows or columns. Because they aren't visible, you must select rows or columns on either side of the hidden area. Do the following:

1. Do one of the following to select rows or columns to unhide:

    • To display hidden rows, select the row heading numbers above and below the hidden area. To display hidden columns, select the column heading letters to the left and right of the hidden area.

- To unhide all rows or columns, click the Select all button to the left of the column headers and above the row headers, or press Ctrl+A.

2. Do one of the following to unhide columns or rows:

   - Right-click the rows or column headings, and choose Unhide.

   - Click the Format menu, choose Row or Column, and then Unhide.

   - Press Ctrl+Shift+((open parenthesis) to unhide rows or Ctrl+Shift+) (close parenthesis) to unhide columns.

Freeze and Unfreeze Rows and Columns

If you have a long worksheet, it might be difficult to decipher what the rows and columns mean when you are scrolling to see the bottom or right end of the range. Often, the labels you need to read are in the first rows or columns that no longer display. To keep these labels visible, you can freeze the rows or columns.

Freeze Rows and Columns

To keep rows and/or columns on the screen when scrolling, do the following:

1. Move the cell pointer below any rows and to the right of any columns you want to freeze.

2. Click the Window menu and choose Freeze Panes.

To unfreeze the rows and columns, click the Window menu and choose Unfreeze Panes.

Split Worksheet

An alternative to freezing the rows or columns is to split the worksheet. Frozen rows and columns remain static on the worksheet, whereas a split worksheet enables you to view different sections of the worksheet side-by-side in separate panes. To split the worksheet, do the following:

1. Move the cell pointer below any rows and to the right of any columns where the split will occur.

2. Click the Window menu and choose Split.

3. Click the mouse pointer in one of the panes and use the scrollbars to move in that pane.

To unsplit the worksheet, click the <u>W</u>indow menu and choose Remove <u>S</u>plit.

You can also split the worksheet by using one of the two split boxes located above the vertical scrollbar or to the right of the horizontal scrollbar. Move the mouse pointer to a split box, and it changes to a double-headed, double-lined pointer. Then drag the split box to where you want the split. While the worksheet is split, you can click each pane or press F6 or Shift+F6 to navigate through the panes. To remove the split, drag the split lines back to the edge of the window.

Change the Zoom Setting

If you can't read your worksheet, you can use zoom to increase the magnification. This only changes the display and not the printing (to magnify the print, see Objective 35, "Change Page Orientation and Scale"). You can also reduce the zoom percentage so you see more of your worksheet at once.

To change the zoom setting, do one of the following:

- Type a value or click the down arrow, and choose a value in the 100% ▼ Zoom box on the Standard toolbar.

- Select a range, click the 100% ▼ Zoom down arrow, and choose Selection to fit the selected range to the screen.

- Click the View menu, and choose Zoom. In the Zoom dialog box, click a percent option, choose Fit Selection, or type a value in the Custom box. Then choose OK.

To return the zoom to normal view, choose 100% in the Zoom box on the standard toolbar or the Zoom dialog box.

Check Spelling

An incorrectly spelled document can distract the reader and undermine your credibility. Before you print and send your workbooks out, check the spelling of each worksheet:

1. Press Ctrl+Home if you want to start at the beginning of the worksheet. If you want to check the entire workbook, go to the first worksheet, hold down Shift, and click the last sheet tab.

2. Do one of the following:

   • Press F7.

   • Click 🔤 Spelling on the Standard toolbar.

   • Click the Tools menu and choose Spelling.

3. If you have any misspelled words, the Spelling dialog box displays. The incorrect word appears at the top of the dialog box beside Not in Dictionary.

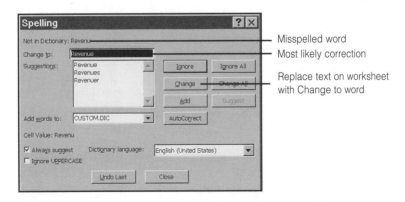

4. Do any of the following to change the settings on what words to check and where words will come from and go to one of the following:

- Check Always suggest to display a list of suggested spellings that are close to what was typed. If this is not checked, click the Suggest button when you want to look up words.

- Check Ignore UPPERCASE to ignore words that are all caps.

- The Add words to drop-down box adds new words to the selected custom dictionary. The spell check will look in the selected custom dictionary and the main dictionary and ignore words found there. To add the word to a new custom dictionary, enter a name for the new dictionary in the Add words to box and click the Add button. To create a list of words for a custom dictionary, use Microsoft Word and press Enter after each new word entry. The new custom dictionary must be saved as a Text only file with a .dic file extension and saved in the file folder containing the main spelling dictionary.

- To use a different language for checking spelling, choose a dictionary language from the Dictionary language drop-down box. To do this, the selected language must have been installed with the Microsoft Office 2000 MultiLanguage Pack.

5. If desired, do either of the following to correct the word:

- Accept or edit the text in the Change to box.

- Click the Suggestions list to select a replacement word.

6. Do any of the following to handle the word displayed by the Not in Dictionary prompt:

- Click Ignore to skip the current occurrence of the word or Ignore All to skip all occurrences of the word in the worksheet.

- Click <u>C</u>hange to replace the current occurrence of the word with the word in the Change <u>t</u>o text box or click Change A<u>l</u>l to replace all occurrences of the word.

- Click <u>A</u>dd to include the word in the dictionary selected in the Add <u>w</u>ords to box. The word will no longer be considered misspelled when you check spelling again for any workbook.

- Click AutoCo<u>r</u>rect to add this word as an AutoCorrect entry. Each time you misspell the word the same way, it will automatically be corrected. To see or modify this list, click <u>T</u>ools and choose <u>A</u>utoCorrect.

7. If you accidentally changed the wrong word, choose <u>U</u>ndo Last.

8. When finished with the spell check, choose Close or Cancel (if you've made no changes).

If you reach the end of the worksheet, you might get a prompt asking if you want to continue checking at the beginning of the sheet or telling you that the spell check is complete for the entire sheet.

The same custom dictionary and AutoCorrect list are used for Word, PowerPoint, and Access.

45

Move Between Worksheets in a Workbook

The sheet tabs on the bottom of the workbook are useful for organizing large amounts of information. You might want to put different time periods or different organizational units on different sheets. When you use multiple worksheets, you can move between them using different methods. To move between worksheets, do one of the following:

- Click the sheet tab if it is visible.

- If the desired sheet tab is not visible, click one of the tab scrolling buttons to the left of the sheet tabs (Top sheet, Previous sheet, Next sheet, Last sheet), and then click one of the sheet tabs. To scroll several sheet tabs at a time, hold down Shift, and click Previous sheet or Next sheet buttons.

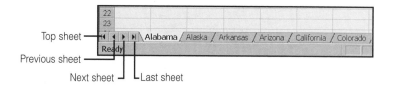

Top sheet ——
Previous sheet ——
Next sheet —┘ └—Last sheet

- To display a list of sheets, right-click a tab scrolling button. Tab scrolling buttons are located to the left of the sheet tabs.

- Press Ctrl+Page Up or Ctrl+Page Down to move to the previous or next sheet.

You can also go to specific areas on the workbook by using <u>G</u>o To (see Objective 2, "Go to a Specific Cell"). In the Name box or Go To dialog box, type the sheet name, an exclamation mark, and the cell reference. For example, click the Name box and type `Arizona!B5` to go to cell B5 on the Arizona sheet.

Rename a Worksheet

The default names for the worksheets are Sheet1, Sheet2, and so on, but you can change the names. When you have multiple worksheets, it is usually easier to navigate and organize your workbook if you name the sheet tabs. To rename a worksheet, follow these steps:

1. Do one of the following:

   - Double-click the sheet tab.

   - Right-click the sheet tab and choose <u>R</u>ename.

   - Click the sheet tab, click the F<u>o</u>rmat menu, choose S<u>h</u>eet, and click <u>R</u>ename.

2. The current name is highlighted. Type the new name over the current sheet tab name.

Insert and Delete Worksheets

The default is for Excel to display three worksheets when you create a new workbook (to change this, click the Tools menu, choose Options, click the General tab, and type the number of sheets you want in the Sheets in new workbook box). If you want to display either more or fewer sheets in the current workbook, you can insert or delete sheets.

To add a new worksheet before the selected worksheets, do the following:

Insert Worksheet

1. If you want to insert multiple worksheets, click the first sheet tab, hold down Shift, and click the number of worksheet tabs you want to add to the workbook. The number of sheet tabs selected indicates the number of new worksheets that will be added.

2. Do one of the following:

   • Right-click a sheet tab, choose Insert, and double-click the Worksheet icon in the Insert dialog box.

   • Click the Insert menu and choose Worksheet.

To remove one or more worksheets, do the following:

Delete Worksheet

1. If you want to remove two or more adjacent worksheets, click the first sheet tab, hold down Shift, and click the tab for the last sheet. To remove two or more nonadjacent worksheets, click the first sheet tab, hold down Ctrl, and click the tabs for the other worksheets.

2. Do one of the following:

- Right-click a sheet tab and choose <u>D</u>elete.

- Click the <u>E</u>dit menu and choose De<u>l</u>ete Sheet.

3. In the prompt asking you to verify that you want to delete the sheets, clickOK.

Move and Copy Worksheets

Sometimes you will want to rearrange your workbook. The sheets might be out of order. You can move and copy these to different locations. However, be careful if you have calculations, charts, or 3D formulas based on worksheet data (see Objective 49, "Link Worksheets and Consolidate Data Using 3D References"). Moving worksheets might cause errors in your data. This is especially true if you move a worksheet at either end of the 3D range.

To drag and drop one or more worksheets, do the following:

Drag and Drop Worksheets

1. If you want to move two or more adjacent worksheets, click the first sheet tab, hold down Shift, and click the sheet tab for the last sheet. To move two or more nonadjacent worksheets, click the first sheet tab, hold down Ctrl, and click the sheet tabs for the other worksheets.

2. Drag the selection or sheet along the sheet tabs. You will see a small triangle where the sheets will go.

3. Release the mouse, and the sheets are in the new location.

If you want to copy a single sheet, hold down Ctrl when you drag. The mouse pointer changes to include a plus sign. The new sheet name will include the original sheet name and a number, so you will probably want to rename the sheet (see Objective 46, "Rename a Worksheet").

**The Move
or Copy
Dialog Box**

You can also move or copy sheets with the shortcut or standard menu. Do the following:

1. If you want to move or copy the sheets to another work-book, open the workbook first.

2. If you want to move or copy two or more adjacent work-sheets, click the first sheet tab, hold down Shift, and click the tab for the last sheet. To move or copy two or more nonadjacent worksheets, click the first sheet tab, hold down Ctrl, and click the tabs for the other worksheets.

3. Do one of the following to display the Move or Copy dialog box:

   • Right-click a selected sheet tab and choose <u>M</u>ove or Copy.

   • Click the Edit menu and choose <u>M</u>ove or Copy Sheet.

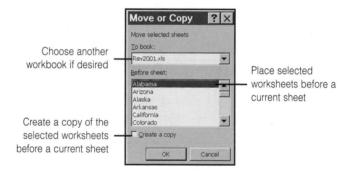

Choose another
workbook if desired

Place selected
worksheets before a
current sheet

Create a copy of the
selected worksheets
before a current sheet

4. To place the selected sheets in another workbook, choose an open workbook from the <u>T</u>o book drop-down list or choose (new book) to create a workbook containing only the copied or moved worksheets.

5. Click the name in the <u>B</u>efore sheet list to choose the loca-tion for the sheets. You can place the moved or copied worksheets before an existing worksheet or select (move to end) to place the worksheets at the end of the open work-book.

6. Check the box if you want to Create a copy of the selected sheets and leave the originals in place. If the box is unchecked, the sheets will be moved.

7. Choose OK.

Link Worksheets and Consolidate Data Using 3D References

When you use multiple worksheets in your workbook, it won't be long before you'll want to create formulas that use references from different sheets or functions that span sheets.

Use Sheet References in a Formula

Using sheet references in a formula isn't much different from using references on the current sheet (see Objective 50, "Enter Formulas in a Cell Using the Formula Bar," and Objective 51, "Enter a Range Within a Formula by Dragging").

To create a formula with a 3D range, do the following:

1. Move to the cell that will contain the formula.

2. Type an equal sign or click the = box on the Formula bar.

3. Click the cell containing the contents to be referenced. If the cell is on a different worksheet, first click the sheet tab and then click the cell containing the contents.

4. Type an arithmetic operator (+, -, *, /, ^).

5. Repeat steps 3 and 4 as many times as necessary.

6. Press Enter or click the Enter button (green check mark) on the Formula bar.

You can also type the references directly in the cell. Use the sheet name first, an exclamation point, and then a cell reference. For example, you can type =Alabama!B5+Alaska!B5. The ! (exclamation point) is an external reference indicator and indicates that the referenced cell is located outside the active worksheet.

If you incorrectly enter the sheet name portion of the cell reference, a File Not Found dialog box will appear. If you incorrectly enter the row and column reference, a #NAME? error message appears in the cell.

While you are creating a function, you can also refer to another worksheet. For example, when you click the AutoSum button, the suggested range is selected. Instead of using the suggested range, click another sheet tab, drag to select the range, and press Enter.

Use 3D References in a Function

If you want the range to span more than one sheet, do the following:

1. Move the cell pointer to the cell where the function is to be placed.

2. Click 𝑓ₓ Paste Function on the Standard toolbar to open the Paste Function dialog box.

3. Choose the Function category and Function name (see Objective 55, "Use Paste Function to Insert a Function") and select OK. The Formula Palette will appear to assist you in building formulas. The Formula Palette displays the name and description of each function, arguments required for the function, and the current result of the function.

4. Type the sheet name and cell reference in each argument box of the Formula Palette, or click the Collapse Dialog Box button and click the desired sheet tab. Then click the cell (or drag the range) you want to select. If you want to span more than one sheet, hold down the Shift key and click the last sheet. When finished, click the Redisplay Dialog Box button.

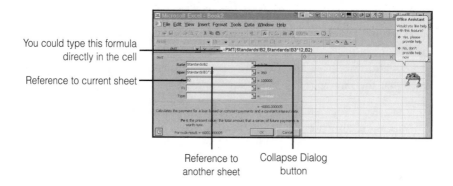

You could type this formula directly in the cell

Reference to current sheet

Reference to another sheet

Collapse Dialog button

5. Repeat step 4 for each argument of the function.

6. Choose OK when you finish.

If you want to type a 3D reference that refers to more than one sheet, type the first sheet name, a colon, the last sheet name, an exclamation mark, and the cell range. An example is =SUM(California:Colorado!B4:F12).

Paste Special

If you want to link to a cell on another sheet, you can also use paste special. Do the following:

1. Select the cell or range to copy on the active worksheet.

2. Click 📋 Copy or choose another method of copying (see Objective 7, "Cut, Copy, Paste, Paste Special and Move Selected Cells, Use the Office Clipboard").

3. Move to the upper-left cell to receive the link on the desired worksheet.

4. Click the Edit menu and choose Paste Special. The Paste Special dialog box opens.

5. Click Paste Link.

TAKE THE TEST

Objectives covered: 40, "Insert and Delete Rows and Columns"; 41, "Hide and Unhide Rows and Columns"; 42, "Freeze and Unfreeze Rows and Columns"; 43, "Change the Zoom Setting."

Task 1

Open practice file 0501P from the enclosed CD and perform the following actions:

1. Select the current region by dragging to select all cells, or press Ctrl+Shift+* (asterisk). Zoom to fit this selection.

2. Unhide all hidden rows and columns.

3. Insert a row, starting in Row 4 (between United States and Alabama), and then insert one every six rows after (between California and Colorado, Florida and Georgia, and so on). The states should be grouped in fives.

4. Delete the rows after Wyoming and Column R.

5. Insert a column before N.

6. Freeze the worksheet so Rows 1 and 2 always show. Scroll to the bottom and scroll to the last column. Notice you cannot read column A.

7. Unfreeze the worksheet and then freeze again so Rows 1 and 2 and Column A always show. Scroll to the bottom to verify.

8. Hide Columns F through I.

Open solution file 0501S from the CD to check your work.

Task 2

Objectives covered: 42, "Freeze and Unfreeze Rows and Columns"; 44, "Check Spelling"; 45, "Move Between Worksheets in a Workbook"; 46, "Rename a Worksheet"; 47, "Insert and Delete Worksheets"; 48, "Move and Copy Worksheets."

Continue with the worksheet from Task 1 or open practice file 0502P from the enclosed CD, and perform the following actions:

1. Spell check the document. Skip any abbreviations in Rows 1 and 2. Spell the state names correctly. Add Colorada as an AutoCorrect entry.

2. Name this sheet Data.

3. Insert a sheet before this one and name it Summary.

4. Copy the Data sheet before Summary, change the name to State Summary, and delete all columns except A (to keep just the state names).

5. Unfreeze the State Summary sheet. Refreeze it at just Rows 1 and 2 (and not Column A).

6. Delete Sheet2 and Sheet3.

7. Reorganize the sheets so they are in the following order: Summary, State Summary, Data.

8. Go to each sheet and view the contents.

Open solution file 0502S from the CD to check your work.

Task 3

Objectives covered: 45, "Move Between Worksheets in a Workbook"; 49, "Link Worksheets and Consolidate Data Using 3D References."

Continue with the preceding worksheet or open practice file 0503P from the enclosed CD, and perform the following actions:

1. On the Summary sheet, type United States in A3, Teachers in B2, Students in C2, and Ratio in D2.

2. Link the values from the Data sheet for Teachers (E3), Students (M3), and Stu/Tea (R3) to the appropriate cells on the Summary sheet (B3, C3, and D3).

3. In B2 of State Summary, type Elementary & Secondary
Students.

4. In B3, create a formula that sums up the two relevant
columns (K and L) on the Data sheet. Copy this formula
for all cells.

5. Format the worksheets as desired.

Open solution file 0503S from the CD to check your work.

Cheat Sheet

Insert and Delete Rows and Columns

Inserting and deleting rows and columns helps you quickly add space for or get rid of extra data.

Select one or more rows or columns, right-click a row or column header, and choose Insert or Delete.

Hide and Unhide Rows and Columns

Hiding rows and columns helps you organize a large worksheet.

To not display a row or column, right-click the header and choose Hide from the shortcut menu.

To redisplay all rows and columns, press Ctrl+A to select the entire worksheet and choose Format, Column, Unhide and Format, Row, Unhide.

Freeze and Unfreeze Rows and Columns

Freezing rows and columns helps you view a large worksheet.

To freeze rows and columns in place, position the cell pointer below the rows to freeze and to the right of columns, and choose Window, Freeze Panes.

To remove the panes, choose Window, Unfreeze Panes.

Change the Zoom Setting

To magnify the view of the worksheet so the text is larger or to shrink it so you can see more cells, use the zoom feature.

`100%` Choose View, Zoom and make a choice on the dialog box.

To see all the selected text, click the down arrow on the Zoom box and choose Selection.

Check Spelling

Spell check can help correct spelling errors in your work.

🔤 Press F7 or choose Tools, Spelling. Choose Ignore to skip the incorrectly spelled word, Change to replace the word, Add to insert the word into the dictionary, or AutoCorrect to replace the word every time you type it incorrectly.

Move Between Worksheets in a Workbook

To select a worksheet, click the tab. If the sheet is not visible, use the tab scrolling buttons to the left of the sheet tabs.

Rename a Worksheet

To rename a worksheet, double-click the tab and type the new name over the current name.

Insert and Delete Worksheets

To insert or delete a sheet, right-click the sheet tab and choose Insert or Delete.

Move and Copy Worksheets

To move a sheet within the current workbook, drag the sheet along the row of sheet tabs to the new location.

To move a worksheet to another workbook, open the workbook that will be receiving the data. Then right-click the sheet tab of the worksheet you want to move, and choose Move or Copy from the shortcut menu. Select the desired To book and Before sheet locations. Click OK.

To copy a sheet, right-click the worksheet tab and choose Move or Copy from the shortcut menu. Select the Before sheet location, and check the Create a copy box. Click OK.

Continued

Link Worksheets and Consolidate Data Using 3D References

You can link a cell on one sheet to a formula or function on another sheet.

Type = in the receiving cell, click the worksheet tab, move to the cell containing the data to be linked, and then press Enter.

Use the f_x Paste Function button to open the Paste Function dialog box. Select a Function category and Function name, and then click OK. The Formula Palette box will automatically open. Use the referenced data in the argument boxes or click the Collapse Dialog button, then click the desired worksheet tab, and select the desired cells or range. Click the Redisplay Dialog Box button, and then click OK.

You can also type a reference to a cell on another sheet by preceding the cell reference with a sheet or sheet range (Sheet1!A1 or Sheet1:Sheet3!A1:A3).

Working with Formulas and Functions

Following is a list of MOUS objectives:

- Enter Formulas in a Cell and Use the Formula Bar
- Enter a Range Within a Formula by Dragging
- Revise Formulas
- Use References (Absolute and Relative)
- Use AutoSum
- Use Paste Function to Insert a Function
- Enter Functions Using the Formula Palette
- Use Basic Functions (AVERAGE, SUM, COUNT, MIN, MAX)
- Use Date Functions (NOW and DATE)
- Use Financial Functions (FV and PMT)
- Use Logical Functions (IF)

Enter Formulas in a Cell and Use the Formula Bar

Creating and using formulas are probably two of the key reasons for using Excel. Formulas enable you to quickly perform numeric calculations and can contain cell addresses or ranges. This is called cell referencing. If you use cell references within a formula and the value in a cell changes, any formula containing that cell reference will automatically recalculate.

Create Formula

To enter a formula in a cell or Formula bar, do the following:

1. Move the active cell pointer to the location where you want the formula result to go.

2. Do one of the following:

   • Type = (equal sign) to indicate the beginning of a formula in a cell.

   • Click ▣ Edit Formula to type in the Formula bar.

3. If needed, type an (opening parenthesis.

4. Type a cell reference or number.

5. Type one of the following operators:

   • + (plus) for addition

   • - (minus) for subtraction

   • * (asterisk) for multiplication

- / (slash) for division
- ^ (caret) for exponentiation (or power of—2^3 means 2*2*2, or 8)

6. Type another cell reference or number.

7. If needed, type a) closing parenthesis.

8. Repeat Steps 3–7 as needed.

9. Do one of the following to complete the formula:

- Press Enter.
- Press Tab or an arrow key to move to another cell.
- Click ✓ Enter.
- If you don't want to enter your formula, press Esc or click ✗ Cancel.

To edit formulas, see Objective 52, "Revise Formulas."

You can type an entire function in the cell as well. For example, you can type =SUM(B3:B30). See Objective 57, "Use Basic Functions (AVERAGE, SUM, COUNT, MIN, MAX)," later in the chapter.

If you make a mistake when typing a formula, you might get an error value such as #NAME?. To interpret the errors and suggestions for fixing them, see Objective 90, "Trace Errors (Find and Fix Errors)."

Order of Preference

In the preceding listed steps, Excel calculates the formula based on an order of precedence and not just left to right. Excel calculates a formula based on the following order of evaluation:

- ( )—Operations inside parentheses are calculated first.
- ^—Exponentiation.

- * /—Multiplication and division.
- + -—Addition and subtraction.

The formula =2+3*2 would evaluate 3*2 first (=6) and then add 2. The total would be 8. If you wanted to add 2 and 3 first and then multiply the sum by 2, change the formula to =(2+3)*2. The result would be 10.

Enter a Range Within a Formula by Dragging

You can also enter a formula by selecting cells with your mouse as you type. This is sometimes easier, and you can verify the cell reference as you click each cell.

To create a formula by using the cell pointer, follow these steps:

1. Move the active cell pointer to the location where you want the formula result to go.

2. Do one of the following:

- Type = (equal sign) to begin typing in a cell.

- Click ▣ Edit Formula to type in the Formula bar.

3. Click a cell or type a number.

A marquee goes around the cell you click, and the cell reference is entered in the active cell and the Formula bar.

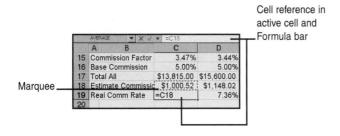

Cell reference in active cell and Formula bar

Marquee

4. Type an operator (+, -, *, /, or ^).

5. Click another cell or type a number.

6. Repeat Steps 3–5 as needed.

7. Do one of the following to complete the formula:

- Press Enter.

- Press Tab or an arrow key to move to another cell.

- Click ✓ Enter.

- If you don't want to enter your formula, press Esc or click ✗ Cancel.

When you create a function, you can type the beginning part of the function =AVERAGE(and then either drag the mouse pointer to select the range or move the mouse pointer with an arrow key, press the . (period) key to anchor the range, use another arrow to finish the range, and press Enter to complete the formula (see Objective 57, "Use Basic Functions (AVERAGE, SUM, COUNT, MIN, MAX)").

Revise Formulas

Revising a formula is similar to editing a cell (see Objective 3, "Edit Cell Content"). The rules for editing a formula are the same, including typing an equal sign first, order of precedence, and having proper cell references.

To edit a cell formula, follow these steps:

1. Move to the cell to be edited.

2. Do one of the following:

   - Click the Formula bar with the I-beam mouse pointer to place the insertion point.

   - Double-click the cell to place the insertion point within the cell.

   - Press F2.

   Each cell reference (or range) in the formula is highlighted in a different color on the worksheet as well as in the Formula bar or cell.

Cell reference
and cell outline
is one color

Drag white
arrow to change
reference

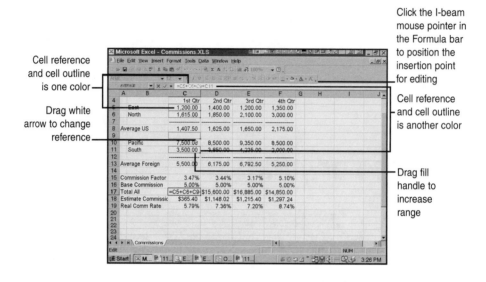

Click the I-beam
mouse pointer in
the Formula bar
to position the
insertion point
for editing

Cell reference
and cell outline
is another color

Drag fill
handle to
increase
range

3. Do one or more of the following:

- With the white arrow mouse pointer, drag the outline of one of the colored cells on the worksheet to a new location.

- If the reference is a range, drag the black plus mouse pointer from the bottom-right corner of the range to contract or expand the range.

- Drag the mouse pointer across text in the Formula bar or cell to select it.

- Press Backspace to delete selected text or characters before the insertion point.

- Press Delete to delete selected text or characters after the insertion point.

- Type characters to replace any selected text and insert the new characters.

4. Then perform one of the following:

- Click ![checkmark] or press Enter or Tab to complete the correction.

- Click ⊟ or press Esc to cancel the changes you made.

If the entire cell contents need to be replaced, you can also move to the cell and start typing. When you press Enter or Tab, the new entry replaces the old.

177

Use References (Absolute and Relative)

Relative References (Default)

When you copy a formula or drag the fill handle from one cell to one or more cells, the cell references that are in the new formula change to reflect the new location of the formula. The change in the formula's cell references depends on the new location of the formula. See Objective 7, "Cut, Copy, Paste, Paste Special and Move Selected Cells, Use the Office Clipboard." For example, if you have the formula =C5+C6 and copy this formula over one column, the formula changes to =D5+D6. This is called *relative referencing*.

Absolute References

If you want a cell reference within a formula to remain constant no matter where you copy or move it, you make the reference absolute by adding dollar signs in front of the column and row reference. If the formula =$C$5+C6 were copied one cell to the right and one down, the copied formula would be =$C$5+D7.

To make a cell reference absolute, do one of the following:

- When you're typing a cell reference or after you click a cell, you can press F4 (Absolute) to change a reference from relative to absolute.

- After you create a formula and are editing in the Formula bar or cell (see Objective 52, "Revise Formulas"), click the I-beam mouse pointer on a cell reference, and press F4 or type dollar signs in front of the column and row reference (or a range name).

A cell reference in a formula can contain both relative and absolute references. This means that either the column or the row part of the cell reference changes, whereas the other part remains constant. For example, C5 in the formula =C$5+C6 is a mixed reference. When you copy the formula over one and down one, the new formula is =D$5+D7.

To make a cell reference mixed, type a dollar sign in front of the column or row reference or click the I-beam in the middle of the cell reference and press F4 until the reference looks like you want it. F4 cycles through the options: absolute ($C$5); column relative, row absolute (C$5); column absolute, row relative ($C5); and relative (C5).

54

Use AutoSum

Instead of adding numerous cells together, AutoSum enables you to quickly total a range of cells together. You can use AutoSum in a single cell, a row or column of cells, and in a range.

One Cell

To use AutoSum, follow these steps:

1. Move the active cell to the location that will have the formula. Usually, this will be below a column of numbers or to the right of a row of numbers.

2. Do one of the following:

   • Click ∑ AutoSum.

   • Press Alt+= (equal sign).

   Excel might suggest a range of numbers by displaying a marquee (blinking dotted line).

   Excel automatically adds an = (equal sign), SUM, and an open and close parentheses around the range.

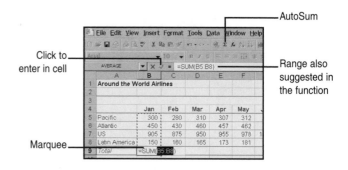

AutoSum

Click to enter in cell

Range also suggested in the function

Marquee

3. If the range is not correct or doesn't display, drag the mouse pointer to select the range or type in a cell reference.

4. If you want the selected cells, press Enter or click ☑.

You can copy the formula to other cells in the row or column or use the fill handle. See Objective 7, "Cut, Copy, Paste, Paste Special and Move Selected Cells, Use the Office Clipboard," and Objective 10, "Work with Series (AutoFill)."

You can create more than one Sum formula with AutoSum. Select the row below or the column to the right of data and click Σ AutoSum.

Row or Column Selected

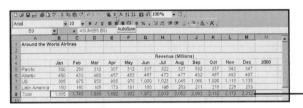

After the row is selected, just one click of AutoSum creates these 12 formulas

---

You can create both row and column sums if your range is in a rectangle. Select the data, a blank row below, and a blank column to the right, and click Σ AutoSum.

Range Selected

Click AutoSum

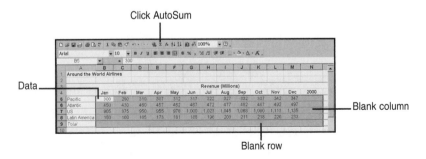

Data

Blank column

Blank row

Use Paste Function to Insert a Function

The AutoSum button enables you to create a SUM function quickly with the equal sign, the name of the function, and parentheses around a range. To create other functions, you can type them in a cell or use the Paste Function dialog box to find the function and a description.

To create a function with Paste Function, do the following:

1. Move the active cell pointer to the cell that will contain the function.

2. Do one of the following to display the Paste Function dialog box:

   • Click 𝒇ₓ Paste Function.

   • Click the Insert menu and choose Function.

   • Press Shift+F3.

3. Choose a Function Category and a Function Name. The Most Recently Used category enables you to choose from functions you use often. Choose All if you don't know the category. A short description at the bottom of the dialog box describes the selected function.

   If you want more detailed help on the function selected in the Function Name box, click the Help button to open the Office Assistant, and choose Help with This Feature and then Help on Selected Function.

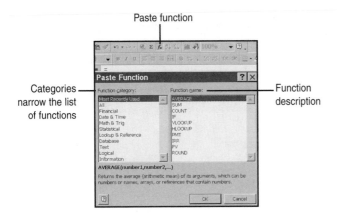

Paste function

Categories
narrow the list
of functions

Function
description

4. Click OK. The Formula Palette opens.

The Formula Palette displays the arguments that the function needs (the items that go between the parentheses). Required arguments are in bold. Nonbolded arguments are optional.

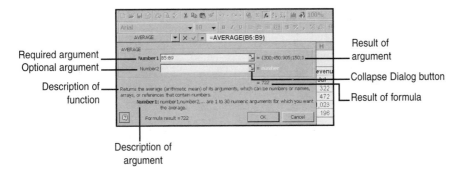

Required argument

Optional argument

Description of
function

Result of
argument

Collapse Dialog button

Result of formula

Description of
argument

5. Fill in each argument in one of the following ways after you move to the text box:

- If the cells are visible onscreen, drag to select them.

- Type a cell address, cell range, or a range name.

- Press F3 and select from a list of range names (see Objective 81, "Use a Named Range in a Formula").

183

- Click the Collapse Dialog button; select the range on the worksheet, a different sheet in the same workbook, or a different workbook. When you finish, click the Redisplay Dialog button.

6. Repeat Step 5 for any arguments you are using, and choose OK when finished.

Enter Functions Using the Formula Palette

In addition to using the Paste Function dialog box to enter the Formula Palette, you can enter it directly through a shortcut key and the most recently used function drop-down list on the Formula bar. The Formula Palette has text boxes for each argument (input) of the function, as well as a description of the arguments and the function.

To enter a function through the Formula Palette, do the following:

1. Click ▣ Edit Formula or type = (equal sign).

2. Click the drop-down list on the left edge of the Formula bar.

List of most recently
used functions

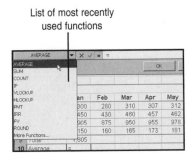

3. Choose one of the functions in the list or select More Functions to go to the Paste Function dialog box (see Objective 55, "Use Paste Function to Insert a Function").

4. The Formula Palette opens, displaying the arguments for the function.

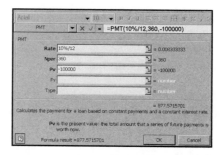

Fill in each argument in one of the following ways after you move to the text box:

- If the cells are visible onscreen, drag to select them.

- Type a cell address, cell range, or a range name.

- Press F3 and select from a list of range names (see Objective 81, "Use a Named Range in a Formula").

- Click the Collapse Dialog button, select the range, and click the Redisplay Dialog button.

5. Repeat Step 4 for any arguments you are using, and choose OK when you finish.

You can also type an equal sign and the function name (for example, =AVERAGE) and press Ctrl+A to display the Formula Palette. Continue with Step 4 in the preceding list.

Use Basic Functions *(AVERAGE, SUM, COUNT, MIN, MAX)*

The most common functions you will probably use are SUM, AVERAGE, COUNT, MIN, and MAX. As with all functions, they require an equal sign, a function name, and parentheses.

Arguments

These functions also require at least one value in parentheses. If you have multiple items that you are totaling, you can separate them with commas.

The items in parentheses can include any of the following:

- A range that is one or more cells (this is the most common).

- Multiple ranges (for example, =MAX(B5:B10, B12:B17, B19:B33).

- An expression =SUM(2*5,3+2,4*B3). In this case, SUM would add these three expressions.

- A number or set of numbers =AVERAGE(3,4,5) would return 4.

- A combination of any of the preceding.

SUM

As seen previously (Objective 54, "Use AutoSum"), you can enter SUM with the AutoSum button. The SUM function is the most common of all functions and calculates the total of the arguments in the parentheses.

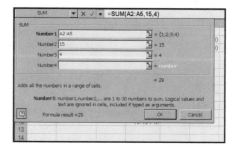

AVERAGE

AVERAGE totals all the items in a list and divides by the number of items in the list. If a cell is blank or contains text, it is ignored and not included in the total or the number of items.

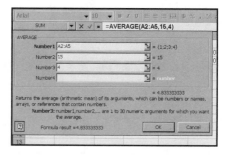

COUNT and COUNTA

COUNT tallies all numbers in the list and gives the number of nontext items.

COUNTA tallies all items in the list and gives the number of numeric and text items.

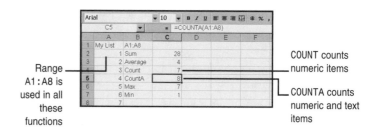

Range A1:A8 is used in all these functions

COUNT counts numeric items

COUNTA counts numeric and text items

MAX returns the largest value among the arguments in a list.   **MAX**

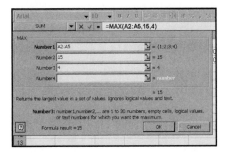

MIN returns the smallest value among the arguments in a list,   **MIN**
ignoring labels and blank cells.

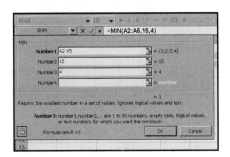

Use Date Functions (*NOW and DATE*)

You might want to use today's date in a worksheet. An example would be if you were finding the number of days since an invoice was mailed. The formula would be today's date minus the invoice date.

NOW and

TODAY

If you want to calculate the current date and time (that is set on your computer's clock), use =NOW(). If you want to include just the date, use =TODAY(). You do not include any arguments in the parentheses.

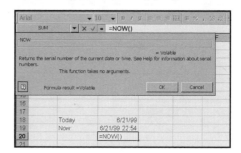

When you open the worksheet, recalculate (with F9), or add to or edit the workbook, NOW and TODAY redisplay the current date and time.

If you want to date-stamp your worksheet with today's date and you don't want it to change, press Ctrl+; (semicolon). If you want to time-stamp with the current time, press Ctrl+Shift+: (colon).

The DATE function returns a number that represents a date. In Excel, the date system starts with 1900 (in Excel for the Macintosh it is 1904). You can use years up to 9999. The DATE function requires three integer arguments (Year, Month, and Day). If the number is not formatted as a date, it will look strange. =DATE(2000,1,1) evaluates to 36526 (the number of days since January 1, 1900). However, when formatted as a date it can look more meaningful (1/1/2000). To format cells, see Objective 24, "Apply Number Formats (Currency, Percent, Dates, and Comma)."

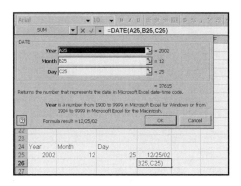

Use Financial Functions (FV and PMT)

The financial functions help make decisions regarding borrowing and lending money. They deal with interest rates and time.

Financial Function arguments

The arguments that you'll see in many of the financial functions include the following:

- Rate—This is the interest rate and usually is expressed in the same time frame that the other arguments or function deal with. Usually, payments are calculated monthly, so the annual rate would be divided by 12.

- Nper—This is the length of the loan (term) and is expressed in the number of payments. Because monthly payments are usually dealt with and the term is often expressed in years, you multiply years times 12.

- PV—Present value is the current value or lump sum amount of the loan.

- FV—Future value is the value of the investment after the term is up at the interest rate calculated.

- PMT—A periodic repeating payment for an amount borrowed.

FV

Future value is generally used to calculate the future value of an investment based on recurring, periodic payments at an unvarying rate of interest. In the example in the figure, if you save $100.00/month for 5 years with an interest rate of 10 percent, you will have $7,743.71 at the end of the period. If you started the investment off with $10,000.00, you would have $24,196.80 at the end of five years.

Rate /12 =
monthly rate

Rate*12 =
number of months

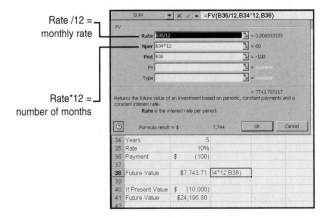

FV requires that you enter the interest rate, number of payment periods, and the periodic payment amount. You can optionally include a PV (present value or starting amount) argument and a Type argument indicating whether you are going to pay the amount at the beginning of each period (1) or the end of each period (0 or blank).

The sign for FV and PMT are opposites (one is a positive number and the other is negative). You can think of it this way—the money for PMTs is going out of your pocket until you get the FV back into your pocket.

PMT

The payment function enables you to calculate the periodic payment amount for a loan on a car, a house, or any other item, based on constant payments and a constant interest rate.

PMT requires that you enter the interest rate, number of periods (length of the loan), and PV (present value, the amount you are borrowing or lending). You can optionally have a future value (cash balance at the end of the loan) and type value (1 if you pay at beginning of period or 0 if you pay at the end of the period).

The sign for PV and PMT are also opposites (one is a positive number and the other is negative). The way to remember is that the money you get for the loan (PV) is going into your pocket, and the money for the PMTs are going out of your pocket.

Use Logical Functions (IF)

The IF function enables you to create a test condition. If the condition is true, you can display one value. If the condition is false, you can display a different value.

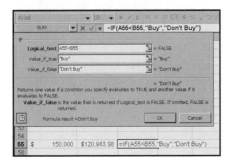

IF requires three arguments:

- **The condition**—Examples are X>35000 and B5<=B6. You can have a condition operator between two values. The condition operators include = (equal to), > (greater than), < (less than), >= (greater than or equal to), <= (less than or equal to), and <> (not equal to).

- **An action to take or value to return if the condition is true**—This can be a value or label. If you want to enter text, include it in quotes.

  For example, =IF (B5>10000,"Bonus","No Bonus").

- **An action to take or value to return if the condition is false**—This can also be a value or label. In the preceding example, if B5 is less than or equal to 10000, No Bonus would be entered in the cell.

Nested Ifs

You can have one function nested inside another one. This is sometimes true of IF functions. In the first argument, you'll test a condition. The second or third arguments, the value if true or false, could have another IF statement. To create this, when you are in the Argument text box for the true or false value, click the function list, choose another function (such as another IF), and continue with that Formula Palette. After you are done with the internal function, you will be returned to the external function.

Current IF function is the argument for the true value for the
First IF function   first function

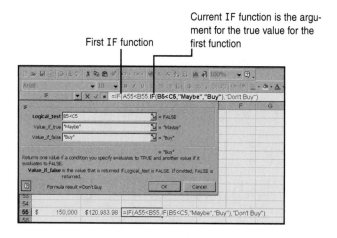

TAKE THE TEST

Objectives covered: 54, "Use AutoSum"; 55, "Use Paste Function to Insert a Function"; 56, "Enter Functions Using the Formula Palette"; 57, "Use Basic Functions (AVERAGE, SUM, COUNT, MIN, MAX)"; 59, "Use Financial Functions (FV and PMT)"; 60, "Use Logical Functions (IF)."

Open practice file 0601P from the enclosed CD, and perform the following actions:

1. Use AutoSum to create the sum of the divisions in Rows 9, 18, and 27 and in Column N.

2. Use Paste Function to create averages for the divisions in Row 10.

3. Use the Function Palette to create averages for the divisions in Rows 19 and 28.

4. Load Factor is Passenger Miles divided by Available Seat Miles. Figure the Load Factor for each of the cells in B32 through O36.

5. If there is no Available Seat Miles, you get an error in the Load Factors; create a formula that says if Available Seat Miles is 0, then put 0 for the Load Factor. Otherwise figure the Load Factor as normal.

6. In Column P, figure the percentage change between 1999 and 2000. (Hint: Figure the difference between 2000 and 1999, and divide this by 1999.)

Check your work against the solution file 0601S.

Task 2

Objectives covered: 54, "Use AutoSum"; 55, "Use Paste Function to Insert a Function"; 57, "Use Basic Functions (AVERAGE, SUM, COUNT, MIN, MAX)"; 58, "Use Date Functions (NOW and DATE)."

Open practice file 0602P from the enclosed CD, and perform the following actions:

1. In C5 show the sum of A5 through A12.

2. In C6 show the average of this range.

3. In C7 show the count of all the numbers, and in C8 show the count of all items (including text).

4. In C9 show the maximum, and in C10 show the minimum.

5. In B1 enter a formula that will automatically put in whatever the date is.

6. In B2 enter a formula that will automatically put in whatever the current time is.

Check your work against the solution file 0602S.

Task 3

Objectives covered: 50, "Enter Formulas in a Cell and Use the Formula Bar"; 51, "Enter a Range Within a Formula by Dragging"; 52, "Revise Formulas."

Open practice file 0603P from the enclosed CD, and perform the following actions:

1. Type =B4+B5 in B6. In C6 type =C4+C5.

2. Use the pointing method to create a formula in B10 to multiply B8 by B9. Do the same in C10 to multiply C8 by C9.

3. In B12 multiply B9 by B6. In C12 multiply C9 by C6.

4. In B14 subtract B12 from B10. In C14 subtract C12 from C10.

5. In B15 divide B9 into B14. In C15 divide C9 into C14.

6. In B17 edit the formula to read B8 instead of B9. In C17 edit the formula to read C8 instead of C9.

Check your work against the solution file 0603S.

Objectives covered: 53, "Use References (Absolute and Relative)"; 54, "Use AutoSum"; 58, "Use Date Functions (NOW and DATE)"; 59, "Use Financial Functions (FV and PMT)."

Task 4

Open practice file 0604P from the enclosed CD, and perform the following actions:

1. In B9 find the total of B4 through B8. In C9 find the total of C4 through C8.

2. Create a formula in C4 that divides B4 by B9 so that when you copy the formula, B9 remains constant. Copy the formula in C4 to C8.

3. The loan amount is in B9, the number of years is in B11, and the annual interest rate is in B12. Figure what the monthly payments should be in B13.

4. Find the future value of an investment in B19 with a three-year term in B16, an annual interest rate in B17, and an annual payment amount in B18.

5. In B25 find the date if the year is in B22, the month is in B23, and the day is in B24.

Check your work against the solution file 0604S.

Cheat Sheet

Enter Formulas in a Cell and Use the Formula Bar

Formulas enable you to create calculations for your data.

Type a formula by starting with an equal sign and typing the cell references, operators, and numbers you need.

Operators include + (addition), - (subtraction), * (multiplication), and / (division).

Enter a Range Within a Formula by Dragging

Begin a formula with an equal sign. When you want to include a cell, click it. When you need a range, drag the range.

Revise Formulas

To edit a formula, double-click the cell, press F2, or click the Formula bar.

Select text, type new text, and press Backspace and Delete while in edit mode.

In edit mode, you can drag the colored outlines surrounding a range or extend the range using the fill handle.

Use References (Absolute and Relative)

Relative referencing means that when a formula is copied, the cell references in the formula adjust to their new location.

Absolute referencing means that when a formula is copied, a cell reference remains constant.

To make a cell reference absolute, place $ (dollar signs) before the column letter and row number. You can also press F4 while building or editing the formula.

Use AutoSum

AutoSum enables you to quickly total one or more columns and rows of data.

Continued

Position the cell pointer in the cell to receive the total or highlight where the totals will go, and click [ic:276] AutoSum or press Alt+= (equal sign).

Use Paste Function to Insert a Function

There are many functions to use to speed up calculation of your data.

fx To choose a function, select Insert, Function (Shift+F3).

Enter Functions Using the Formula Palette

After you choose a function, you enter the Formula Palette, which describes the function and has text boxes for arguments required in the function.

Use Basic Functions (AVERAGE, SUM, COUNT, MIN, MAX)

The basic functions start with an (=) equal sign, followed by the name of the function, and then generally a range within parentheses.

AVERAGE totals the values in the range and divides by the number of items.

SUM totals the values in the range.

COUNT gives the number of numeric items in a range.

MIN gives the smallest number in the range.

MAX gives the largest number in the range.

Use Date Functions (NOW and DATE)

=NOW() will put the current day and time in the cell.

DATE requires three arguments (the year, the month, and the day) and will calculate a date value.

Use Financial Functions (FV and PMT)

Financial functions generally deal with the time value of money and need the interest rate, number of payments, loan or investment amount, and payment amount.

Continued

Make sure all time periods are the same (usually monthly or annually).

FV (future value) calculates the value of an investment given periodic payments, an interest rate, and a term.

PMT (payment) finds how much money you'll have to pay if you borrow a certain amount at an interest rate and term.

Use Logical Functions (IF)

IF enables you to look at a condition and place one result in the cell if the condition is true and another answer if the condition is false.

Using Charts and Objects

Following is a list of MOUS objectives:

- Use Chart Wizard to Create a Chart
- Modify Charts
- Insert, Move, and Delete an Object (Picture)
- Create and Modify Lines and Objects
- Preview and Print Charts

Use Chart Wizard to Create a Chart

Charts enable you to graphically display your data. You or your audience might see patterns that are not evident when you're looking at the raw data. You can create many different kinds of charts, from simple line charts and pie charts to bubbles and pyramids.

Quick Chart (F11)

The quickest way to create a chart is with the F11 function key. Do the following:

1. Position your cell pointer in your data.

2. Press F11 or Alt+F1.

A default chart is created on a new sheet. To modify the chart, see Objective 62, "Modify Charts."

Chart Wizard

The Chart Wizard leads you through chart creation and helps you pick chart settings including data location, type of chart, titles, legends, and other information.

To use the Chart Wizard, follow these steps:

Begin Chart

1. Select the data for the chart through one of the following methods:

   • Drag the mouse over the range that will include the x-axis labels, legend, and data. Generally, you do not include year or company totals if you're including monthly or division data.

- Hold down the Shift key and use the arrow keys to select the range.

- Select the first range, hold down the Ctrl key, and drag to select additional noncontiguous ranges.

2. Click ▥ or click the Insert menu and choose Chart.

3. Choose Chart Type.

4. The Chart Wizard opens.

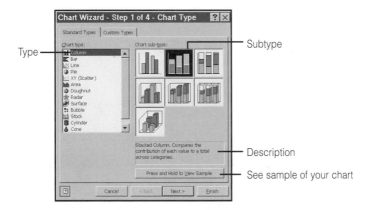

Do one of the following to select the kind of chart you want:

- Click the Standard Types tab. In the Chart Type list, select the basic type of chart you want and then select the Chart sub-type.

- For other, less common types of charts, click the Custom Types tab. Click User-defined or Built-in and choose from the Chart Type list.

When you choose a Chart Type, a sample of the chart displays and a description of the chart type or subtype appears.

5. If desired, hold the mouse button down on Press and Hold to View Sample to see what your data will look like in the chart type.

6. Choose Data Source.

7. Choose Next to go to the second step of the wizard. The Data Range tab indicates the data you selected. Generally, the first row you selected will be the x-axis labels, and the first column will be the legend labels for each bar, line, or other item on the chart. The second row and each row after are the data series (values for the lines, bars, or other chart types).

If you selected the wrong range, you can type a new Data Range or use the Collapse Dialog button to select a new range.

If the data does not look correct, you might need to change the option to plot the data series from the rows or columns. Click Columns rather than Rows if the data series values are vertical rather than horizontal in the range.

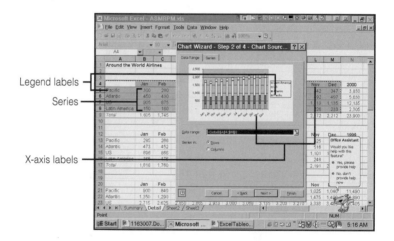

8. If necessary, click the Series tab to change the range for each series of data or the legends. Do one or more of the following if part of the data range is incorrect:

- If the x-axis labels are incorrect or missing, choose Category (X) Axis Labels and type a new range. Alternatively, use the Collapse Dialog button and select the desired cells in the worksheet.

Series label

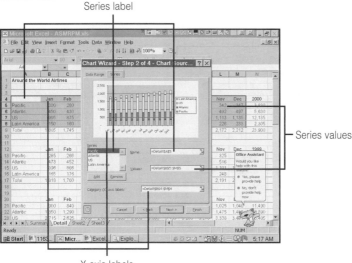

Series values

X-axis labels

- If you need to delete a <u>S</u>eries, select it from the list and click <u>R</u>emove.

- If you need to modify the range for a <u>S</u>eries, choose it in the list; in the <u>N</u>ame box, type text or a cell reference for the legend label, and type a cell reference or select a range for the <u>V</u>alues of the series.

- If you need to add another bar, line, or other chart item, click <u>A</u>dd; in the <u>N</u>ame box, type text or a cell reference for the legend label, and type or select a range for the <u>V</u>alues of the series.

Choose Chart Options

9. Click Next to go to the third step of the wizard and do any of the following:

   - If you want to add labels to your chart, click the Titles tab and type a Chart <u>T</u>itle, <u>C</u>ategory (X) Axis, and/or a <u>V</u>alue (Y) Axis.

Title at top of chart

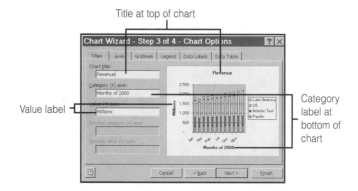

Value label

Category label at bottom of chart

- If you don't want labels or values for the axes, click the Axes tab and clear the Category (X) Axis or Value (Y) Axis check boxes.

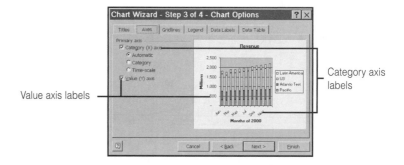

Value axis labels

Category axis labels

- If you want to add or remove horizontal and vertical lines on your chart to help identify data, click the Gridlines tab. Select or clear Category and Value check boxes as desired. Category (X) Axis, Major Gridlines are lines between the category values. Minor Gridlines are lines going through category values. Value (Y) Axis, Major Gridlines are lines going through the major divisions in value units (usually 10s, 100s, or power of 10). Minor Gridlines are lines dividing the major divisions.

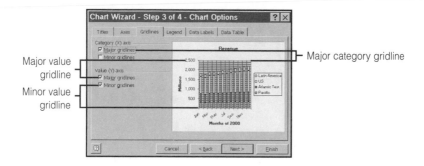

Major value gridline

Minor value gridline

Major category gridline

- If you don't want to display the legend, click the Legend tab and clear the Show Legend check box. If you want to display the legend, select the Show Legend check box and choose a Placement location: Bottom, Corner, Top, Right, or Left.

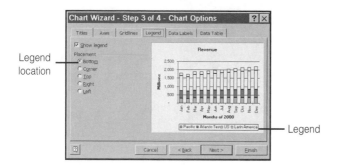

Legend location

Legend

- The data labels are descriptive text or values that appear next to bar, line, or chart items. On the Data Labels tab you can Show Value of the data or Show Labels (legend text). If the chart is a pie chart, you can also Show Percent or Show Label and Percent and show legend colors next to the label with or without lines leading to the label.

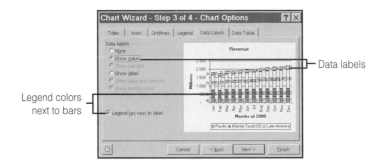

Data labels

Legend colors
next to bars

- If you also want to see the data with the chart, click the Data Table tab and check Show Data Table. You can include the colors assigned to the chart items by checking Show Legend Keys.

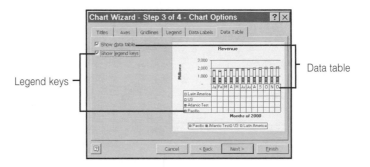

Legend keys

Data table

Choose Chart Location

10. Click Next to go to the fourth step of the wizard, and choose whether you want to place the chart As New Sheet (and the name if desired) or on an existing sheet by selecting As Object In and choosing the sheet name.

New chart
sheet name
Existing work-
sheet name

11. If necessary, click Back to return to any of the tabs or settings in Steps 3–7. Click Finish when you are finished.

210

The chart either is created on a new sheet or is an embedded object in an existing sheet. If you need to make any changes on the chart, see Objective 62, "Modify Charts." If the chart is embedded, see Objective 63, "Insert, Move, and Delete an Object (Picture)."

If you created a chart sheet, you can navigate and rename the sheet tab as you do worksheet tabs (see Objective 45, "Move Between Worksheets in a Workbook," and Objective 46, "Rename a Worksheet").

Modify Charts

After you create a chart with the Chart Wizard, you can use the Chart toolbar, Chart Wizard, or menu choices to change the chart.

Chart Toolbar

The Chart toolbar displays after you create a chart or when you click a chart sheet tab or a chart object on a worksheet. Use the buttons on the toolbar as follows:

1. If the toolbar does not display, right-click an existing menu or toolbar, and choose Chart.

2. Click a part of the chart or choose the part from the Chart Objects drop-down box on the toolbar.

   The chart object name also appears in the Name Box.

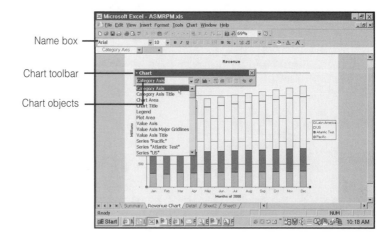

3. Use one of the other buttons on the toolbar:

🖼 **Format Selected Object**—The actions of this button change depending on the object selected:

- If the object is text, you can change the font, border, and area surrounding the text object and the alignment of the text.

- If the object is a data series, you can change the color, pattern, and series order, display data labels, or change the spacing between bars.

- If the object is an axis, you can change the font of the axis text, style of line, scaling of the axis (upper and lower value and tick marks), formatting of numbers, and orientation of the text.

- If the object is the legend, you can change the font of, fill pattern behind, border around, and placement of the legend.

- If the object is the chart area, you can change the fill pattern for the background and the font for all items on the chart.

Instead of clicking this button, you can also click the Format menu and choose Selected (Object) or press Ctrl+1 to change the preceding options.

🖼 **Chart Type**—Select a different chart type.

If anything but a series is selected, all the data changes to that chart type. However, if you select a single data series, just that series changes to the chart type.

🖼 **Legend**—Turn on or off the display of the chart legend.

🖼 **Data Table**—Turn on or off the display of chart data contained in a grid attached to the bottom of the chart.

🖼 **By Row**—Change the data series to rows of data.

🖼 **By Column**—Change the data series to columns of data.

[象] Angle Text Downward—Rotates selected text down at a 45 percent angle.

[象] **Angle Text Upward**—Rotates selected text up at a 45 percent angle.

Titles

If you want to edit a title, follow these steps:

1. Select a title by clicking it or selecting it in the Chart Objects box. You can also press an arrow key until the chart item is selected.

2. Position the I-beam mouse pointer in the text. Type to add new text, or press Backspace to delete characters before or Delete to delete characters after the insertion point.

3. If you want to add a second line to the title, move to the end, press Enter, and type additional text.

You can also click the Chart menu, choose Chart Options, and click the Titles tab to add or edit titles.

If desired, you can select a title or any text and use Font and Font Size boxes on the Formatting toolbar to change the typeface and size of the font (see Objective 20, "Apply Font Styles (Typeface, Size, Color, and Styles)").

Unattached Text

If you want to add new text on the chart unattached to a title, do the following:

1. Click the chart background or select Chart Area in the Chart Objects box.

2. Type the new text and press Enter.

3. The new text appears in a box in the middle of the chart. With the four-headed arrow, drag the border of the text box to the desired location.

Chart Wizard

You can also click [⊞] Chart Wizard and change any of the preceding options in Objective 61, "Use Chart Wizard to Create a Chart."

The Chart menu also goes to specific steps of the Chart Wizard:

- Click the Chart menu and choose Chart Type to change the kind of chart you want (see Step 3 of Objective 61, "Use Chart Wizard to Create a Chart").

- Click the Chart menu and choose Source Data to change the designated data for the chart (see Steps 5–6 of Objective 61, "Use Chart Wizard to Create a Chart").

- Click the Chart menu and choose Chart Options to change settings for the titles, axes, gridlines, legend, data labels, and data table (see Step 7 of Objective 61, "Use Chart Wizard to Create a Chart").

63

Insert, Move, and Delete an Object (Picture)

In addition to Excel charts, you can also insert pictures, WordArt, organizational charts, and other items on your worksheets and chart sheets. After you insert an object, you can change the size, move it, or delete it.

**Insert
Object
Using Copy
and Paste**

If you have an object created somewhere else in Excel or a different application, you can copy and paste the object to Excel.

Do the following to copy a graphic object:

1. Move to the application and select the object.

   If you want to, copy a chart on a chart sheet and place it as an embedded object on a worksheet. Click the chart sheet and choose the chart area.

2. Do one of the following (these options might not be available, depending on the application):

   • Click 📋 Copy.

   • Press Ctrl+C.

   • Click Edit and choose Copy.

   • Right-click the object and choose Copy.

3. Move to the location in Excel where you want to place the copy.

4. Do one of the following:

   • Click 📋 Paste.

   • Press Ctrl+V.

- Click <u>E</u>dit and choose <u>P</u>aste.

- Right-click the location and choose <u>P</u>aste.

If you want to add clip art to a worksheet, do the following:

1. Click the <u>I</u>nsert menu, choose <u>P</u>icture, and click <u>C</u>lipArt.

2. On the Picture tab of the ClipArt dialog box, choose a category. A preview of the available pictures in the selected category displays.

Back button

Click to go to category

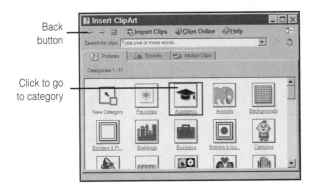

3. If you want to go back to the list of categories, click Back and repeat Step 2.

4. Click the picture you want and choose Insert Clip.

Close

Insert Clip

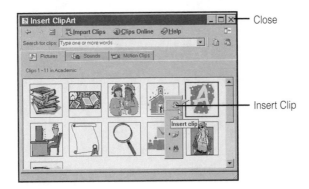

5. Click the Close (×) button to close the ClipArt window.

You can also insert other kinds of objects by clicking <u>I</u>nsert and choosing <u>O</u>bject.

217

Move an Object

After you've inserted a picture, you can move it by clicking and dragging the object with the four-headed arrow to the new desired location.

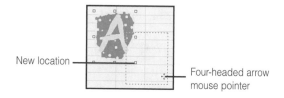

You can also use cut (Ctrl+X) and paste (Ctrl+V) to move the object.

Delete an Object

To remove the object, click it to select it and press Delete.

If your object is difficult to select or if you want to get rid of all objects on the workbook, follow these steps:

1. Press Ctrl+G, press F5, or click the Edit menu and choose Go To.

2. On the Go To dialog box, click the Special button.

3. Select Objects and choose OK.

Size Object

If you need to change the size of your object, you can drag a size handle. Follow these steps:

1. Select the object.

2. Move to one of the square handles on the corner or center edge of the object. The mouse pointer changes to a double-headed arrow. Choose a corner handle to change both the width and height at the same time.

3. Drag the mouse pointer away from or toward the center of the object to make it larger or smaller.

Create and Modify Lines and Objects

In addition to borders (see Objective 26, "Apply Cell Borders and Shading"), you can draw lines and other shapes on your worksheet or chart.

To draw a shape, do the following:

1. If necessary, click 🔲 to turn the Drawing toolbar on.

2. Choose one of the following tools to draw with and drag the mouse pointer to create the object. If you want to draw multiple times, double-click the tool.

   - 🔲 **Line**—Drag opposite ends.

   - 🔲 **Arrow**—Drag from tail to head of arrow.

   - 🔲 **Rectangle**—Drag opposite corners. Hold down Shift as you drag for a square.

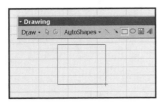

   - 🔲 **Oval**—Drag diameter. Hold down Shift as you drag for a circle.

Draw a Shape

- ▣ **Text box**—Drag opposite corners. Hold down Shift as you drag for a square. Type text after the text box has been created.

- Click AutoShapes, choose a category, click the shape you want, and drag to draw the shape.

If you are drawing several shapes, you can drag the top of the AutoShape menu or top of each set of AutoShapes and tear off to create a toolbar.

Drag to show
AutoShapes toolbar

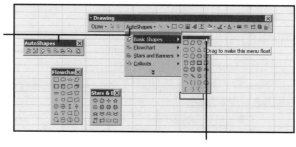

Drag to display
the toolbar

3. If you double-clicked a tool in Step 2, continue drawing. When you finish, click the tool again or press Esc.

4. While the shape is still selected (if it isn't, you can click the shape), do any of the following to change the style of the shape:

- ▣ **Fill Color**—Click to choose the current color or click the down arrow to select a color for rectangles, ovals, text boxes, and AutoShapes.

- ▣ **Line Color**—Click to choose the current color or click the down arrow to select a color for the border of an object or the line.

- ▣ **Font Color**—Click to choose the current color or click the down arrow to select a color for the text in a text box.

- 📑 **Line Style**—Click to select a thickness or multiple lines for the line or border.

- 📑 **Dash Style**—Click to select a pattern for the line or border.

- 📑 **Arrow Style**—Click to select one or two arrow heads (or no heads) for lines and arrows.

- 📑 **Shadow**—Click to add a shadow and direction for the shadow.

- 📑 **3-D**—Click to turn the object into 3D and choose the direction of the third dimension.

Modify Shapes

After you create the shape, you can modify the size, move it, or change the style.

Click the shape to select it, and do any the following to change the drawing item:

- Press Delete to remove it.

- Drag the shape with the four-headed arrow to move it.

- Drag a handle on the ends, corners, or sides to change the size of the shape.

- Choose one of the buttons on the Drawing toolbar mentioned in Step 4 of the preceding list to modify the shape.

- Press Ctrl+1 or click the Format menu and choose the selected item name for additional options for colors, patterns, borders, positioning, protecting, and text for the picture while it is loaded in a Web browser.

Preview and Print Charts

To print and preview a chart, you must select it first. Select the chart by clicking a chart sheet tab or clicking a chart that is on a worksheet.

When the chart is selected, do any of the following:

- If you want to print it without previewing or changing settings, click 🖨.

- If you want to preview the chart, click 🔍 or click File and choose Print Preview. While in the preview window, click Settings to change the orientation, margins, or other options. Click Print to go to the Print dialog box in the next bullet or Close to return to the workbook.

- If you want to choose a number of copies or other print options, press Ctrl+P or click File and choose Print. On the Print dialog box, you can choose the Number of Copies, Go to Preview (see preceding bullet). If you entered the dialog box from a chart tab, you can choose to print the Entire Workbook or this Active Sheet. Click OK to print.

For additional options on printing, previewing, and setting up the page, see Chapter 4, "Page Setup and Printing."

TAKE THE TEST

Task 1

Objectives covered: 61, "Use Chart Wizard to Create a Chart"; 62, "Modify Charts."

Open practice file 0701P from the enclosed CD and perform the following actions:

1. On a new chart sheet, create a column chart by month from the Revenue section of the Detail worksheet for each of the divisions. Include Revenue as the title and Millions as the Value title.

2. Label this sheet Revenue.

3. On a new chart sheet, create a line chart by month from Passenger Miles for each of the divisions. Include Passenger Miles as the title and Millions as the Value title. Place the legend on the bottom of the chart.

4. Label this sheet RPM.

5. On the Summary worksheet, create an embedded pie chart showing the ASMs for each division. Show percentages next to each pie slice and include the title Available Seat Miles.

Check your work against the solution file 0701S.

Task 2

Objectives covered: 61,"Use Chart Wizard to Create a Chart"; 62, "Modify Charts"; 63, "Insert, Move, and Delete an Object (Picture)"; 65, "Preview and Print Charts."

Open practice file 0702P from the enclosed CD and perform the following actions:

1. On the Summary tab, there is a pie chart for ASM (Available Seat Miles). Change this to a 3D pie chart.

2. On the Summary tab, create two more pie charts for RPM (title: Revenue Passenger Miles) and Revenue. These charts should be pie charts with 3D visual effects and percent data labels.

3. On the Summary tab, create a cylinder chart for Load (title: Load Factor).

4. Place the Revenue pie chart to the right of the data. Remove the legends for ASM, RPM, and Load charts and move them below the data so you can see as much of the charts and data in the screen as possible.

5. Preview and print the two chart sheets, the Summary worksheet, and the Load Factor chart on the Summary worksheet.

Check your work against the solution file 0702S.

Objectives covered: 61, "Use Chart Wizard to Create a Chart"; 62, "Modify Charts"; 63, "Insert, Move, and Delete an Object (Picture)"; 64, "Create and Modify Lines and Objects"; 65, "Preview and Print Charts."

Task 3

Open practice file 0703P from the enclosed CD and perform the following actions:

1. Create a new column chart sheet (named Revenue by Year) that shows 1998, 1999, 2000 (in that order) as the legend and each division along the category axis.

2. Add a text box and an arrow pointing to the US data for 1999 that says TTT Airlines went out of business in June.

3. Format the text box with a light yellow background and the text as 14-point italic.

4. Add a clip art figure and size it so it displays on the chart.

5. Preview and print the chart.

Check your work against the solution file 0703S.

You can create the chart for 1998 (using data in column O12:O16), then add the data for 1999 (O4:O8), and then add the data for 2000 (N12:N16).

Cheat Sheet

Use Chart Wizard to Create a Chart

A chart can visually help you understand your data.

Click the data and press F11 to create a quick chart.

For more options, click 🔲 Chart Wizard or choose Insert, Chart, and follow the steps on the Chart Wizard.

Modify Charts

Select a chart; then click 🔲 Chart Wizard to change options on the chart, or use items on the Chart or Format menus to change the chart.

Click a title and use the I-beam mouse pointer to position the insertion point for editing.

Insert, Move, and Delete an Object (Picture)

Click an object in a chart or on a worksheet to select it.

Press Delete to remove a selected item.

Drag the item to a new location.

Create and Modify Lines and Objects

Click 🔲 to turn on or off the Drawing toolbar.

Click a Drawing toolbar button or choose an item from a submenu of the AutoShapes menu, and drag to create the object.

Click formatting tools on the Drawing toolbar to change the color, line, shadow, or 3D effect of the object.

Preview and Print Charts

Click an embedded chart on a workbook to select it.

Click the chart sheet tab to select the chart.

With a selected chart, click 🔲 Print Preview or choose File, Print Preview to see what the chart will look like when printed.

With a selected chart, click 🔲 to print the chart.

Expert Objectives

Expert objectives take you one step further into the use of the program and move beyond the basic skills necessary for program operation.

This part covers more advanced skills, including the following topics:

- Importing and Exporting Data
- Using Templates
- Using Multiple Workbooks
- Formatting Numbers
- Printing Workbooks
- Working with Named Ranges
- Working with Toolbars
- Using Macros
- Auditing a Worksheet
- Displaying and Formatting Data
- Using Analysis Tools

Importing and Exporting Data

Following is a list of MOUS objectives:

- Import Data from Text Files (Insert, Drag and Drop)
- Import from Other Applications
- Import a Table from an HTML File (Insert, Drag and Drop—Including HTML Round Tripping)
- Export to Other Applications

Import Data from Text Files (Insert, Drag and Drop)

There are a number of ways to get information from another application into Excel. You can open, insert, copy, drag and drop, and get external data. The method you use depends on the type of data, if you are starting a new workbook, if you are adding to an existing workbook, and your personal preferences. This section covers text files, whereas Objective 67, "Import from Other Applications," covers importing from other applications.

Open Text File

If you are starting a new workbook, you can open a text file. Follow these steps:

1. Do one of the following to choose the Open dialog box:

   - Press Ctrl+O or Ctrl+F12.

   - Click 🖼 Open.

   - Click the File menu and choose Open.

2. If necessary, choose a different location.

3. Click the Files of Type drop-down and choose Text Files (for example, *.prn, *.txt, *.csv).

4. Double-click the file in the list, or select the file and choose Open.

   The Text Import Wizard dialog box opens.

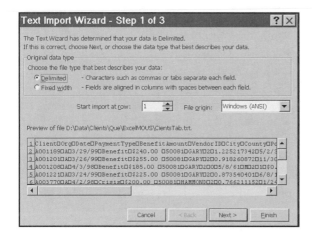

5. If your file appears to contain odd-looking characters (other than small squares), try one of the other options on the File Origin drop-down.

6. Usually the top row(s) of the file contain text. You might or might not want to include this text. Change the Start Import at Row box to specify the first row of data you want to import.

7. Depending on the layout of the text file, continue with the Delimited or Fixed Width. Choose Next and continue with one of the following:

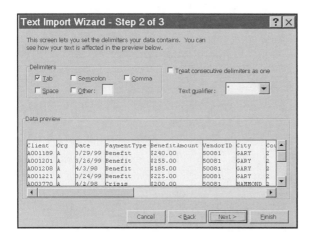

- Delimited text files usually have commas, colons, tabs, semicolons, or other characters between fields and quotes around text. On the Text Import Wizard (Step 2 of 3), set the type of delimiters your data contains (Tab, Semicolon, Comma, Space, Other—type in the character). The Data Preview pane will show a preview of where the columns will be separated. If the Data Preview doesn't show the columns separated correctly, choose another delimiter. If your data contains a delimiter of more than one character between data fields or multiple delimiters, you might need to check Treat Consecutive Delimiters as One. Text is usually identified with quotes. Choose the Text Qualifier drop-down if you want to choose an apostrophe or {none}.

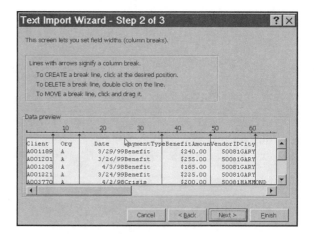

- Fixed width files do not have a delimiter. The starting point of a column is determined by the position in the text file. If you have an export choice in your other application, choose delimited; usually the results are more reliable. However, if the file is fixed width, Step 2 of the wizard shows you a Data Preview of the file, and Excel attempts to configure the column separation. You can drag a line to change the column position, double-click a line to remove it, or click a position to create a column.

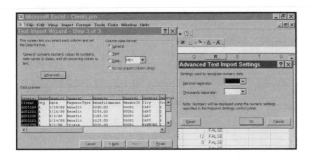

8. Choose Next to get the third step of the Text Import Wizard. This step enables you to select each column under the Data Preview pane and choose a data format from the Column data format list. General is the default format and is recommended because it will convert numbers, dates, and all remaining values to text. However, if you've tried this or the columns don't look correct, change to one of the other options in the Column Data Format section. Click the column, choose Text or Date, and choose the order for the digits in your dates—M (month), D (day), Y (year). If you don't need the column, choose Do Not Import Column (Skip).

   If you need to change the decimal and thousands separator, click the Advanced button and make changes on the Advanced Text Import Settings dialog box.

9. Choose Finish.

Excel imports the text format file into a blank worksheet. To work with and save Excel's features, save this file as a workbook (in the Save As dialog box, click Save as Type and choose Microsoft Excel Workbook).

Link to Text File

If you are continually updating the text file from another source, you might want to link to the file instead of opening it. Then, if the data changes, you can refresh the link to see the changes.

To create a link to the file in the current workbook, follow these steps:

1. Click the Data menu, choose Get External Data, and click Import Text File.

2. If necessary, change to the location of the file.

3. Change the Files of Type to All Files if your filename does not have a .txt extension.

4. Double-click the file or select the file and choose Import. You will go through the same Text Import Wizard as the previous steps.

5. After you finish using the wizard, the Import Data dialog box displays. Choose the location on the Existing Worksheet, or click New Worksheet and choose OK.

When you want to see the changes or updates that were made to the original text file, click Refresh 🔯 on the External Data toolbar. For more information on external data, see Objective 100, "Query Databases."

Copy and Paste

If you open a file in a text-editing program, you can copy and paste the data.

To copy and paste, do the following:

1. Open the other application and select the data to copy.

2. Choose one of the methods in the other application to copy. Any of the following methods could be available:

    • Click the Edit menu and choose Copy.

    • Press Ctrl+C.

    • If there is a Copy button, click it.

3. Move back to Excel, and click in the cell where you want the copy to start.

4. Choose one of the following:

    • Click 📋 Paste.

    • Press Ctrl+V.

- Click the Edit menu and choose Paste.

- Right-click the cell and choose Paste.

5. If the data goes all in one column, you will probably want to parse it. Click the Data menu and choose Text to Columns. The same Text Import Wizard opens as mentioned in the beginning of this chapter. Choose the Fixed Width option, and continue with the wizard as previously described.

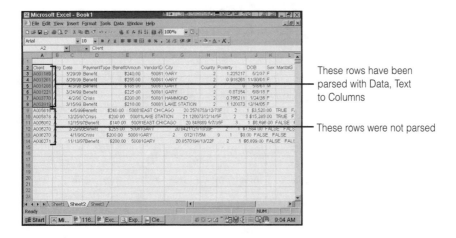

These rows have been parsed with Data, Text to Columns

These rows were not parsed

Drag and Drop

Depending on your text application, you might also be able to drag and drop the data to Excel. After you select the data, drag the mouse pointer to Excel. If the Excel window is not visible, drag the mouse pointer to the Excel icon on the Windows taskbar, and Excel opens. Then let go of the mouse pointer in the cell where you want to start the copy.

In Word, you will need to hold down Ctrl as you drag or the text will be moved out of Word and into Excel.

After you copy the data, you might need to parse it. Click the Data menu and choose Text to Columns. See Step 5 in the preceding procedure.

Import from Other Applications

In addition to importing from a text file, you can import data from other spreadsheets and databases. If you want to link your data, especially to Microsoft Access, see Objective 100, "Query Databases."

To import data from another application, follow these steps:

1. Do one of the following to choose the Open dialog box:

   • Press Ctrl+O or Ctrl+F12.

   • Click 📧 Open.

   • Click the File menu and choose Open.

2. If necessary, choose a different location.

3. Click the Files of Type drop-down and choose the application file type.

   The other files include different versions of Excel, other spreadsheet programs (Lotus 1-2-3, Quattro Pro), databases (dBase), and others (Data Interchange Format, Symbolic Link). Before you import, the converter might need to be installed.

   Importing from Web pages is discussed in Objective 68, "Import a Table from an HTML File (Insert, Drag and Drop—Including HTML Round Tripping)."

4. Double-click the file in the list, or select the file and choose Open.

The file will load in Excel. To work with and save Excel's features, save this file as a workbook (in the Save As dialog box, click Save as Type and choose Microsoft Excel Workbook).

Depending on the applications, you might have to do some formatting (see Chapter 3, "Formatting Worksheets") and formula verifying (see Chapter 6, "Working with Formulas and Functions").

Change font if desired

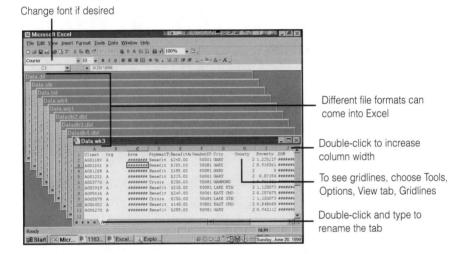

Different file formats can come into Excel

Double-click to increase column width

To see gridlines, choose Tools, Options, View tab, Gridlines

Double-click and type to rename the tab

68

Import a Table from an HTML File (Insert, Drag and Drop—Including HTML Round Tripping)

You can work with Web (HTML) documents in a variety of ways. You can save an Excel workbook as a Web file, display it in a Web browser, and then save it again as another Excel workbook. This is called HTML round-tripping. You can also open an HTML file or drag and drop data from a Web document that is open in a browser into Excel.

HTML Round Trip

The HTML round trip is when you save a document as a Web page, display it in a Web browser, and save it again in Excel.

To make the HTML round trip, follow these steps:

1. In an open Excel workbook, click File and choose Save as Web Page.

2. Choose a location and give the document a name. If you are publishing directly to a Web server, choose 🔘 Web Folders and select the site folder.

3. Click **P**ublish. The Publish as Web Page dialog box opens.

   You can also choose **S**ave to store the document as an HTML file. You can save an entire workbook and open this document in a browser, but this does not give you the interactivity that would enable you to change the worksheet and save the file as Excel.

4. Check **A**dd Interactivity with and choose Spreadsheet Functionality (for the other options, see Objective 108, "Create Interactive PivotTables for the Web"). You can add interactivity to only a single worksheet and not the workbook.

5. If desired, click the C**h**ange button to add a title to the top of the Web page.

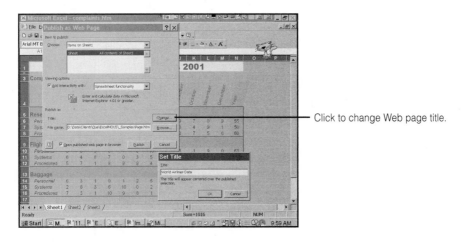

Click to change Web page title.

6. If desired, change the File **N**ame and location.

7. Check **O**pen Published Web Page in Browser, and click **P**ublish.

8. The Web browser launches, and the document displays with an Excel toolbar (for information on how to use work with these pages, see Objective 18, "Save a Worksheet/Workbook as a Web Page," and Objective 108, "Create Interactive PivotTables for the Web").

   After you make any desired changes in the document, click the Export to Excel button.

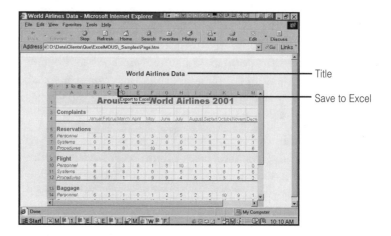

9. The worksheet returns to Excel. Click File, choose Save
   As, and change the Save as Type back to Microsoft Excel
   Workbook. Choose a location and filename, and choose
   Save (see Objective 13, "Use Save As (Different Name,
   Location, and Format").

Drag and Drop

You can also select text in a Web document and drag it into an
open Excel workbook. Web tables convert into rows and
columns.

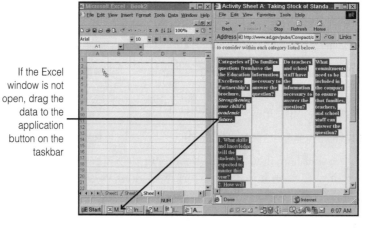

If the Excel
window is not
open, drag the
data to the
application
button on the
taskbar

Export to Other Applications

You can export your Excel data to another application's file type. This is helpful if another user has a file format besides Excel and you want to share data. Before you email a file to someone, check to see what application she uses or what formats she can use, and convert the file for her (see Objective 17, "Send a Workbook via Email").

The closer the file format is to the current version of Excel, the more features and formatting are saved. For a description of features that are not saved, click the Office Assistant, type `Formatting and features not transferred in file conversions`, and choose Search. Then click Features Not Transferred in File Conversions. Note: Many of the file types do not support multiple sheets, so only the active worksheet will be saved.

To save the file as a different type, do the following:

1. If necessary, open the workbook, click the worksheet, and click the area where the data is located.

2. To open the Save As dialog box, do one of the following:

   • Click the File menu and Choose Save As.

   • Press F12 or Alt+F2.

3. In the Save as Type drop-down, choose a desired file format type. Available file types include other versions of Excel, Lotus 1-2-3, Quattro Pro, dBase, text files, and others.

Save File as Type

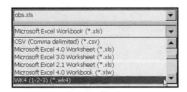

The file converters might need to be installed before you save.

4. Choose the location, type the File Name, and choose Save.

5. If the application does not support multiple worksheets, you will get a prompt with instructions; choose OK.

6. You will also get another prompt indicating that formats might not be saved. Choose Yes.

Access

You can also convert a data list in an Excel worksheet to an Access database. Although you could import a worksheet from within Access, you can also export from Excel into a table of an Access database.

You will probably first have to install the Access Links Add-in. Click the Tools menu, choose Add-Ins, check Access Links, and click OK. This adds a new item on the bottom of your Data menu. Then follow these steps:

1. Click the Data menu and choose Convert to MS Access.

2. In the Convert to MS Access dialog box, choose whether to create a New Database or Type or Browse for an Existing Database Location and File Name and click OK.

3. After a moment, Access opens into the Import Spreadsheet Wizard. If the first row of your worksheet included labels for columns, check First Row Contains Column Headings. Choose Next.

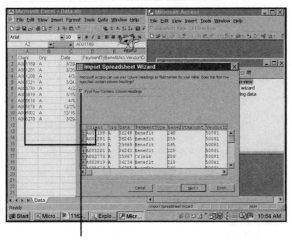

First row labels in worksheet

4. On the second dialog box of the wizard, do one of the following:

   • Choose a name In an E̲xisting Table drop-down and choose F̲inish. Skip the rest of the steps in this procedure.

   • Click to store your data In a N̲ew Table and choose N̲ext.

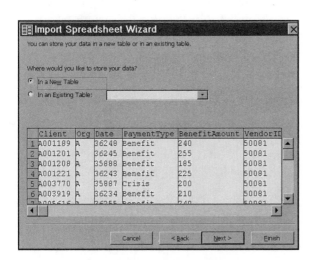

5. If you chose a new table, continue with these steps. In the third dialog box of the wizard, type a Field Name for each field and whether you want the field Indexed, or check Do Not Import Field (Skip). Choose Next.

6. The next dialog box of the wizard is where you specify the table's primary key. You can let Access assign the primary key, choose your own primary key, or choose to not use a primary key. The primary key is a unique identifier for each record and enables you to retrieve information more quickly. Choose Next.

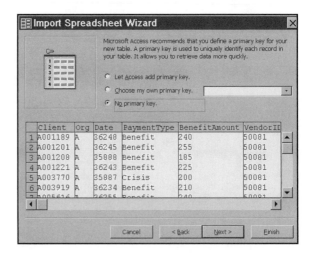

7. On the last step of the wizard, give the table a name and choose Finish.

You will be in Access and ready to work with the table.

TAKE THE TEST

Objectives covered: 66, "Import Data from Text Files (Insert, Drag and Drop)"; 68, "Import a Table from an HTML File (Insert, Drag and Drop—Including HTML Round Tripping)"; 69, "Export to Other Applications."

1. Open the text file 0801P.txt. Import the data to Excel.

2. Format the worksheet as desired, and save the file as an Excel workbook.

   Check your work against 0801s1.xls.

3. Save the Excel file as an interactive Web page (change the title to World Airlines 2000 Data.)

   Check your work against 0801s.htm.

4. Open the file in your Web browser, and change the value of Jan Pacific Rev to 999.

5. Save the Web file as an Excel workbook.

   Check your work against 0801s2.xls.

6. Save the Excel workbook in a new Access database in a new table. When prompted, name the first field Division and the second field Data and let Access assign a primary key.

   Check your work against 0801s.mdb.

Objectives covered: 66, "Import Data from Text Files (Insert, Drag and Drop)"; 67, "Import from Other Applications"; 68, "Import a Table from an HTML File (Insert, Drag and Drop—Including HTML Round Tripping)."

1. Import 0802p1.prn (a fixed-width file) using the text labels in Row 1 as a guide for where the columns should go (you'll have to adjust the columns), and save it as an Excel workbook.

   Check your work against 0802s1.xls.

2. Import 0802p2.wk4. Go to BU4 and see that some of the formulas did not convert.

3. Save as an Excel workbook.

   Check your work against 0802s2.xls (including cell BU4).

4. Create a new workbook in Excel and open 0802p3.htm in your Web browser.

5. Drag the text from the Web browser to the new workbook.

   Check your work against 0802s3.xls.

Cheat Sheet

Import Data from Text Files (Insert, Drag and Drop)

You can import text files whether they are delimited, fixed width, or straight text.

🖼 Choose File, Open (Ctrl+O), change the Files of Type to Text files, and follow the steps on the wizard.

Alternatively, you might be able to drag the text and choose Data, Text to Columns.

Import from Other Applications

You can also import from other versions of Excel, database, and spreadsheet programs.

🖼 Choose File, Open (Ctrl+O) and change the Files of Type.

Import a Table from an HTML File (Insert, Drag and Drop—Including HTML Round Tripping)

In Excel, you can save a file as an interactive Web document, make changes in a Web browser, and then save the changes as a new Excel workbook.

From Excel, choose File, Save As Web Page, and choose Publish.

In Internet Explorer, click the Export to Excel button.

Export to Other Applications

You can also save to a text file, spreadsheet, or database application.

Choose File, Save As (F12) and change the Save as Type.

To save as an Access table, install the Access Links add-in and choose Data, Convert to MS Access.

Using Templates

Following is a list of MOUS objectives:

- Create Templates
- Apply Templates
- Edit Templates

Create Templates

A template is a stored file that serves as a blueprint for a new file. When you use a template, a copy of the file is opened so that the original template is not overwritten.

The first step in creating a template is to create a workbook with all the data, formatting, and settings you want included. Because the following features can be saved with a template, first create your file by doing any of the following:

- Add, delete, and rename worksheets (see Chapter 5, "Working with Worksheets and Workbooks").

- Type any data you want included (see Objective 1, "Enter Text, Dates, and Numbers").

- Create formulas (see Chapter 6, "Working with Formulas and Functions").

- Change formats (see Chapter 3, "Formatting Worksheets").

- Create common charts (see Chapter 7, "Using Charts and Objects").

- Change settings for printing (see Objectives 34, "Set Page Margins and Centering"; 35, "Change Page Orientation and Scaling"; 36, "Set Up Headers and Footers"; 37, "Insert and Remove a Page Break"; 38, "Set Print Titles and Options (Gridlines, Print Quality, and Row and Column Headings").

- Create and attach toolbars and macros to the workbook (see Chapters 14, "Working with Toolbars," and 15, "Using Macros").

- Add passwords and protection to the workbook (see Objective 111, "Apply and Remove Worksheet and Workbook Protection," and Objective 113, "Apply and Remove File Passwords")

After you've created your workbook, save it as a template by following these steps:

1. Click the File menu and choose Save As.

   The Save As dialog box displays.

2. Click the Save as Type drop-down and choose Template.

3. The location automatically changes to the default file where Office templates are stored. Do one of the following:

   - Change type to Template. Location changes to where templates are stored.

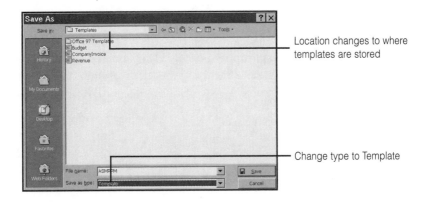

Location changes to where templates are stored

Change type to Template

   - If you want to have this file available when you choose File, New, keep this folder.

   - If you want to create a default workbook, change to the XLSTART folder or the alternative startup location.

To determine the XLSTART folder, right-click the Start button, choose Find, and type XLSTART in the Named text box. To set the alternative startup folder, click Tools, choose Options, click the General tab, and type the folder in Alternative Startup File Location.

- Store the file in any location.

To use it as a template, you'll have to go to that folder in Windows Explorer and double-click.

4. Name the workbook so you can use it again as a default workbook, default sheet, or template in the New dialog box. Do one of the following:

- Type any name in the File Name text box. If this location is where the templates are stored, it will display in the New dialog box.

- If you type the name Book and the folder is XLSTART or the alternative startup folder, this file becomes the default when you start Excel or when you click [□].

- If the workbook is only one sheet, you type the name Sheet, and the folder is XLSTART or the alternative startup folder, this file becomes a default worksheet inserted when you click Insert and choose Worksheet (see Objective 47, "Insert and Delete Worksheets").

5. Choose Save.

Apply Templates

After you save a template, you can create a new workbook based on the template. Do one of the following:

- If you saved it in the templates location, click the <u>F</u>ile menu and choose <u>N</u>ew. The new dialog box opens. Double-click the template.

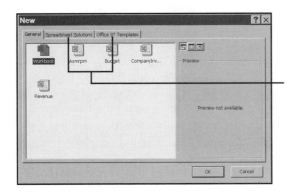

You might have additional folders that have templates that come with Excel or from previous versions

- If you saved the template as Book in the XLSTART or alternative start location, a new file based on the template will automatically open when you start Excel or click □ on the Standard toolbar.

- If you saved the template as Sheet in the XLSTART or alternative start location, a new sheet based on the template is inserted when you click the <u>I</u>nsert menu and choose <u>W</u>orksheet.

- If you right-click a sheet tab and choose Insert, the Insert dialog box opens with the templates you've saved in addition to the standard templates. Even if your template is more than one sheet, you can use it here and all sheets are inserted.

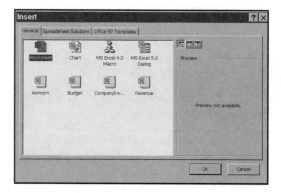

- If you saved the template to some other folder, you must find the folder through the Windows Explorer and double-click the template to launch Excel and create a new file based on the template.

When you create a new file based on the template, the default name is the name of the template with a number after the name (the number of workbooks created during this session). Edit the workbook as you would any other. When you save the workbook, changes you make do not affect the underlying template.

Templates That Come with Excel

Depending on your installation, Excel comes with four templates:

- Expense Statement.
- Invoice.
- Purchase Order.
- Village Software. This is the company that created these three templates. You can contact them for more templates if you want.

These templates are on the Spreadsheet Solutions tab of the New and Insert dialog boxes. The templates contain macros that help you input data and graphics.

You can also get templates from other third-party companies as well at Microsoft's Web site: www.microsoft.com.

Edit Templates

To edit a template, you cannot open the file through Windows Explorer (or you will create a new workbook). You can, however, open the template through Excel.

1. Do one of the following to choose the Open dialog box:

   - Press Ctrl+O or Ctrl+F12.

   - Click 📂 Open.

   - Click the File menu and choose Open.

2. Change the Files of Type to Templates.

3. If necessary, choose a drive and folder. The default location where templates are stored is
   `C:\os\Profiles\`*user_name*`\ApplicationData\Microsoft\`
   `Templates` where *os* is the operating system folder—for example, `Windows`. You might also see templates in
   `C:\WINDOWS\Application Data\Microsoft\Templates`. If you can't find the templates, right-click the Start button, choose Find, and look for `*.xlt` files.

4. Double-click the file in the list, or select the file and choose Open.

The template file opens, enabling you to edit it like a normal workbook (see Objective 3, "Edit Cell Content," and the other cross-references mentioned in Objective 70, "Create Templates"). When you're finished editing the template, use one of the following to save it again:

- Click 💾 Save.
- Press Ctrl+S or Shift+F12.
- Click <u>F</u>ile and choose <u>S</u>ave.

TAKE THE TEST

Task 1

Objective covered: 70, "Create Templates."

Open practice file 0901P from the enclosed CD and perform the following actions:

1. In A1, type Around the World Airlines.

2. In B2, type the current year and notice the changes in column N.

3. While still in B2, click the Data menu, choose Validation, and click the Input Message tab. In <u>T</u>itle, type Is year correct? For the Input message, type Input the current year here (in cell B2). Click OK.

4. Leave your cell pointer in B2 so the message comes up when the user starts a new file.

5. Save the file as a template with the name of ASMRPM.

Check your work against the template solution file 0901S.xlt.

Task 2

Objectives covered: 71, "Apply Templates"; 72, "Edit Templates."

1. Open a new file based on the ASMRPM.xlt template you did in Task 1 or the 0902P.xlt template on the CD.

2. Save the new workbook.

3. Open one of the templates, ASMRPM.xlt (on your hard drive) or 0902P.xlt (on the CD), to edit it.

4. In A1, change the name of the company to Around the Region Airlines.

5. Save the template as AsmRpmRe.

6. Open a new workbook based on the template.

7. Close the workbook without saving.

Check your work against the template solution file 0902S.xlt.

Cheat Sheet

Create Templates

Templates can contain text, formatting, and many other features.

Create a workbook, and then when you save it in the Save As dialog box's File of Type, choose Template.

Apply Templates

Create new workbooks based on a template.

Choose File, New and select the template.

Alternatively, double-click the filename in the Windows Explorer window.

Edit Templates

If necessary, right-click the Start menu and choose Find to search for the location of the templates folder. Return to Excel and click ▣ Open, change the location to where the templates are, and open the template file.

Edit and save the template like any other workbook.

Using Multiple Workbooks

Following is a list of MOUS objectives:

- Use a Workspace
- Link Workbooks

Use a Workspace

A workspace is a saved set of workbooks including window sizes and screen positions. You use a workspace when you need to open a group of workbooks simultaneously during an Excel session. A workspace works well in conjunction with linked workbooks because it is easier to create the links when both the source and the target workbooks are open.

Arrange Windows

If you want to arrange your windows before saving the workspace, follow these steps:

1. Click <u>W</u>indow and choose <u>A</u>rrange.

   The Arrange Window dialog box opens.

2. Choose one of the following:

   • To show multiple windows in blocks across the screen, choose <u>T</u>iled.

   • To show windows in strips running back and forth across the screen, choose H<u>o</u>rizontal.

   • To show windows in strips running up and down the screen, choose <u>V</u>ertical.

- To show windows one on top of each other with the title bars showing, choose Cascade.

- If you've opened one workbook in more than one window with Window, New Window, check the Windows of Active Workbook check box to arrange only those windows.

3. Choose OK.

4. You can drag the title bar of any window to move it to the desired position.

To save a workspace, do the following steps after opening and arranging your workbooks:

Save Workspace

1. Click the File menu and choose Save Workspace.

The Save Workspace dialog box displays. Notice that Save as Type shows Workspaces.

2. If desired, choose a drive and folder for the file (see Objective 13, "Use Save As (Different Name, Location, Format)").

3. Type the File Name in the text box.

4. Choose Save.

After you save the workspace, you still need to save any changes in the individual workbooks.

To open the workspace file with all the workbooks at one time, do the following:

Open Workspace

1. Do one of the following to choose the Open dialog box:

- Press Ctrl+O or Ctrl+F12.

- Click ⬚ Open.

- Click the File menu and choose Open.

2. If necessary, choose a drive and folder.

3. If desired, change the Files of Type to Workspaces (Microsoft Excel Files and All Microsoft Excel Files also work).

4. Double-click the file in the list, or select the file and choose Open.

Link Workbooks

Moving Between Workbooks

To work with multiple workbooks in this section, you might need to review how to get to each workbook. First, open the workbooks (see Objective 14, "Locate and Open an Existing Workbook"). If you saved several workbooks as a workspace, see Objective 73, "Use a Workspace."

To move between workbooks, do one of the following:

- Click the workbook button on the Windows taskbar (pause the mouse pointer over the button to see the file-name). To make sure this option is turned on, click the Tools menu, choose Options, click View Tab, and select the Windows in Taskbar check box.

- Click the Window menu and choose an open file.

Use Another Worksheet's Reference in a Formula

While you are creating a formula, you can refer to a reference on another workbook. For example, when you click the AutoSum button, the suggested range is selected. Instead of using the suggested range, click another workbook, select the worksheet, drag to select the range, and press Enter.

If you want to use references in another workbook in a formula, follow these steps:

1. Move the cell pointer to the cell where the formula is to be placed.

2. Start your formula by doing one of the following:

- Type = or click ■ Edit Formula on the Formula Bar.

- Type =, a function name, and an open parenthesis.

- Click 𝒇𝒙 Paste Function, choose the function, and choose OK to move to the arguments for the function. Click the Collapse Dialog button.

3. Move to the workbook and worksheet, and then click the cell or drag the range you want.

4. Add any operators or move to another argument text box and repeat Step 3 as necessary.

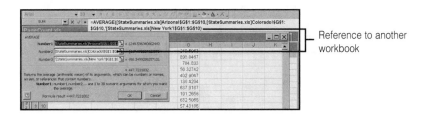

Reference to another workbook

5. When you finish with a formula, press Enter or choose OK.

After you finish the formula, the workbook reference is included.

Instead of using the preceding pointing method, you could type the formula including the workbook. The following are two examples:

Typing Workbook References

```
=[obs.xls]Colorado!B30+[obs99.xls]Arizona!C33
```

Add B30 from the Colorado worksheet in the obs.xls workbook to C33 from the Arizona worksheet in the obs99.xls workbook.

```
=SUM([obs.xls]Colorado!B33:B40)
```

Sum up cells B33 through B40 on the Colorado worksheet in the obs.xls workbook.

The name of the workbook goes before the sheet name and is enclosed in brackets. To work with formulas on multiple worksheets of a workbook, see Objective 49, "Link Worksheets and Consolidate Data Using 3D References."

Paste Special

If you want to link to a cell on another workbook, you can also use Paste Special. Follow these steps:

1. Select the cell or range to copy on the active worksheet.

2. Click ▣ Copy or choose another method of copying (see Objective 7, "Cut, Copy, Paste, Paste Special and Move Selected Cells, Use the Office Clipboard").

3. Move to the workbook and the upper-left cell to receive the link on the desired worksheet.

4. Click the Edit menu and choose Paste Special. The Paste Special dialog box opens.

5. Click Paste Link.

Change Links

If you move your workbooks to another location or change the filename after you close the file, the formulas will no longer be valid. The link can be changed in one of three ways:

- When you open the file, you get a message asking if you want to update links. Choose Yes. If Excel cannot find the workbook, it will open the File Not Found dialog box and enable you to choose the location and name of the file.

- Click the Edit menu and choose Links to open the Edit Links dialog box. Click the Source file, choose Change Source, and choose the location and name of the file.

- Edit the reference to the workbook. The following formula includes a reference to a drive and folder:

```
=AVERAGE('D:\Data\[StateSummaries.xls]Arizona'!$G$1
➡:$G$10)
```

Notice the apostrophe before the name of the drive (D) and the apostrophe after the sheet name.

TAKE THE TEST

Objectives covered: 73, "Use a Workspace"; 74, "Link Workbooks."

Open practice file 1001P from the enclosed CD and perform the following actions:

1. Open the following workbooks: 1001pAL.xls, 1001pAK.xls, 1001pAZ.xls, 1001pAR.xls, and 1001pCA.xls.

2. Tile all these workbooks.

3. Save this as a workspace.

4. Create links to the totals in cell B15 of the 1001pAL.xls, 1001pAK.xls, 1001pAZ.xls, and 1001pAR.xls worksheets in 1001P.xls cells B3 (Alabama), B4 (Alaska), B5 (Arizona), B6 (Arkansas).

5. In B7 (California) of 1001P.xls, create a linked formula that sums up the range B3:B14 from the 1001pCA.xls workbook.

6. Save all the workbooks as a workspace. Close all workbooks, and then open the workspace file.

7. Close all workbooks and move the location of 1001pCA.xls to a different folder. Open 1001P.XLS and change the linked file to the new location.

Check your work against the solution files 1001S.XLS and 1001S.XLW.

Cheat Sheet

Use a Workspace

A workspace is a stored file containing a group of workbooks and their windows positions.

You can arrange workbooks before saving a workspace. Choose Window, Arrange.

To save a workspace, choose File, Save Workspace. Open the workspace as you would any other file.

Link Workbooks

Linked workbooks enable you to reference values from another workbook.

When you would normally choose a cell or range reference, go to the other workbook and choose the cell or range.

If you want to type a workbook reference, type the workbook name in square brackets and place this before the sheet name.

If you need to include a drive and folder, type an apostrophe, the path, the workbook name in brackets, the sheet name, another apostrophe, an exclamation, and the range reference. For example:

```
=AVERAGE('D:\Data\[StateSummaries.xls]Arizona'!$G$1:$G$10)
```

Formatting Numbers

Following is a list of MOUS objectives:

- Apply Number Formats (Accounting, Currency, Number)
- Create Custom Number Formats
- Use Conditional Formatting

Apply Number Formats (Accounting, Currency, Number)

Formats for numbers do not change the value of a number, but they do change the way a number is displayed. A formatted number is often easier to read than an unformatted number. For example, 1234567 is hard to read without counting the digits, but with commas added to 1,234,567, it is easier to tell that the 1 is a million. You can type an entry with the format $25.00, or it is often easier to type numbers without formatting and then format after you've entered all the data.

You can format numbers using the Formatting toolbar, but you have more options when you use the Number tab of the Format Cells dialog box.

Formatting Toolbar

Select the cells you want to format and click one of the following buttons on the Formatting toolbar:

Toolbar	Button Name	Shortcut	Description
$	Currency Style	Ctrl+Shift+$	Adds a dollar sign, commas, and two decimal places. 25 becomes $25.00.

Toolbar	Button Name	Shortcut	Description
%	Percent Style	Ctrl+Shift+%	Multiplies the number by 100 and adds a per-cent sign. 1 becomes 100% and .5 becomes 50%.
,	Comma Style	Ctrl+Shift+!	Adds a comma for every three digits to the left of the decimal place (thousands, millions, and so on) and two decimal places. 1234 becomes 1,234.00.
.00	Increase Decimal		Adds more places after the decimal point.
.00	Decrease Decimal		Decreases digits after decimal point.

Additional Shortcuts

In addition to the previously mentioned shortcuts, you can also use the following shortcut keys to apply number formats (for a description, see the items in the following section, "Format Cells Dialog Box—Number Tab"):

- Ctrl+Shift+~—General number format (no formatting).

- Ctrl+Shift+^—Exponential number with no decimal places.

- Ctrl+Shift+#—Date format with day, three-letter month, two-digit year (1-Jan-00).

- Ctrl+Shift+@—Time format with Hour:Minute A.M. or P.M. (12:00 AM).

Format Cells Dialog Box— Number Tab

The Format Cells dialog box gives you many more options than the options on the Formatting toolbar. Follow these steps:

1. Move to the cell or select the range.

2. Press Ctrl+1, or click the Format menu and choose Cells.

The Format Cells dialog box displays.

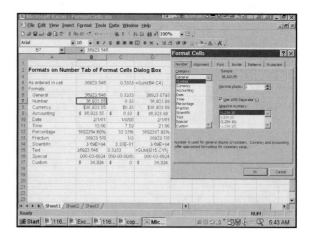

3. Click the Number tab.

4. Choose a <u>C</u>ategory. The right side of the dialog box changes depending on the choice:

- **General** —There are no additional choices, numbers have no commas or symbols, and they display the number of decimal places you entered.

- **Number** —Lets you choose <u>D</u>ecimal Places, select the <u>U</u>se 1000 Separator (,) check box if you want a comma, and choose whether you want <u>N</u>egative Numbers displayed in red or in parentheses.

- **Currency** —Gives you the same choices as Number and lets you choose a currency <u>S</u>ymbol.

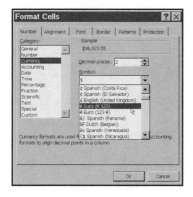

- **Accounting**—Also lets you choose a currency <u>S</u>ymbol. Both the symbols and the decimal places are lined up in a column. In currency format, just the decimal places are lined up. You can also choose the number of decimal places to display.

- **Date** —Lets you choose examples that display the date in different formats. These formats display numbers (1–12) or the name for the month. You also choose the order and whether you have slashes or dashes separating month, day, and year. Some options also include the time as well as the date.

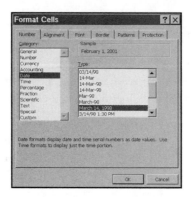

• **Time** —Choose from different time formats that give
you the option of showing seconds, AM or PM, and
a 12-hour or 24-hour clock. Time format also has
date options.

• **Percentage** —Like the Percent button on the
Formatting toolbar, this multiplies the number by
100 and adds a percent sign. This also gives you the
option to specify the number of decimal places displayed.

• **Fraction** —Lets you choose a fraction format including the number of digits in the denominator and
whether the display represents halves, eighths, quarters, sixteenths, tenths, or hundredths.

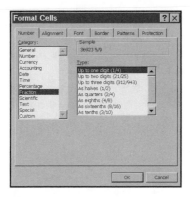

- **Scientific** —Displays in scientific format. 123 becomes 1.23E02. 1200 becomes 1.2E03. 0.01 becomes 1E-02. For every unit past the ones, a positive number is added. For the first significant units to the right of the decimal place, a negative number is added. You can also choose the number of decimal places.

- **Text** —Displays a number or formula as it is in the Formula bar rather than evaluating a result. For example, =SUM(A1:A10) will display in the cell rather than the value.

- **Special** —Lets you choose Zip Code, Zip Code+4, Phone Number, or Social Security Number formats. If Social Security Number were applied to the entry with a value of 123456789, 123-45-6789 would display.

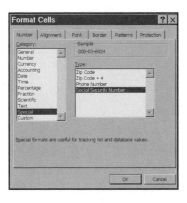

275

- **Custom** —Lets you be more specific when choosing
  the format in the Type list, or you can type your own
  characters, especially if one of the formats you want is
  not listed above. For example, you might want to
  spell out the entire month when working with dates
  (see Objective 76, "Create Custom Number
  Formats").

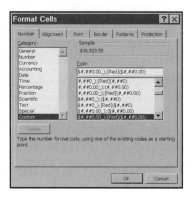

5. When you finish, choose OK.

Create Custom Number Formats

If you want to display a number in a special way that is not obtainable using one of the predefined formats in the preceding section, you can use the Custom format choice on the Number tab of the Format Cells dialog box.

Custom Formats for Numbers

You can choose up to four sections in the Type text box. Each section is separated by a semicolon. An example is `[Blue]#,###.00_)`; `[Red](#,###.00)`; `0.00_)`; `"No sale"`. The four sections are the following:

- **Format for positive numbers**—3456.789 will be 3,456.79 and blue with extra space for a closing parenthesis to line up with negative numbers.

- **Format for negative numbers**—3456.789 will be (3,456.79) in red.

- **Format for zeros**—0 will be 0.00 with extra space for a closing parenthesis to line up with negative numbers.

- **Replace format if any text is typed**—abc will turn into No sale.

The characters you use help describe how you want to deal with decimal places, the thousands separator, and color.

Decimal places

An *insignificant* number means a 0 before numbers or after decimal places. The insignificance term means that it does not contribute to the value of the number. 03456.70 evaluates to 3456.7. Some ways to handle insignificant numbers follow:

> #—Type a pound sign to show a number without display-ing insignificant zeros. The pound sign acts as a place-holder, and decimal fractions are rounded up to the number of placeholders to the right of the decimal. The preceding number with #,###.00 would be 3,456.70.

> 0—Type a 0 (zero) when you do want to show insignifi-cant zeroes if a number is not present. The zero acts as a placeholder and decimal portions round up to number of zeros to the right of the decimal. The .6 formatted with the above formatting would be .60. If you used 0.0, .6 would become 0.6.

> ?—Use ? as a placeholder to correctly align numbers with the decimal place. The ? adds spaces and removes insignificant zeros. If the format was ??.???, the numbers 1.2, 3.45, and 123.456 would all line up on the decimal point.

Thousands Separator

Use the comma with characters after it to show thousands. The format #,### shows thousands, millions, and so on. 1234 becomes 1,234. 1234567 becomes 1,234,567.

Use the comma with no digits after it to scale a number by thousands. The format #, divides a number by 1,000. 1234 becomes 1, and 1234567 becomes 1235. If you typed 23, noth-ing would display. If you used 0.0,, the numbers 1234 would display as 0.0 and 12345678 would display as 12.3.

Color

In any one of the four preceding positions, you can use a color. The example at the beginning of this section has positive num-bers in blue and negative numbers in red. Enclose the name of the color in square brackets before the other codes in the sec-tion. You can use the following colors:

[Black]	[Blue]	[Cyan]	[Green]
[Magenta]	[Red]	[White]	[Yellow]

If you use white in a normal cell, the number will not display.

Conditions

Conditional formatting is discussed in Objective 77, "Use Conditional Formatting." However, you can also apply conditions as part of the formatting. You also enclose conditions in square brackets. An example is the following:

```
[Blue][>1000]#,##0.00;[Red][<=-500]-#,##0.00;0.00
```

This will show only positive numbers greater than 1,000 in blue and negative numbers less than or equal to 500 in red.

The following table shows how numbers display with the preceding formatting characters:

Entered As	Display	Color
456	456.00	black
1234	1,234.00	blue
.5	0.50	black
0	0.00	black
-678	-678.00	red
-234	-234.00	black

Fractions

You can also use the ? in fractions that have varying numbers of decimals and leave space for the slashes to line up. # ??/?? would show the following numbers formatted as fractions:

Entered As	Display
1	1
.5	1/2
13.25	13 1/4
2.567	2 55/97

Custom Formats for Dates and Times

Dates and times use letter characters to indicate whether to use numbers or digits and whether to include the AM or PM after times.

For months, use the following:

Type	To Display	Example	Displays
m	one digit (1–12)	m/d/yy	11/2/00
mm	two digits (01–12)	mm/d/yy	01/2/00
mmm	three letters (Jan–Dec)	mmm d	Jan 12
mmmm	four letters (January)	mmmm d, yy	January 12, 99

For days, use the following:

Type	To Display	Example	Displays
d	one digit (1–12)	m/d/yyyy	11/2/2000
dd	two digits (01–12)	m/dd/yy	1/02/00
ddd	three letters (Sun–Sat)	ddd m/d/yy	Sat 1/12/99
dddd	four letters (Sunday)	dddd, m/d	Saturday, 1/22

For years, type yy to display the two-digit year and yyyy to display the four-digit year.

If the data is time, type h for hours, mm for minutes (00–59), ss for seconds (00–59), and AM/PM to display the hour based on the 12-hour clock. For example, type h:mm:ss AM/PM to display 5:06:15 PM.

Use Conditional Formatting

If you want to format values differently depending on the value of the contents, use conditional formatting. For example, you could add a yellow fill to all customers whose revenue was over $10,000.

You can use the brackets in custom formatting as mentioned previously (see Objective 76, "Create Custom Number Formats"), but that is limited to a color for the font. Conditional formatting gives you substantially more choices.

To use conditional formatting, follow these steps:

1. Select the cells, columns, or rows to format.

2. Click the Format menu and choose Conditional Formatting.

   The Conditional Formatting dialog box opens.

3. If you want to base the conditions on values, choose Cell Value Is in the first drop-down box and continue with the following:

   • In the second drop-down box, choose Between or Not Between and type values or cell references in the second two text boxes. You can also use the Collapse Dialog button to choose a cell that has a value in it.

   • If you choose any of the other operator choices in the second drop-down box (such as Equal To or Greater Than), one additional text box (instead of two) appears. Type a value or cell reference in the text box or use the Collapse Dialog button to choose a cell.

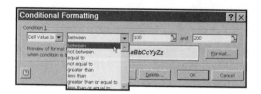

4. Click the Format button. The Format Cells dialog box opens with Font, Border, and Patterns tabs. Some of the options that you might see on this dialog box if you were to enter it through the Format menu (see Chapter 3, "Formatting Worksheets") are not available. Choose the formatting options you want. For example, to change the color of the font, click the Font tab and choose a Color. To change the background color of the cell, click the Patterns tab and choose a Color in the palette.

5. If you want to add more formatting conditions, click Add and repeat Steps 3 and 4.

6. If you want to remove a formatting condition, click Delete and select the check box for the formatting condition that you want to remove.

7. When you finish with the Conditional Formatting dialog box, choose OK.

You cannot apply conditional formatting after you share a workbook (see Objective 115, "Create a Shared Workbook").

If you want to find cells that have conditional formatting, click the Edit menu, choose Go to, click the Special button, and choose Conditional formats (see Objective 2, "Go to a Specific Cell").

Using a Formula in Conditional Formatting

Instead of using a value in Step 3, you can use a formula. In most cases, you will want to click the first cell that will have this formula and then set the conditional formatting. In the first drop-down box, choose Formula Is. In the text box, type a formula such as =E2>Average(E2:E1000). Then continue as previously in choosing the format. When you return to the worksheet, use the Format Painter button to copy this conditional format to the rest of the cells in the range (see Objective 28, "Use the Format Painter").

TAKE THE TEST

Task 1

Objectives covered: 75, "Apply Number Formats (Accounting, Currency, Number)"; 76, "Create Custom Number Formats."

Open practice file 1101P from the enclosed CD and perform the following actions:

1. Format Column A in 3/14/1998 format.

2. Format A2 to show the day of the week, long month name, day, and four-digit year (for example, Sunday, June 20, 1999).

3. Format Column B as time with AM/PM (for example, 1:30 PM).

4. Format Column E as Currency with two decimal places.

5. Format Column F with commas and zero decimal places.

6. Format Column G with percent and three decimal places.

Check your work against the solution file 1101S.

Task 2

Objectives covered: 76, "Create Custom Number Formats"; 77, "Use Conditional Formatting."

Open practice file 1102P from the enclosed CD and perform the following actions:

1. Format Column H as a fraction with up to one digit.

2. Format Column I as a social security number.

3. Format each Column C using the currency symbol mentioned in Column D with two decimal places. Hint: Use Column D as a guide for the currency symbol. Use Ctrl to select all the US Dollar entries, and then format these noncontiguous cells. Repeat for Pounds and Euros.

4. If items in Column F are over 50,000, make the font color blue, and if they are under 10,000, make the color red.

5. If items in Column G are between .4 and .6, make the background of the cell yellow.

Check your work against the solution file 1102S.

Cheat Sheet

Apply Number Formats (Accounting, Currency, Number)

Number formatting displays numbers and dates with options for decimal places, a thousands separator, negative numbers, currency symbols, and date and time digits or words.

Choose Format, Cells (Ctrl+1), Number tab to set number formats.

Create Custom Number Formats

Custom formats enable you to more precisely define formats for your numbers.

Choose Format, Cells (Ctrl+1), Number tab, Category Choose Custom to set custom number formats.

To display significant digits, type a #, for insignificant digits type a 0, for thousands type a comma, and for negative numbers type parentheses or a dash.

For dates, you can type m, mm, mmm, and mmmm to display months; d, dd, ddd, and dddd to display days; and yy and yyyy to display years.

Use Conditional Formatting

Conditional formatting enables you to change the format of a cell based on the value of the contents of the cell.

Choose Format, Conditional Formatting, identify the rules for formatting, and click the Format button to open the Format Cells dialog box and make your format choices.

Printing Workbooks

Following is a list of MOUS objectives:

- Print and Preview Multiple Worksheets
- Use the Report Manager

Print and Preview Multiple Worksheets

You can use each worksheet of a workbook for different categories, divisions, time frames, or even notes. For example, you might have a separate sheet for each state's sales. Dealing with multiple worksheets of a workbook is covered in Chapter 5, "Working with Worksheets and Workbooks." This section covers printing multiple worksheets.

Print Workbook

If you want to print or preview all sheets, the task is easy. Follow these steps:

1. Click the <u>F</u>ile menu and choose <u>P</u>rint.

2. On the Print dialog box, choose <u>E</u>ntire Workbook.

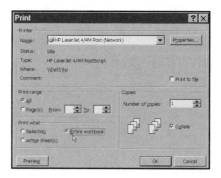

3. To print right now, choose the OK button.

4. To see what the print will look like when printed, choose Preview.

5. While in Print Preview, click the mouse pointer to zoom in or out of view, choose the Next or Previous button to move to different pages, click to Print, or choose Close to return to the workbook.

If you want to print more than one sheet, you can select the sheets you want by using the sheet tabs at the bottom of the screen.

Print Multiple Worksheets

To print more than one worksheet, do the following:

1. Select worksheets through one of the following methods:

- To select contiguous worksheets, click the first worksheet, hold down Shift, and click the last worksheet (see Objective 45, "Move Between Worksheets in a Workbook").

- To select noncontiguous worksheets, click the first worksheet, hold down Ctrl, and click any other worksheets you want. To deselect all except the first selected worksheet, click the chosen worksheets while holding down Ctrl.

- Right-click a sheet tab and choose Select All Sheets.

- Click the first sheet. Hold down Shift and Ctrl and press Page Up or Page Down to select multiple sheets.

2. If you want to include a consistent, built-in header and footer across all sheets, click File and choose Page Setup. Click the Header/Footer tab, choose the drop-down arrow for Header or Footer, and select an item. If the item has page numbers, they will appear sequentially among all pages that you choose.

3. After the sheets are selected, do one of the following:

- Click 🖨 Print.

- Click 🔍 Print Preview.

- Click File, choose Print, click Active Sheet(s), and then choose Preview or OK to print.

See also Chapter 4, "Page Setup and Printing," for more information about headers and footers, margins, and printing and previewing.

If you want to save sets of sheets for printing, see Objective 79, "Use the Report Manager."

Use the Report Manager

If you have different parts of your workbook that you print frequently, you can go to a named range (see Objective 80, "Add and Delete a Named Range") and then print the selection. However, you might have different areas of your workbook that have different page setup settings. You can use Report Manager to create reports with selected print settings and custom views. You can also use the Report Manager to print different scenarios (see Objective 104, "Work with Scenarios") and views with the workbook.

You can save a number of settings with a view and use the view with or without the Report Manager. First, set up the workbook as desired with any of the following settings:

Views

- Column widths (see Objective 27, "Modify Size of Rows and Columns").

- Hidden rows and columns (see Objective 41, "Hide and Unhide Rows and Columns").

- Hidden sheets (click the Format menu, choose Sheet, click Hide; to redisplay, choose Unhide).

- Split windows or frozen panes (see Objective 42, "Freeze and Unfreeze Rows and Columns").

- Filters (see Objective 98, "Apply Data Filters").

- Page setup (see Chapter 4, "Page Setup and Printing").

- If desired, select a worksheet and range that you want selected when the view is chosen.

To create the view, do the following:

1. Click the <u>V</u>iew menu and choose Custom <u>V</u>iews.

2. On the Custom Views dialog box, click <u>A</u>dd.

3. Select each check box if you want to include <u>P</u>rint Settings and/or Hidden <u>R</u>ows, Columns and Filter Settings.

4. Type a <u>N</u>ame for the view and choose OK.

To display a view, click the <u>V</u>iew menu, choose Custom <u>V</u>iews, choose the view from the list of defined views, and click Show.

Create Report

The Report Manager enables you to choose the view and scenarios you want and save them for printing.

Before you use the Report Manager, you must first load the Report Manager add-in program. Click the <u>T</u>ools menu, choose Add-<u>I</u>ns, select the Report Manager check box, and choose OK.

To create a report, follow these steps:

1. Click the <u>V</u>iew menu and choose <u>R</u>eport Manager.

2. On the Report Manager dialog box, click the <u>A</u>dd button.

3. The Add Report dialog box opens. Type in a <u>R</u>eport Name.

4. In the <u>S</u>heet drop-down box, choose one of the worksheets of the workbook.

5. If desired, select the <u>V</u>iew check box and choose a view, and select the <u>S</u>cenario check box and choose a scenario.

6. Click <u>A</u>dd to include this worksheet in the Report.

7. Repeat Steps 4–6 for as many different worksheets as you want in the report.

8. If you want to change the order of the worksheets, click

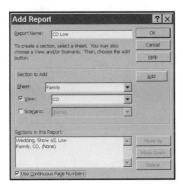

the Sections in This Report box and choose Move Up, Move Down, or Delete.

9. If you want page numbers to continue across worksheets, select the Use Continuous Page Numbers check box.

10. Choose OK when you finish with the report.

11. Repeat Steps 2–10 for any reports you want to create.

After you create one or more reports, do the following:

1. Click the View menu and choose Report Manager.

2. On the Report Manager dialog box, do any of the

Manage Reports

following:

- Choose <u>P</u>rint. Enter the number of copies, and choose OK.

- Choose <u>A</u>dd or <u>E</u>dit, and do the steps in the preceding procedure.

- To remove the report, choose <u>D</u>elete.

3. When you finish, choose OK.

Objectives covered: 78, "Print and Preview Multiple

TAKE THE TEST

Worksheets."

Task 1

Open practice file 1201P from the enclosed CD and perform the following actions:

1. Print the entire workbook.

2. Preview Wedding and Friends sheets.

3. Preview all sheets in the workbook.

There is no solution file.

Objectives covered: 79, "Use the Report Manager."

Task 2

Open practice file 1202P from the enclosed CD and perform the following actions:

1. Go to the Family worksheet. In the State drop-down list in Cell E2, select CA. Save this as view CA. Do the same thing to create views for CO and AZ.

2. Change the State drop-down to All and save this view as All Family.

3. Go to the Wedding worksheet. Create a Show All view. Hide rows 3:16, 19:24, 27:34, and select E39. Save this view as Summary. Return to Show All view.

4. Create a report called CA High that includes the Wedding worksheet, High scenario, Family worksheet, and CA view.

5. Create a report called CO Low that includes the Wedding worksheet, Low scenario, Family worksheet, and CO view.

6. Create a report called Everyone Summary that includes the Wedding worksheet, High scenario, and Summary view; and the Family worksheet and the All Family view.

7. Edit all reports to show continuous page numbers.

8. Delete the CO Low report and print the Everyone Summary report.

Check your work against the solution file 1202S.

Cheat Sheet

Print and Preview Multiple Worksheets

To print all the worksheets in the workbook, choose File, Print, Entire Workbook, OK.

To print or preview multiple contiguous worksheets, select the first sheet, hold down Shift, select the last sheet, and then click 🖨 Print or 🔍 Preview.

To print or preview multiple noncontiguous worksheets, select the first sheet, hold down Ctrl, select the sheets you want, and then click 🖨 Print or 🔍 Preview.

Use the Report Manager

The Report Manager can save multiple worksheets with views and scenarios as a collection of named reports. Then, you can select the name of the report you want to print.

To create a view, set up the workbook as desired, choose View, Custom Views, Add and give the view a name.

To create a report, choose View, Report Manager, Add, give the report a name, and choose the sheet, view, and scenario.

Working with Named Ranges

Following is a list of MOUS objectives:

- Add and Delete a Named Range
- Use a Named Range in a Formula
- Use Lookup Functions (HLOOKUP or VLOOKUP)

80

Add and Delete a Named Range

Range names help in several ways. If you use the same range repeatedly for formatting or printing, it might be easier to name the range and select it whenever you need it (see Chapter 3, "Formatting Worksheets," and Objective 32, "Print a Selection"). In more complex formulas, it is easier to understand your workbook when arguments are named rather than just using cell addresses (see Chapter 6, "Working with Formulas and Functions"). Finally, range names are good bookmarks in the workbook. You can use them to quickly go to places you often use (see Objective 2, "Go to a Specific Cell").

Use Name Box

The Name Box is the easiest way to define and go to a named range.

To name a range with the Name Box, follow these steps:

1. Select the range you want to name.

2. Click and type in the Name Box.

3. Press Enter.

Type range name in Name Box

To go to a named range, click the drop-down arrow in the Name Box and select the name (see also Objective 2, "Go to a Specific Cell").

Choose range to go to

You can also create a range name by using the Define Name dialog box. This gives you the opportunity to see the other names in the workbook and define several names at once.

Define Name

To define a range name, follow these steps:

1. Select the range you want to name.

2. Click the Insert menu, choose Name, and click Define.

3. In the Define Name dialog box, type the name of the range in the Names in Workbook text box.

4. If you want to change the range, edit the range in the Refers to text box or click the Collapse Dialog button to the right of the text box, select the range, and click the Redisplay Dialog box button.

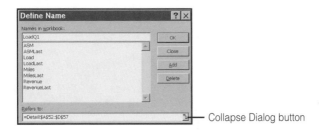

Collapse Dialog button

5. Click Add.

6. Repeat Steps 3 and 4 for each range you want to name. When you finish, choose OK.

Delete Name

To remove a range name, do the following:

1. Click the Insert menu, choose Name, and click Define.

2. In the Names in Workbook list, select the name and click Delete.

3. Choose OK.

Create Names Using Labels

If you've already created your worksheet with labels identifying the rows and columns, you can use the labels to create multiple range names at one time.

To create names using labels, follow these steps:

1. Select the range of labels and values you want to include in range names.

2. Click the Insert menu, choose Name, and click Create.

3. In the Create Names dialog box, choose any of the following:

    • If you want to use labels from the first row of the selected range to name the columns, select the Top Row check box.

    • If you want to use the labels from the left column of the selected range to name the rows, select the Left Column check box.

    • Less commonly, you can also select the Bottom Row or Right Column check boxes to name the column or ranges.

4. Choose OK.

If you created a number of range names and want to convert cell references in formulas to the range names, you can do the following:

Apply Names to Existing Ranges

1. Click the Insert menu, choose Name, and click Apply.

2. The Apply Names dialog box opens. In the Apply Names list box, select one or more names (they might already be selected for you).

3. If you want to replace references regardless of whether they are relative or absolute, select the Ignore Relative/Absolute check box; otherwise, clear this box to have the named references convert to relative, absolute, or mixed.

4. If you want to name cells a combination of the row and column labels if no name exists for the cell (for example, Benefits Jan), select the Use Row and Column Names check box.

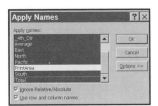

5. Choose OK when you finish.

81

Use a Named Range in a Formula

After you create range names (see Objective 80, "Add and Delete a Named Range"), you can use them in formulas to make your workbook easier to understand (see Chapter 6, "Working with Formulas and Functions").

To use a range name in a formula, do the following.

1. Start your formula by doing one of the following:

   • Type = or click ▣ Edit Formula on the Formula Bar.

   • Type =, a function name, and an open parenthesis.

   • Click ƒₓ Paste Function, choose the function, and choose OK to move to the arguments for the function.

2. When the formula is ready for a cell or range reference that you have a range name for, do one of the following:

   • Type the name of the range.

   • Press F3 to open the Paste Name dialog box, select the name, and click OK.

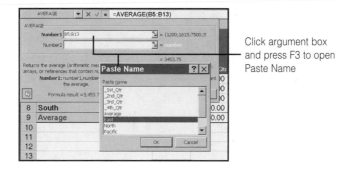

Click argument box and press F3 to open Paste Name

3. Add any operators or move to another argument text box and repeat Step 2 as necessary.

If you want to use natural language formulas where you can use the labels at the top or left of columns in formulas (without naming the ranges), click the Tools menu, choose Options, click the Calculation tab, and select the Accept Labels in Formulas check box.

82

Use Lookup Functions (HLOOKUP or VLOOKUP)

Sometimes, you will need to look up a value from a list of items. For example, you might need to look up a tax rate for a specific state. Usually, this will be necessary when you need to use this value in a formula for further calculations. These functions are easier to create if you use the Lookup Wizard add-in.

Lookup Wizard

Before you use the Lookup Wizard, you must first load the Lookup Wizard add-in. Click the Tools menu, choose Add-Ins, select the Lookup Wizard check box, and choose OK.

To use the Lookup Wizard, do the following:

1. Create a table that has rows and columns identifying the data to look up. If you are going to want to look up values in the table between rows or columns, make sure the column and row identifiers are sorted.

2. Click the Tools menu, choose Wizard, and click Lookup.

3. The Lookup Wizard Step 1 of 4 dialog box opens. Type a range name or cell reference or select the range of the table you created in Step 1, and choose Next.

Table range to look up

The Collapse Dialog button looks different on these dialog boxes

4. On the Lookup Wizard Step 2 of 4, select the Which Column Contains the Value to Find? drop-down list and choose the column label.

Note: If the columns don't match exactly and you want to find the closest match, choose No Column Labels Match Exactly, and then choose the column label.

5. Select the Which Row Contains the Value to Find? drop-down list and choose the row label.

Note: If the rows don't match exactly and you want to find the closest match, choose No Row Labels Match Exactly, and then choose the row label.

6. Choose Next to go to Step 3 of the Lookup Wizard and choose if you just want the value from the table (Copy Just the Formula to a Single Cell) or if you want to copy the value and the row and column headings (Copy the Formula and Lookup Parameters).

7. Choose Next to go to Step 4 of the wizard, type or select a cell where you want the result to go, and choose Finish.

Excel creates a long formula that uses the INDEX, MATCH, VLOOKUP, or HLOOKUP functions, depending on your choices in the wizard.

HLOOKUP

You can create the HLOOKUP or VLOOKUP functions using the Paste Function dialog box instead if you want.

The HLOOKUP function stands for Horizontal lookup. This means that you find a cell in the first row and then look up a value in a row of that column by moving down a certain number of rows.

To create an HLOOKUP function, follow these steps:

1. Create a table with only the first row identifying the columns (and not a column for labeling for the rows— or at least don't include the column in the Table_Array range in Step 5).

2. Position the cell pointer where you want the function to go.

3. Click f_x Paste Function, choose the Function Category Lookup and Reference (or All), choose the Function Name HLOOKUP, and choose OK.

4. The Function Palette opens with the arguments for the HLOOKUP function. In Lookup_Value, type or select the cell that contains the value that matches the first row in the table.

5. In the `Table_Array` argument, type the range reference or name of the table, or if named, press F3 and select the range name.

6. In the `Row_Index_Num` argument, type how many rows you want to move down (including the row labels). The first row below the labels would be numbered 2.

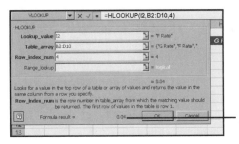

Use the Formula result area to verify you have the correct arguments

7. If you want to find the closest value, type `TRUE` in `Range_Lookup` or leave this blank. Type `FALSE` if an exact match is required.

VLOOKUP

The VLOOKUP function stands for Vertical lookup. This means that you find a cell in the first column and then look up a value in a column of that row by moving right a certain number of columns.

To create a VLOOKUP function, do the following:

1. Create a table with only the first column identifying the rows (and not a row for labeling for the columns—or at least don't include the row in the `Table_Array` range in Step 5).

2. Position the cell pointer where you want the function to go.

3. Click ☑ Paste Function, choose the Function category Lookup and Reference (or All), choose the Function Name VLOOKUP, and choose OK.

4. The Function Palette opens with the arguments for the VLOOKUP function. In Lookup_Value, type or select the cell that contains the value that matches the first column in the table.

5. In the Table_Array argument, type the range reference or name of the table, or if named, press F3 and select the range name.

6. In the Col_Index_Num argument, type how many columns you want to move right (including the column labels). The first column to the right of the labels would be numbered 2.

7. If you want to find the closest value, type TRUE in Range_Lookup or leave this blank. Type FALSE if an exact match is required.

TAKE THE TEST

Task 1

Objectives covered: 80, "Add and Delete a Named Range"; 81, "Use a Named Range in a Formula."

Open practice file 1301P from the enclosed CD and perform the following actions:

1. Name the range A1:F9 Print.

2. Use the labels in Column A and Row 4 to name the ranges in Rows 4 through 8 (East, North, and so on) and Columns B through E (_1st_Qtr and so on).

3. Replace the cell references in average and total formulas with the range names.

4. Instead of _1st_Qtr as a range name, change the name to Qtr1 and delete the range name _1st_Qtr. Do this for all four quarters. Correct the formulas as necessary.

5. Type Total in A10 and create sums in cells B10 through E10 that refer to the range names. Adjust column widths if necessary.

Check your work against the solution file 1301S.

Task 2

Objectives covered: 80, "Add and Delete a Named Range"; 81, "Use a Named Range in a Formula"; 82, "Use Lookup Functions (HLOOKUP or VLOOKUP)."

Open practice file 1302P from the enclosed CD and perform the following actions:

1. Name the range A2:D10 Rates.

2. Create a formula in H3 that looks up the G Rate for CO from the Rate table. You can use the Lookup Wizard, VLOOKUP, or HLOOKUP.

3. Create formulas in the rest of H3 through J10 that look up the appropriate Rate for each state. Hint: If you want, look at the formula and replace text references with cell references to the values in Column G and Row 2.

Check your work against the solution file 1302S.

Cheat Sheet

Add and Delete a Named Range

Range names help select and go to cells or ranges you use frequently. Select a range and type a name in the range box to create a name.

You can also create range names through Insert, Name and using either Create or Define.

Use the Define Name dialog box to also Delete range names.

Use a Named Range in a Formula

Range names help make formulas easier to understand.

Whenever a cell or range is called for in a formula, type a range name or press F3 and choose the range name.

Use Lookup Functions (HLOOKUP or VLOOKUP)

The lookup functions enable you to find values in a table.

The easiest way to create lookup functions is through the Lookup Wizard add-in, which first much be turned on through Tools, Add-Ins.

To use the Lookup Wizard, choose Tools, Wizards, Lookup and follow the dialog boxes.

Working with Toolbars

Following is a list of MOUS objectives:

- Hide and Display Toolbars
- Customize a Toolbar
- Assign a Macro to a Command Button

Hide and Display Toolbars

Toolbars enable you to quickly do most common tasks. The default toolbars, Standard and Formatting, display when you start Excel. Depending on the feature used, other toolbars might display as well. However, you can hide and display toolbars when you want.

To hide and display toolbars, do one of the following:

- Right-click the menu or toolbar, and click a toolbar. If the toolbar is already on, it will turn off. If the toolbar is off, it will turn on.

- Click the View menu and choose Toolbars. Click a toolbar to turn it on or off.

- With either of the preceding two options, if the toolbar name is not displayed, click Customize to bring up the Customize dialog box. You can also click Tools and choose Customize. On the Toolbars tab, place a check mark next to each toolbar you want to see, clear the check box for each toolbar you want to hide, and click Close.

Customize a Toolbar

Because the menu bar is considered a toolbar, there is only one procedure to customize a toolbar or a menu bar. Because toolbars are so useful, there are many ways to customize them. You can add or delete buttons, create a new toolbar, copy a toolbar to a workbook, and choose options on how the toolbars look on the screen.

There are two different ways to add buttons to toolbars.

Office 2000 has a new feature that appears at the end of each of the docked toolbars and in the upper-left corner of floating toolbars. The More Buttons icon is a button that enables you to add additional built-in buttons. This button changes appearance and location, depending on whether there is not enough room to show all current buttons or whether the toolbar is floating or docked.

Use More Buttons to Add Buttons to Toolbars

Indicates additional current buttons not visible ⌐

More Buttons icon ⌐

Click to add or
remove more ⌐
buttons to toolbar

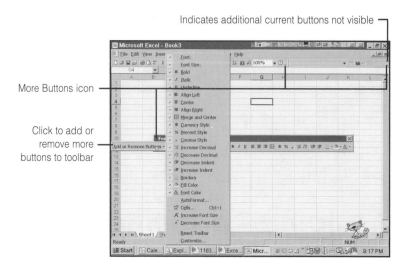

Click the More Buttons icon to display the rest of the buttons, and make a choice from the current icons. If the More Buttons icon has two right arrows, click to use a button that is on the current toolbar but doesn't fit in view. In all cases, the More Buttons icon has a menu choice called Add or Remove Buttons.

To add or remove a button through the More Buttons icon, do the following:

1. Click More Buttons.

2. Choose Add or Remove Buttons.

3. Select or clear the check boxes preceding the buttons you want to add or remove.

4. Click outside the button list to return to the worksheet.

Use Customize Dialog Box to Add Buttons to Toolbars

You can add any button to any toolbar (regardless of whether it is on the More Buttons list) with the following procedure:

1. Click the Tools menu and choose Customize, or right-click a toolbar and choose Customize.

2. The Customize dialog box opens. Click the Commands tab.

3. Click a category of commands in the Categories list and drag a button from the Commands list to an existing toolbar. The button can be an icon or a menu item.

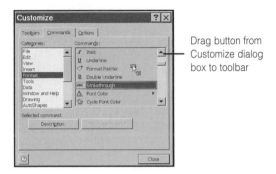

Drag button from Customize dialog box to toolbar

To customize the button image or text display options, right-click the button and choose from items on the shortcut menu.

You can even create a new menu on an existing toolbar, menu bar, or menu. In the Categories list, choose New Menu and drag New Menu from Commands onto a toolbar or menu bar, or click a menu and drag down to where you want the sub-menu to go. Right-click the menu and type a Name. For the hotkey (Alt+letter choice), type an ampersand before the letter (for example, Ne&w Company). Add items to the menu with the preceding procedure.

If you want to return a built-in toolbar to its default settings, click the Toolbars tab in the Customize dialog box, select the name in the Toolbars list, and choose Reset. Click OK at the prompt, and the toolbar will be returned to its original form.

Reset Toolbars

You can create an entirely new toolbar by the following:

Create New Toolbar

1. Open the Customize dialog box in one of the ways mentioned earlier (one way is to click the Tools menu and choose Customize).

2. If necessary, click the Toolbars tab.

3. Click New.

4. In the text box, type the name of your toolbar and click OK.

5. Click the Commands tab and use the preceding procedure to add buttons to the toolbar.

> You can save this toolbar with the current workbook. Click the Toolbars tab and choose Attach. Click the toolbar in the Custom Toolbars list and click Copy. The toolbar will be added to the workbook.

Options

Click the Options tab of the Customize dialog box to select options for displaying and using toolbars.

- To put the Formatting toolbar on the same row as the Standard toolbar, check Standard and Formatting Toolbars Share One Row. Clear this check box to place them on two rows. You can also drag the handle on the left edge to move a toolbar. See the following section, "Move a Toolbar."

- A new option for Office 2000 is Menus Show Recently Used Commands First. If this check box is cleared, menus will show all choices. If this check box is selected, the menus will show only basic and frequently used choices. Double-click the menu word or click the double arrow at the bottom to expand the menu. If you want to pause your mouse pointer on the menu to show the complete menu, select the Show Full Menus After a Short Delay check box.

- Excel will keep track of the menu items and toolbar choices you use frequently and place them on the short menus and toolbars. If you want to return the settings to the default ones, choose Reset My Usage Data.

- To increase the size of toolbar buttons, check Large Icons.

- To make the Font button list operate more quickly, clear the List Font Names in Their Font check box; otherwise select this check box to show a preview of the font.

- To show the onscreen descriptions of the buttons when you pause your mouse on a button, select the Show ScreenTips on Toolbars check box.

- You can make the menus appear to slide down or unfold if you choose Slide or Unfold in the Menu Animations list.

When you finish with the Customize dialog box, click Close.

Move a Toolbar

You can drag a toolbar where you would like it to go. If a toolbar is docked, drag the handle on the left edge of the toolbar (the mouse pointer becomes a four-headed arrow). You can drag the toolbar to any edge of the screen, and it will dock.

If you leave the toolbar in the middle of the screen, it is called floating. A floating toolbar has a title bar and a close (×) button. You can drag the title bar to move the toolbar or double-click the title bar to return it to its most recently docked position.

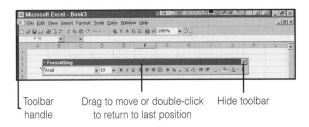

Toolbar handle   Drag to move or double-click to return to last position   Hide toolbar

Assign a Macro to a Command Button

In addition to running macros by using the Macro dialog box and keyboard shortcuts (see Objective 87, "Run Macros"), a convenient way is to attach a macro to a button or menu item. Obviously, you first must create the macro (see Objective 86, "Record Macros").

To attach a macro to a command button, follow these steps:

1. Click <u>T</u>ools and choose <u>C</u>ustomize to open the Customize dialog box (or choose one of the other ways mentioned at the beginning of the chapter).

2. Click the <u>C</u>ommands tab.

3. Although you can assign a macro to any toolbar button, you will generally create a new button. In the Categories list, choose Macros.

4. From the Comman<u>d</u>s list, you generally drag the Custom Menu Item to a menu or the Custom Button to a toolbar.

5. Right-click the button or menu item and choose Assign <u>M</u>acro.

6. In the Assign Macro dialog box, select the desired macro and click OK.

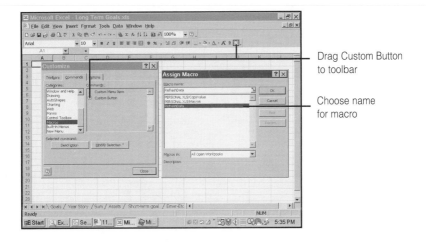

Drag Custom Button to toolbar

Choose name for macro

7. To change the image, right-click the button and do one of the following:

- Choose Change <u>B</u>utton Image and select an image.

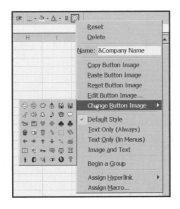

- Choose <u>E</u>dit Button Image and draw your own image.

- From another button, choose <u>C</u>opy Button Image (or copy from a graphics program), and on this button, choose <u>P</u>aste Button Image.

- To return the button to its original image, choose Re<u>s</u>et Button Image.

8. Click Close when you finish with the Customize dialog box.

323

TAKE THE TEST

Task 1

Objectives covered: 83, "Hide and Display Toolbars"; 84, "Customize a Toolbar"; 85, "Assign a Macro to a Command Button."

Open practice file 1401P from the enclosed CD and perform the following actions:

1. Put the Formatting and Standard toolbars on one line.

2. Create a new toolbar named MyTools.

3. On the new toolbar, add the Double Underline, Strikethrough, Cycle Font Color, and Angle Text Upward buttons.

4. Add two new buttons, and assign the macros NameAndCompany and Budget to the buttons. Change the Image Faces to a Heart and Diamond. Name the buttons the same as the macro name. Using the More Buttons icon, add the Increase Font Size button to the Formatting toolbar.

5. First, click the NameAndCompany button and then click the Budget button. Select B5:M5. Click the Angle Text Upward buttons on MyTools and the Increase Font Size, Align Center, and Align Left buttons on the Formatting toolbar.

6. Attach the MyTools toolbar to the workbook, and save and close the workbook.

7. Delete the MyTools toolbar, reset the Formatting toolbar, and change the Formatting and Standard toolbars to two rows.

Check your work against the solution file 1401S. You'll have to display MyTools. The workbook created in Step 5 is 1401SA. If you open 1401S to check the solution, make sure you delete the MyTools toolbar.

Cheat Sheet

Hide and Display Toolbars

If you need additional functionality, you can display other toolbars. When you no longer need a toolbar, you can hide it.

Right-click a toolbar and select a toolbar name to turn the toolbar on or off.

Customize a Toolbar

You can create a new toolbar and add or remove buttons from any toolbar.

To open the Customize dialog box, choose Tools, Customize; View, Toolbars, Customize; alternatively, right-click a toolbar and choose Customize.

On the Toolbars tab of the Customize dialog box, you can turn on and off toolbars, choose New to create a new toolbar, Delete a toolbar, Attach a toolbar to the workbook, and Reset a toolbar to its default settings.

On the Commands tab of the Customize dialog box, you can drag buttons to a toolbar or menu.

On the Options tab of the Customize dialog box, you can choose to place the Formatting and Standard toolbars on one line as well as change the appearance of all toolbars.

Assign a Macro to a Command Button

You can place macros on command buttons on a toolbar.

On the Commands tab of the Customize dialog box, choose Macros in the Categories list and drag Custom Button to a toolbar.

Right-click the Custom Button, change the Name, and choose Assign Macro.

Using Macros

Following is a list of MOUS objectives:

- Record Macros
- Run Macros
- Edit Macros

Record Macros

If you perform the same task repeatedly, you might be able to reduce your time spent if you record a macro. Macros are recorded series of instructions that perform tasks in a specified order. The instructions are recorded in Visual Basic for Applications programming language and stored as modules.

To record a series of actions and save the results as a macro, do the following:

1. If necessary, prepare the workbook or position the cell pointer in the workbook where you want it to be when the macro starts.

2. Click the Tools menu, choose Macro, and click Record New Macro.

3. The Record Macro dialog box appears. Type the name of the procedure in Macro Name. The first character of a macro name must be a letter.

4. If you want to run this macro by pressing shortcut keys, type the Shortcut Key. If you use a lowercase letter, it is Ctrl+the letter. If you use an uppercase letter, it is Ctrl+Shift+the letter. Try not to use a common shortcut key you would normally use (such as Ctrl+C for copy or Ctrl+O for open).

   If you want to run a macro from a toolbar button, see Objective 85, "Assign a Macro to a Command Button."

5. In the Store Macro in drop-down box, choose one of the following locations as a place to store the macro:

- **This Workbook**—If you want to use this macro only when this workbook is open.

- **New Workbook**—If you want to use the macro for some of your workbooks (but not all). The new workbook must be open to run the macro.

- **Personal Macro Workbook**—If you want to use the macro in all workbooks. This is a hidden file that is always available after you record your first macro in it.

6. By default, Description displays your name and system date. It is a good idea to change the Description and describe the macro: Type the changes in the text box.

7. Choose OK. You are returned to your worksheet, the Stop Recording toolbar appears, and the status bar says Recording.

8. By default, Excel will record your movements to the actual cells. If you want to record locations relative to where the cell pointer is, click ▦ Relative Reference. For example, the macro will record down two over three rather than D3.

9. Type the text and perform whatever actions you want to record. Make sure you add a new workbook if necessary and/or move to the correct starting cell before you start typing (in case your cell pointer is somewhere different when you start the macro).

10. When you finish recording, do one of the following:

- Click ■ Stop Recording.

- Click the Tools menu, choose Macro, and click Stop Recording.

To run this macro, see Objective 87, "Run Macros." To edit the macro, see Objective 88, "Edit Macros."

Run Macros

To run a macro that you've recorded (or that has been created manually in the Visual Basic Editor), follow these steps:

1. Press Alt+F8; alternatively, click the Tools menu, choose Macro menu, and click Macros.

2. The Macro dialog box opens. If you want to limit the list of macros to a specific workbook, choose the workbook from the Macros in drop-down. To see all macros, choose All Open Workbooks.

 — The description of the selected macro

3. In the Macro Name list, double-click the macro, or click the macro and choose Run.

If the macro has been assigned a shortcut key combination, you can also press the key combination to run the macro.

If the macro is assigned to a button or menu item, you can also click the button or choose the menu item (see Objective 85, "Assign a Macro to a Command Button").

Edit Macros

After you create a macro, you can use the Visual Basic Editor to make changes. Visual Basic programming is quite involved. This section covers only a rudimentary description of how to edit a simple macro.

Edit Procedure

To edit a macro, do the following:

1. Press Alt+F8; alternatively, click the Tools menu, choose Macro menu, and click Macros.

2. The Macro dialog box opens. If you want to limit the list of macros to a specific workbook, choose the workbook from the Macros in drop-down. To see all macros, choose All Open Workbooks.

3. In the Macro Name list, click the macro and choose Edit.

4. The Visual Basic Editor opens with a module window opened and your macro displayed.

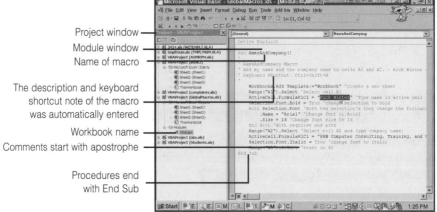

Project window
Module window
Name of macro
The description and keyboard
shortcut note of the macro
was automatically entered
Workbook name
Comments start with apostrophe
Procedures end
with End Sub

5. If you want to add a comment in the macro on a line by itself or after a line of programming, type an apostrophe, and then type the text.

6. Edit the macro as you would a document. Click to position the insertion point. Press Backspace to delete before the insertion point and Delete to delete after the insertion point. Select text, and then type new text or press Delete to remove it.

7. The name of the macro is after the keyword Sub. If you want to change the name of the macro, edit this text.

8. Type text in the body of the macro in quotes (`""`).

9. You are generally working with objects such as Range("A1"), properties (characteristics of the objects), and methods (actions either the object performs or to perform on the object). Type an object, a period, and then a property or method. For example, type
`Range("A1").Select` or `Selection.Font.Bold = True`.

10. When you finish editing the macro, click 🖫 Save, press Ctrl+S; or click File, and choose Save Filename.

11. Exit the Visual Basic Editor by clicking the Close (|) button, by pressing Alt+Q, or by clicking File and choosing Close and Return to Microsoft Excel.

If you want to edit macros recorded in the Personal Macro Workbook, you'll have to unhide the workbook first. Click the Window menu and choose Unhide. When you finish editing, click Window and choose Hide

---

If you want to add or modify the shortcut key combination associated with a macro, follow these steps:

Keyboard Shortcut

1. Press Alt+F8 or click the Tools menu, choose Macro menu, and click Macros.

2. The Macro dialog box opens. If you want to limit the list of macros to a specific workbook, choose the workbook from the Macros in drop-down. To see all macros, choose All Open Workbooks.

3. In the Macro <u>N</u>ame list, click the macro and choose <u>O</u>ptions.

4. The Macro Options dialog box opens. Type the new Shortcut <u>K</u>ey.

5. If desired, type a new <u>D</u>escription.

6. Choose OK.

7. Click Cancel on the Macro dialog box to return to the workbook, or choose <u>E</u>dit to go to the macro. If you want, you can edit the comments showing the description and keyboard shortcut.

TAKE THE TEST

Objectives covered: 86, "Record Macros"; 87, "Run Macros"; 88, "Edit Macros."

Create a new workbook and perform the following actions:

1. Save the workbook as mymacros.

2. Create a macro named MyInfo in the current workbook with a keyboard shortcut of Ctrl+Shift+O.

3. The macro should create a new workbook and place My Name in cell A1 of the new workbook, My Company Name in A2, and today's date in A3. Format A1 as bold 16 point font, and Times New Roman. Format A2 as Italic.

4. Exit the new workbook. Save mymacros with the macro.

5. Run the macro MyInfo.

Check your work against the solution file 1501S. The macro might not match exactly, depending on the exact procedures you followed.."

Objectives covered: 88, "Edit Macros."

Open practice file 1502P from the enclosed CD and perform the following actions.

Edit the MyInfo macro with the following changes:

1. Change the macro name to NameCompany.

2. Delete the comments on who created the macro, and add a comment with your name and today's date.

3. Type your own name and company name where it says My Name and My Company Name.

4. Instead of a date hard-coded in A3, have the macro type in the formula =Today().

5. At the end of the macro, have the cell pointer go to A5.

6. Test your macro.

Check your work against the solution file 1502S.

Cheat Sheet

Record Macros

Macros enable you to automate tasks that you do often. The easiest way to learn how to create macros is to record them.

Record a macro by clicking Tools, Macro, Record New Macro.

If you want the macro to be available to all workbooks, click Store Macro in and choose Personal Macro Workbook.

Click ■ Stop Recording when you finish recording the macro.

Run Macros

To run a macro, press Alt+F8 or choose Tools, Macros to display the Macro dialog box. Then double-click the macro.

If you recorded a keyboard shortcut for the macro, open the workbook if necessary and press the key combination.

Edit Macros

You edit macros in the Visual Basic Editor.

Choose Alt+F8; alternatively, click Tools, Macro, Macros, select the macro, and choose Edit.

Auditing a Worksheet

Following is a list of MOUS objectives:

- Work with the Auditing Toolbar
- Trace Errors (Find and Fix Errors)
- Trace Precedents (Find Cells Referred to in a Specific Formula)
- Trace Dependents (Find Formulas that Refer to a Specific Cell)

Work with the Auditing Toolbar

Use the Auditing toolbar to graphically trace the relationship between cells and formulas, identify and circle invalid data, or trace errors.

Display the Auditing Toolbar

Unlike the other toolbars, the Auditing toolbar is not listed on the shortcut menu when you click a toolbar.

To turn on the Auditing toolbar, do one of the following:

- Click the Tools menu, choose Auditing, and click Show Auditing Toolbar.

- Click the Tools menu, choose Customize, click the Toolbars tab, check Auditing, and choose Close.

- Click the View menu, choose Toolbars, choose Customize, click the Toolbars tab, check Auditing, and choose Close.

Buttons on the Toolbar

The toolbar has the following buttons:

- Trace Precedents **Trace Precedents**—Shows cells that are referenced by a formula (see Objective 91, "Trace Precedents").

- Remove Precedent Arrows **Remove Precedent Arrows**— See Objective 91, "Trace Precedents."

- `⚡ Trace Dependents` **Trace Dependents**—Shows formulas that reference a cell (see Objective 92, "Trace Dependents").

- `⚡ Remove Dependent Arrows` **Remove Dependent Arrows**—See Objective 92, "Trace Dependents."

- `⚡ Remove All Arrows` **Remove All Arrows**— Removes error, precedent, and dependent arrows.

- `◇ Trace Error` **Trace Error**—Finds cells that make up a formula with an error (see Objective 90, "Trace Errors").

- `⬚ Comment` **Comment**—Adds a note to the cell (see Objective 110, "Create, Edit, and Remove a Comment").

- `⊞ Circle Invalid Data` **Circle Invalid Data**—Finds cells that no longer meet validation rules (see Objective 101, "Use Data Validation").

- `⊞ Clear Validation Circles` **Clear Validation Circles**— See Objective 101, "Use Data Validation."

As you can see, most of these buttons are referenced in this chapter or elsewhere in the book.

The Auditing Toolbar Doesn't Work

If the buttons on the Auditing toolbar are dimmed or don't work, check one of the following:

- When the buttons are dimmed, objects are hidden. Click the Tools menu, choose Options, click the View tab, and in the Objects section, click Show All.

- When the buttons don't work, the sheet might be protected. Click the Tools menu, choose Protection, and click Unprotect Sheet (see Objective 111, "Apply and Remove Worksheet and Workbook Protection").

90

Trace Errors (Find and Fix Errors)

If your active cell has a formula that displays an error value, you can use Trace Error to find the cell that causes the error value.

To find the source of the error, follow these steps:

1. Move the active cell pointer to the cell with the error.

2. Do one of the following:

   • Click ⟨ Trace Error ⟩ Trace Error on the Auditing toolbar.

   • Click the Tools menu, choose Auditing, and click Trace Error.

3. Tracer arrows show the cells referenced in the formula or the cell causing the problem. Double-click a blue arrow's head to go to the cell that contains the problem causing the error.

Blue tracer arrow shows references in formula

Red tracer arrow shows location causing the error

4. Edit the cell, or type in a new value.

The type of errors that you will see in a cell include the following:

- #VALUE!—You have the wrong kind of argument or operand in a function. For example, the function =ROUND(B2,A1) would produce #VALUE! if A1, which should be a number, has text instead. In this case, change the value of A1 or edit the formula so the second argument refers to a cell with a number.

- #DIV/0!—Divide by zero; for example, =A1/A2 where A2 is 0, blank, or text. This usually happens when you've made an error and put the wrong cell reference in the divisor. If the cell is blank or contains text, this counts as zero. Fix the number or the cell reference under the divide-by symbol (/).

- #NAME?—You've typed a formula that has text that is not a recognized cell reference or range name; for example, =ddd1/D11. The reference to ddd1 doesn't refer to anything (unless you have a range name ddd1 that refers to a single cell). Correct the typo or fix the cell reference.

- #N/A—This error occurs when a value is not accessible to a function or formula and is often done on purpose to avoid turning in a worksheet that has incomplete data. If you are waiting for some data, type #N/A in the cell instead of a number. Then, all formulas that refer to the cell display #N/A. To fix, type a value in the cell.

- #REF!—The reference to the cell is not valid. This usually happens when you delete a row or column containing the formula. You'll have to edit the formula to include valid cell references.

- #NUM!—There is a problem with a number in a formula or function. The result could be too large or too small (the number would have to be greater than 10^308 or less than -10^308). Another possibility is that a formula that uses iteration such as IRR can't find the answer.

- #NULL!—This is uncommon and appears when you're specifying two ranges that don't intersect. Verify your cell and range references.

- #####—Usually, this doesn't mean that there is an error. It just means that the column isn't wide enough to display the number as formatted. Widen the column (see Objective 27, "Modify Size of Rows and Columns"), change the format of the number (see Objective 24, "Apply Number Formats"), or adjust the number of decimal places (see Objective 25, "Adjust the Decimal Place").

  You can also get this error if you are subtracting dates or times that produce a negative number. Excel automatically uses a date or time format. Click the 🟦 Comma Style button to see the negative number.

If these explanations cannot solve the preceding errors, there are more thorough explanations in online help. In the Office Assistant, type errors and choose Troubleshoot Formulas and Error Values.

Trace Precedents (Find Cells Referred to in a Specific Formula)

You might need to evaluate a formula because of an error or to understand your worksheet. You can find the cells referenced by the formula. These can include cells directly in the formula or cells that refer to other cells within the formula.

To find cells precedent to a formula, follow these steps:

1. Move the active cell pointer to the cell containing the formula.

2. Do one of the following:

   - Click [⁞ Trace Precedents] Trace Precedents on the Auditing toolbar.

   - Click the Tools menu, choose Auditing, and click Trace Precedents.

   Tracer arrows show the cells referenced in the formula.

3. If you want to continue finding cells that are precedents of these new cells, repeat Step 2.

4. If the cell being referenced is on another sheet, a worksheet icon appears on the page with a black arrow leading to the selected cell. If you want to go to that cell, move the white arrow mouse pointer to the black arrow pointing to the icon, and double-click. The Go To dialog box appears. Choose a reference and click OK.

Trace Precedents ─┐   ┌─ Remove Precedent
                             arrows

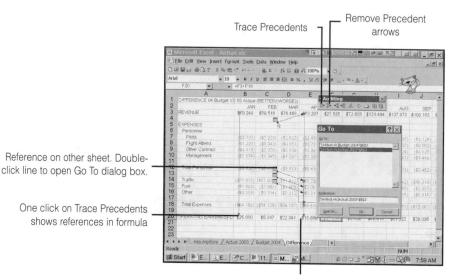

Reference on other sheet. Double-
click line to open Go To dialog box.

One click on Trace Precedents
shows references in formula

Multiple-click on Trace Precedents
shows direct and indirect references

Remove Trace Arrows

To remove the arrows on the worksheet, do one of the
following:

- Click `Remove Precedent Arrows` Remove Precedent
  Arrows.

- Click `Remove All Arrows` Remove All Arrows.

- Click the Tools menu, choose Auditing, and click
  Remove All Arrows.

Select Precedent Cells

An alternative is to select the precedent cells instead of drawing
arrows to them. Select a formula and do one of the following:

- Press Ctrl+[(open bracket) to select cells that directly are
  referenced by the formula.

- Press Ctrl+Shift+{ (open brace) to select cells that are
  directly or indirectly referenced by the formula.

- Press F5, press Ctrl+G, or click the Edit menu and
  choose Go To. The Go To dialog box opens. Click the
  Special button and choose Precedents.

Trace Dependents (Find Formulas That Refer to a Specific Cell)

You might be wondering what would happen if you changed a single cell in a worksheet. What are the ripple affects throughout the whole workbook? You can find the formulas that are dependent on this cell. This can include formulas that directly reference the cell or formulas that use other formulas that refer to the cell.

To find formulas dependent to a cell, follow these steps:

1. Move the active cell pointer to the cell.

2. Do one of the following:

   - Click [Trace Dependents] Trace Dependents on the Auditing toolbar.

   - Click the Tools menu, choose Auditing, and click Trace Dependents.

   Tracer arrows show the formulas that have references to cell.

3. If you want to continue finding formulas that are dependents of these selected formulas, repeat Step 2.

4. If the formula with reference to the cell is on another sheet, a worksheet icon appears on the page with a black arrow leading to the selected cell. If you want to go to that cell, move the white arrow mouse pointer to the black arrow pointing to the icon and double-click. The Go To dialog box appears. Choose a reference and click OK.

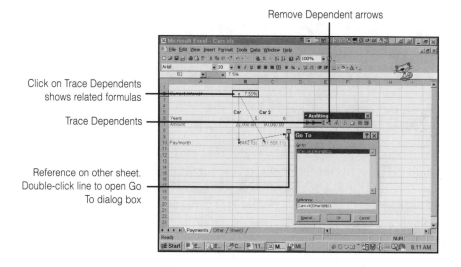

Remove Dependent arrows

Click on Trace Dependents shows related formulas

Trace Dependents

Reference on other sheet. Double-click line to open Go To dialog box

Remove Trace Arrows

To remove the arrows on the worksheet, do one of the following:

- Click [Remove Dependent Arrows] Remove Dependent Arrows.

- Click [Remove All Arrows] Remove All Arrows.

- Click the Tools menu, choose Auditing, and click Remove All Arrows.

Select Dependent Cells

An alternative is to select the dependent cells instead of drawing arrows to them. Select a cell and do one of the following:

- Press Ctrl+] (close bracket) to select formulas that have direct references to the cell.

- Press Ctrl+Shift+} (close brace) to select formulas that directly or indirectly reference the cell.

- Press F5, press Ctrl+G, or click the Edit menu and choose Go To. The Go To dialog box opens. Click the Special button and choose Dependents. Under this option button, choose whether you want to select Direct Only or All Levels of Dependent Formulas.

You can also quickly see all formulas that refer to the cell by typing #N/A in the cell. All formulas that refer to this cell at any level will display #N/A (see Objective 90, "Trace Errors").

TAKE THE TEST

Task 1

Objectives covered: 89, "Work with the Auditing Toolbar"; 90, "Trace Errors (Find and Fix Errors)."

Open practice file 1601P from the enclosed CD and perform the following actions:

1. Turn on the Auditing toolbar.

2. Use [⊘ Trace Error] Trace Error on each formula error to find the location of the error.

3. Fix the errors on the worksheet. For the Educational Savings Goal, there is a row missing that states that the number of months is 60.

Check your work against the solution file 1601S.

Task 2

Objectives covered: 91, "Trace Precedents (Find Cells Referred to in a Specific Formula)"; 92, "Trace Dependents (Find Formulas That Refer to a Specific Cell)."

Open practice file 1602P from the enclosed CD and perform the following actions:

1. Trace all the precedents to the formula in B15.

2. Clear all the arrows.

3. Trace just one level of precedents in D15.

4. Trace two levels of dependents to C6.

When you save the file, the auditing arrows disappear. To check your work, go to Microsoft Explorer and double-click the solution file 1602S.pcx. Change the zoom percentage to 100 percent.

Cheat Sheet

Work with the Auditing Toolbar

The Auditing toolbar enables you to see the source of errors, references to formulas, formulas in which a cell is referenced, and comments.

Choose Tools, Auditing, Show Auditing Toolbar to turn the toolbar on or off.

| ◢ Remove All Arrows | Choose Tools, Auditing, Remove All Arrows to remove all error, precedent, and dependent auditing arrows.

Trace Errors (Find and Fix Errors)

A worksheet might have different kinds of formula errors.

Click | ◇ Trace Error | Trace Error to find references to the error in a formula.

Trace Precedents (Find Cells Referred to in a Specific Formula)

Precedents are cells that are referenced in a formula.

| ◱ Trace Precedents | Choose Tools, Auditing, Trace Precedents.

Trace Dependents (Find Formulas That Refer to a Specific Cell)

Dependents are formulas that refer to a cell.

| ◲ Trace Dependents | Choose Tools, Auditing, Trace Dependents.

Displaying and Formatting Data

Following is a list of MOUS objectives:

- Apply Conditional Formats
- Perform Single and Multilevel Sorts
- Use Grouping and Outlines
- Use Subtotaling
- Use Data Forms
- Apply Data Filters
- Extract Data
- Query Databases
- Use Data Validation

93

Apply Conditional Formats

If you want to automatically apply formatting attributes based on the value of the contents, use conditional formatting. For example, you could add a yellow fill to all customers whose revenue was over $10,000.

To use conditional formatting, follow these steps:

1. Select the cells to format by doing any of the following:

   - Click a cell.

   - Drag the mouse pointer over a range.

   - Hold down Shift and use the keyboard to select a range.

   - Click a column header, or drag along multiple column headers to select multiple columns.

   - Click a row header, or drag along multiple row headers to select multiple rows.

2. Click the Format menu and choose Conditional Formatting.

   The Conditional Formatting dialog box opens. The number of input fields will vary depending on which operator is chosen.

3. If you want to base the conditions on values, choose Cell Value Is in the first drop-down box and continue with the following to define the formatting attributes:

- In the second drop-down box, choose Between or Not Between, and then type values or cell references in the second two text boxes. You can also use the Collapse Dialog button to choose a cell that has a value in it.

- If you choose any of the other choices in the second drop-down box (such as Equal To or Greater Than), one additional text box (instead of two) appears. Type a value or cell reference in the text box or use the Collapse Dialog button to choose a cell.

4. Click the Format button. The Format Cells dialog box opens with Font, Border, and Patterns tabs. Some of the options that would be available if you were to enter it through the Format menu (see Chapter 3, "Formatting Worksheets") are not in this dialog box. Choose the formatting options you want. For example, to change the color of the font, click the Font tab and choose a Color in the drop-down list. To change the background color of the cell, click the Patterns tab and choose a Color in the palette.

5. If you want to add more formatting conditions, click Add and repeat Steps 3 and 4.

6. If you want to remove a formatting condition, select the cells containing the conditional formatting, click Format, click Conditional Formatting, and then click the Delete button. Select the conditions to delete from the Delete Conditional Formatting dialog box and click OK.

7. When you finish with the dialog box, choose OK.

355

You cannot apply conditional formatting after you share a workbook (see Objective 115, "Create a Shared Workbook").

If you want to find cells that have conditional formatting, click the Edit menu, choose Go To, click the Special button, and choose Conditional Formats (see Objective 2, "Go to a Specific Cell").

Using a Formula in Conditional Formatting

Instead of using a value in Step 3, you can use a formula. In most cases, you will want to click the first cell that will have this formula, and then set the conditional formatting. In the first drop-down box, choose Formula Is. In the text box, type a formula such as =E2>Average(E2:E1000). Then continue as previously in choosing the format. Then, when you return to the worksheet, use the Format Painter button to copy this conditional format to the rest of the cells in the range (see Objective 28, "Use the Format Painter").

Perform Single and Multilevel Sorts

Sorting orders a list of data by one or more fields. Sorting can either be ascending (1–9 and A–Z) or descending (Z–A and 9–1). When you sort, the whole row in the list is moved based on which column you are sorting.

To sort a list, do the following:

1. Save your workbook before you sort.

2. Depending on the organization of the data, do one of the following:

    • If there are no blank columns or rows, position the cell pointer in the list.

    • If there are blank rows or columns or if you only want to partially sort a range within the list, select the rows and columns you want to sort.

3. Do one of the following:

    • Click [A↓] Sort Ascending to sort in alphabetical order.

    • Click [Z↓] Sort Descending to sort in reverse order.

If you want to undo the sort, click [↰] Undo, press Ctrl+Z, or click the Edit menu and choose Undo.

If you select only some of the columns, the surrounding columns will not be sorted.

Multilevel Sorts

If you want to sort more than one column, you can use the Data menu. For example, you might have 100 entries in one city. If the city is the only field you sort, it will be hard to find information. Therefore, you might want to sort City, Last Name, and then First Name.

To perform a multilevel sort, follow these steps:

1. Click the list of data or select the range you want to sort (see the preceding procedure).

2. Click the <u>D</u>ata menu and choose <u>S</u>ort.

3. The Sort dialog box opens. If your list has a row of labels at the top, choose Header <u>R</u>ow so the field name levels will not be included in the sort; otherwise choose No Header Ro<u>w</u>.

4. In the Sort By drop-down list, choose the name of one of the labels in the header row or the column letter by which you want to sort.

5. Choose <u>A</u>scending to sort in normal order or <u>D</u>escending to sort in reverse order.

6. If desired, repeat Steps 4 and 5 in the second and third sets of boxes.

7. Choose OK.

Sort Options

In the Sort dialog box, there is an <u>O</u>ptions button that you might use occasionally if you do custom sorting. This button brings up the Sort Options dialog box and enables you to specify custom sort orders for selected fields.

You can change your sort through any of the following options:

- In the First Key Sort Order drop-down list, choose one of the items from your custom lists. For example, to sort in order by month names, choose the abbreviations or month names in the list. Otherwise, your list will be organized alphabetically starting with Apr, Aug, and Dec. To add your own customized list, choose the Tools menu, choose Options, and select Custom Lists (see also Objective 10, "Work with Series (AutoFill)").

- Check the Case Sensitive check box to sort on capitalization.

- The default orientation is Sort Top to Bottom (moving the rows to sort). If you want to reorganize the columns, choose Sort Left to Right. If you choose this option, when you return to the Sort dialog box, you will choose rows instead of columns.

95

Use Grouping and Outlines

Outline view enables you to view portions of your worksheet and hide or display levels of detail. You can hide or display columns and rows.

Auto Outline

If you already have a worksheet with subtotals and totals in either the rows or columns, Excel can automatically create an outline with a couple of steps.

To automatically create an outline, do the following:

1. Position the cell pointer in the data area.

2. Click the Data menu, choose Group and Outline, and click Auto Outline.

   Excel will create an outline for rows and/or columns and add outline symbols to the left of rows and/or above columns. See the following section on how to navigate within the outline.

When you use subtotals, Excel also automatically creates an outline (see Objective 96, "Use Subtotaling").

Outline View

Regardless of whether you created your outline with Auto Outline, Subtotals, or manually with Group, you hide and display rows and columns the same way.

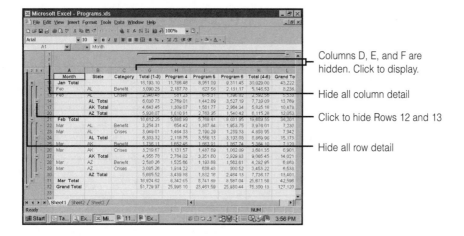

Columns D, E, and F are hidden. Click to display.

Hide all column detail

Click to hide Rows 12 and 13

Hide all row detail

To hide and display items in outline view, do the following:

- Click a level of detail you want to see. Click outline button 1 to show just the grand totals. This shows the least level of detail. Button 2 will show the highest-level category under the grand total. In the figure, click the 4 to the left of the rows to see all row detail and the 3 above the columns to show all column detail.

- Click the + (plus) outline button to the left of any row or above any column to show the detail that makes up those totals.

- When detail shows, the outline button is a – (minus). Click this button to hide the detail for that section.

If you don't have totals in your workbook, you can use the Group command to manually create an outline.

Create Group

Do any of the following to group rows or columns:

- Click multiple row or column headings. Click the Data menu, choose Group and Outline, and click Group.

- Click multiple row or column headings and press Alt+Shift+Right.

- Select a range of cells. Click the Data menu, choose Group and Outline, and click Group. The Group dialog box appears. Choose to group in Rows or Columns.

Undo Group

Select the rows or columns you want to remove from grouping and press Alt+Shift+Left. Alternatively, click the Data menu, choose Group and Outline, and click Ungroup. If you select a range or the entire worksheet (click the Select All button above the row headers or press Ctrl+A), Excel will open a dialog box similar to the Group dialog box. Choose Rows or Columns to ungroup.

Remove Outline

To remove all grouping at once, click the Data menu, choose Group and Outline, and click Clear Outline.

Use Subtotaling

Subtotals enable you to total a numeric column (or count a text column) by category. You can have multiple layers of subtotals. For example, you could subtotal by country, and within each country you could have subtotals by company.

To create subtotals, you must first sort by the columns you want to group for totals. If you are using the preceding example, the primary sort would be by country, and the secondary sort (the first Then By line on the Sort dialog box) would be by company (see Objective 94, "Perform Single and Multilevel Sorts").

Create Subtotals

After you sort, create subtotals by doing the following:

1. Click the Data menu and choose Subtotals.

2. On the Subtotal dialog box, choose the highest sort level field in the At Each Change In drop-down list.

3. In the Use Function list, the most likely choice, Sum, is selected. You can also use other functions such as Count, Min, and Max. See Objective 57, "Use Basic Functions (AVERAGE, SUM, COUNT, MIN, and MAX)."

4. In the Add Subtotal to List box, place a check mark next to each column containing values that you want to total.

5. If you already have done subtotals before on this worksheet and you want to wipe out the existing subtotals and put new ones in, check Replace Current Subtotals. If you leave this check box blank, Excel will add another line at each break in the category field you chose in Step 2.

6. If you want a page break for each change in category of the field in Step 2, check P̲age Break Between Groups.

7. If you want to place the summary function and line below when the value of each category changes, check S̲ummary Below Data. If you clear this box, the summary will appear above each group.

8. Choose OK.

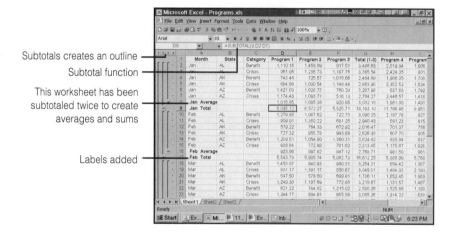

Subtotals creates an outline

Subtotal function

This worksheet has been subtotaled twice to create averages and sums

Labels added

Excel will create formulas in the worksheet and labels showing where the subtotals are. The actual function used is SUBTOTAL. The first argument of the function determines whether the values will be summed, averaged, or another summary function. This procedure also automatically creates an outline (see Objective 95, "Use Grouping and Outlines").

Remove Subtotals

To remove subtotals from a list, click the D̲ata menu, choose Sub̲totals, and click the R̲emove All button. The outline and all associated page breaks will also be removed.

Use Data Forms

You can enter data in a list like any other worksheet (see Objective 3, "Edit Cell Content"), or you can use a form. The worksheet must be set up like a database, with the first row in the range being labels identifying the columns (fields). There should be no blank rows, and each row describes characteristics of one object (record).

Instead of your data going across the screen in a row of a worksheet, you can show each record to be in a dialog box going down the screen. You can use the form for data entry or for searching records.

Input Data with Data Forms

To see the data in a form, follow these steps:

1. Position the active cell pointer in the data range.

2. Click the Data menu and choose Form.

   The Data form opens. The title bar of the form is the name of the sheet.

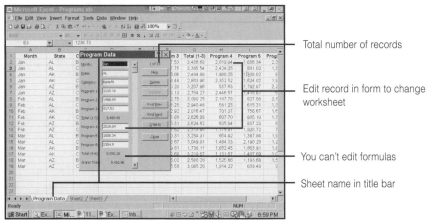

Total number of records

Edit record in form to change worksheet

You can't edit formulas

Sheet name in title bar

3. Do any of the following to move to a record you want to edit (see also the following section, "Find Data"):

   - To move to the same field on the next record, click the down scroll arrow in the middle of the form or press the down-arrow key.

   - To move to the same field on the previous record, click the up scroll arrow in the middle of the form or press the up-arrow key.

   - To move to the first field in the next record, press Enter.

   - To move to the first field in the previous record, press Shift+Enter.

   - To move to a new, blank record, click New or press Ctrl+Page Down.

   - To move to the same field 10 records forward, click below the scroll box or press Page Down.

   - To move to the same field 10 records previous, click above the scroll box or press Page Up.

   - To move to the first record, drag the scroll box to the top of the form or press Ctrl+Page Up.

4. Do any of the following to move to a field within the record:

   - Click the field.

   - Press Alt+ the underlined letter of the field name.

   - Press Tab to go to the next field or next button on the form.

   - Press Shift+Tab to go to the previous field or button on the form.

5. Use the following to edit a field:

   - If the text is selected, type new text or press Delete to remove the text.

   - Position the insertion point and type new text, press Backspace to remove previous characters, or press Delete to remove characters after the insertion point.

- Press Home or End to move the insertion point to the beginning or end of the field. Hold down Shift to select from the insertion point to the beginning or end of the field.

- Press the right arrow key or the left arrow key to move the insertion point one character at a time. Hold down Shift to select characters one at a time.

- If you change your mind and want to return the record as it is on the worksheet, click Restore.

6. To remove an entire record, click Delete. You will be prompted to confirm the deletion. Choose OK.

7. When you finish editing the fields and records, choose Close.

If you want to find a record before you go into the data form, you can use the Find command (see Objective 9, "Use Find and Replace"). However, you can also use the data form's search capabilities to look for a record.

Find Data

To find data on a form, do the following:

1. Click the Data menu and choose Form.

2. In the data form, click the Criteria button.

   The data form changes and all fields now have blank text boxes you can use to enter search criteria.

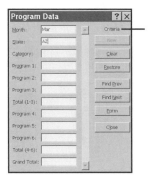

The label here indicates that this is the Criteria view of the data form

3. Move to the field the same way as mentioned in Step 4 of the preceding procedure.

4. Type the text you want to find. If you want to search for data that has to match more than one field, you can type in multiple text boxes. You can also use wildcards to help fine-tune your search.

5. If you want to remove all search criteria, click the Clear button.

6. Click the Find Next button to search forward or the Find Prev button to search backward through the records.

7. You return to the data form and can edit the found record or click the Find Next or Find Prev button to continue looking through the records.

If Excel doesn't find a match, it beeps but still goes to the last record you found in Step 6.

Apply Data Filters

If your worksheet is set up like a database, you can use either
AutoFilter or the Advanced Filter command to view only the
data you need to look at. After the data is filtered, you can edit
(see Objective 3, "Edit Cell Content") or print the worksheet
(see Objective 31, "Preview and Print Worksheets and
Workbooks").

AutoFilter is a quick way to select only the items you want to
see in a list.

To turn on AutoFilter, do the following:

**Set
AutoFilter**

1. Position the active cell pointer in the data list.

2. Click the Data menu, choose Filter, and click AutoFilter.

Each field name now has an arrow that you can use to select
the data you want.

To turn off AutoFilter, click the Data menu, choose Filter, and
click AutoFilter again.

When AutoFilter is turned on, you can display the data you
want by doing any of the following:

**Use
AutoFilter**

• Click the filter arrow and choose a value in the list. Only
   the rows that match the value in this field display.

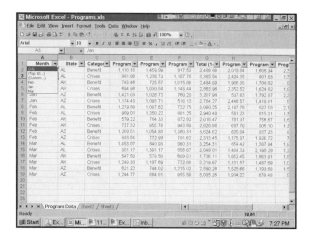

- You can also move the active cell pointer to a field and press Alt+Down to activate the filter list. Press Home to select the first item (All), Down or Up to select the next or previous item, or End to select the last item. Press Enter when the item you want in the list is selected.

The arrow turns blue to indicate that the field is selected

The rows also turn blue to indicate that not all data is visible

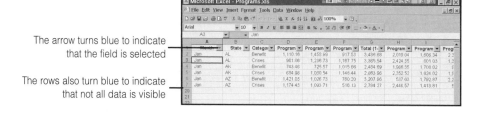

- To display all values for the field, click the filter arrow and choose All.

- To select the largest or smallest values in a numeric field, click the arrow and choose Top 10. A dialog box opens. Choose Top or Bottom in the first drop-down, choose the number in the second text box, and choose whether you want the number of Items or Percent of items in the third box. When you finish, choose OK.

- To set your own criteria, click the filter arrow and choose Custom. The Custom AutoFilter dialog box displays. Click the first drop-down and choose a comparison operator such as equal or greater than. Type the text or value in the second text box, or choose a value from the drop-down list. If you use text, you can use an asterisk for a wild card. For example, Ben* would find Ben, Benjamin, and Benefits. If you want another condition, choose And for both conditions to be true. Choose Or for either condition to be true. Choose OK to apply the filter.

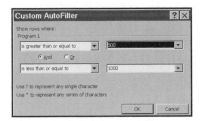

- If you have any blanks for a field, click the filter arrow and choose Blanks to display records with nothing in the field or NonBlanks to display only records than have an entry in the field.

To see all the records, click the Data menu, choose Filter, and click Show All.

Display All Records

Extract Data

You can apply multiple conditions with the AutoFilter by selecting an item in each filter list. However, if you want to copy records from the database into another part of the worksheet, you can use the advanced filter feature.

You will have three areas of the worksheet you are working with: the data list (database), a criteria range that indicates which records you want, and an extract range that indicates where and what columns you want.

To set up the criteria range, follow these steps:

1. Copy or type the field labels from the data list to another area of the worksheet.

2. Type criteria under the labels. For example, if you want to choose a company name, type the name on the row under the company label.

3. If you use more than one row, the records meet any of the criteria. (This is an OR.)

4. If you type data on the same row, the records must match all the criteria. (This is an AND.)

5. You can also type a greater-than sign (>) or the less-than sign (<), with or without an equal sign (=), and then a number to select data.

6. It is helpful to name this range Criteria. Select the range and type Criteria in the Name Box (see Objective 80, "Add and Delete a Named Range").

To set up the extract range, do the following:

1. If you want to choose only specific columns of data, copy or type labels from the data list to another area of the worksheet.

2. Do one of the following to select the extract range:

    • If you want all columns from the data list, you can just select the upper-left corner of where you want to start the extract.

    • If you want all the records that match the criteria, select the field names only.

    • If you want to limit the number of records that are extracted, select the field names and the number of blank rows you want copied.

3. It is helpful to name this range. Type Extract in the Name Box.

To extract records, do the following:

1. Click the data list.

2. Click the Data menu, choose Filter, and click Advanced Filter.

3. Choose Copy to Another Location. (Note that if you want to see the records in their current location, choose Filter the List, In Place. This produces the same result as AutoFilter.)

4. Because you started in the data list in Step 3, the List Range should automatically filled in. If it is not, type the range address, a range name, or use the Collapse dialog button to select the range.

5. In the Criteria Range dialog box, type Criteria. Generally if you named the ranges Criteria and Extract, the cell references might already be identified for you.

6. In the Copy To text box, type Extract.

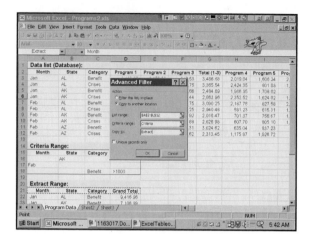

7. If there are duplicate records, you can choose to see only one copy of the record by checking the <u>U</u>nique Records Only box.

8. Choose OK.

Although you do not have to name the criteria and extract ranges, it is easier to work with them if you do. If you don't name the ranges, in Steps 5 and 6 type the cell addresses or use the Collapse dialog button, and select the ranges when prompted in the Extract dialog box.

Query Databases

You aren't limited to using data from Excel. You can use data from other database and text files. The database can be on your local hard drive, on a network drive, or even on a mainframe computer. This objective deals with making a link and using that external data. If you want to copy data into Excel or take the data from Excel into the other application, see Chapter 8, "Importing and Exporting Data."

To retrieve information from a database, you can set up a query. The query answers a set of questions about the location, file-name, data type, fields, records, and possibly tables, a user ID, and password, and enables you to exclude unwanted data.

This section gives an overview of how to use one data source, Microsoft Access, to create a link to an external database. If you want more detail, see Que's *Special Edition Using Microsoft Excel 2000*.

To create a link from external data to the current workbook in Excel, follow these steps:

1. Click the Data menu, choose Get External Data, and click New Database Query.

2. The Choose Data Source dialog box opens. On the Databases tab is the list of database applications you can use, such as another Excel file, dBase, FoxPro, and Access. You can also use <New Data Source> to connect to data in Oracle, SQL Server, and other ODBC databases (if you have the drivers). These steps discuss how to use an Access database. Choose MS Access Database.

Database Queries

The Query Wizard uses Microsoft Query, an optional feature in Excel, so Microsoft Query must be installed. If it isn't, use the CD or network install to get it.

When you use external data, this is a one-way link between Excel and Access. Any changes to the Access database are reflected in the Excel worksheet; however, if you make a change to the Excel data, it is not reflected in the Access database. If you want to change the data from Excel and Access, do the following: From within Access, choose File, Get External Data, Link Tables and choose an Excel file.

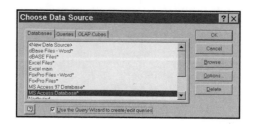

3. The procedure is easier if you use the Query Wizard rather than Microsoft Query. Keep U̲se the Query Wizard to Create/Edit Queries checked, and click OK.

4. The Select Database dialog box opens. Click the Dri̲ves drop-down list to select the local or previously mapped network drive, or click the Network button, choose a drive letter, and type the network path for the folder (such as \\accounting\data).

5. If necessary, choose the folder in the D̲irectories list.

6. Choose the file in the Database N̲ame list.

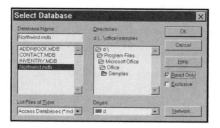

7. In Access, you can open a file so no one else can work in the database while you have the file open. Check E̲xclusive if you need this option.

8. If you don't want to make changes to the database (which you wouldn't anyway from Excel), check R̲ead-Only.

9. Choose OK. The Query Wizard—Choose Columns dialog box displays. On the left side is a list of available tables and columns. Click the + next to a table to display the list of fields in the table.

+ to show
fields

- to hide
fields

Click to
show first
values in
fields

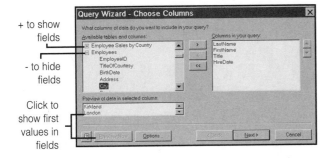

10. Double-click each field you want. To remove all fields and start over, click <<. Select the fields you need and choose Next.

11. The Query Wizard—Filter Data dialog box displays. If you want to see only certain records, choose a field in the Column to Filter list, choose a comparison operator in the first drop-down, and choose or type a value in the second drop-down list. If you want more conditions, choose And to require both conditions or choose Or to require either condition, and repeat this step. Choose Next.

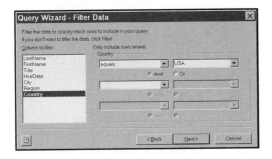

12. The Query Wizard—Sort Order dialog box displays. If you want to specify the order of the records, choose the fields and whether you want them Ascending or Descending. Choose Next.

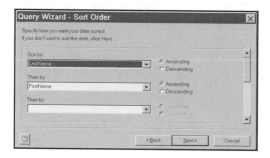

13. The Query Wizard—Finish dialog box displays. If you want, click Save Query and enter a filename you want to use. Click Save to save the query as a .dqy file and add the query to the list of available queries.

14. Choose Return Data to Microsoft Excel, and click Finish.

15. The Returning External Data to Microsoft Excel dialog box opens. Choose a cell on Existing Worksheet for the upper-left corner of the data or choose New worksheet and choose OK.

The data appears in the worksheet.

You can sort, format, edit, add subtotals to, and outline the data. However, when you refresh the data, it removes these settings and brings in just the data.

You can also create a PivotTable in Step 15 (see Objective 105, "Use Data Analysis and PivotTables").

Edit Query

You can change your query settings if you forgot a column, selection criteria, or sort order. Click ▦ Edit Query on the External Data toolbar and repeat Steps 9–14 of the preceding list.

If other people are working on the database, you can click ▮ Refresh Data to get the latest changes from the database to the active data list or click ▮ to update all external data sources for the whole workbook.

Refresh Data

Use Data Validation

Data validation enables you to specify what data is valid for a range of cells as it is entered into the worksheet. You can prevent entry of invalid data, specify valid data entries, or give users a warning message if they enter the wrong data.

To add data validation, set up your text labels first, and then do the following:

1. Generally, the same data rules will need to be applied to a column of data, so click the column header. Alternatively, select the range that will have the validation.

2. Click the Data menu and choose Validation.

3. The Data Validation dialog box opens. The Settings tab is where you'll tell Excel what is acceptable data. Do one of the following:

   • The default under the Allow drop-down is Any Value. You can type anything you want in the range (no data validation). To remove everything from the dialog box and return to this setting, click the Clear All button.

   • For numbers, dates, and times, click Allow and choose Whole Number (no decimals allowed), Decimals, Date, or Time. Under the Data drop-down list, choose a comparison operator. If you choose Between or Not Between, two text boxes appear, one for a Minimum and one for a Maximum value. Type the numbers or a cell reference, or use the Collapse Dialog button. If you select any other choices (such as Equal To or Less Than) in the Data drop-down, one text box appears for the number or cell reference.

- For text, you can click <u>A</u>llow, choose Text length, and choose the length between, equal to, greater than, and so on.

- If you want to permit a limited number of valid text entries, click <u>A</u>llow and choose List. In the Source text box, type the range reference to the valid values. If you check <u>I</u>n-cell Dropdown, the active cell will have a down arrow, which you can use to choose one of the items from the list. You can also press Alt+Down to access this list from the active cell.

- If you want to base the validation on a calculation, click <u>A</u>llow and choose Custom. In the Formula text box, type a formula starting with an equal sign.

Cell reference will change for each cell in range

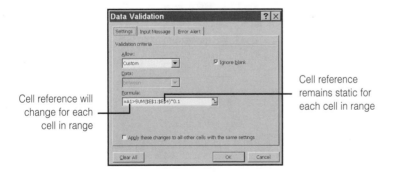

Cell reference remains static for each cell in range

4. Choose Ignore <u>B</u>lank to stop error messages from displaying when a cell is blank. If this is unchecked, you will get an error message when you edit a restricted cell or reference. The message does not appear when you press Delete.

381

5. Check Apply These Changes to All Other Cells with the Same Settings when you are editing a data validation rule if you want other cells with the same rule to match your edits.

6. Click the Input Message tab, and type a title for the message and a message. The message will appear as a ScreenTip when the active cell is in the validation range if the Office Assistant is not on. If the Office Assistant is on, a bubble appears with the message.

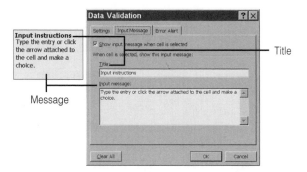

7. Click the Error Alert tab. If you want to show an error message, check Show Error Alert After Invalid Data Is Entered and choose a Style:

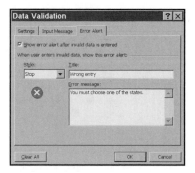

- ⊗ Stop displays a red circle with an × and will not enable the user to continue until the entry is fixed.

- ⚠ Warning displays a yellow triangle with an exclamation point and will prompt the user to reply
  whether he wants to continue. He can choose Yes to
  continue, No to go into edit mode, or Cancel to erase
  the entry.

- ⓘ Information gives a bubble with the letter "i."
  The user can choose OK to go to the next cell or
  Cancel to enter the value but remain in the cell.

  If the Office Assistant is on, the message will appear
  as a bubble with the Assistant. If the Office Assistant
  is off, the message appears as a dialog box.

8. When you finish with the dialog box, choose OK. Now,
   when you enter data, the input message appears when you
   go into the cell. The error message appears if you don't
   follow the rules defined in the Settings tab.

If you want to find cells that no longer meet validation rules,
click the Tools menu, choose Auditing, and click Show
Auditing Toolbar. Then click Circle Invalid Data
⊞ Circle Invalid Data .

TAKE THE TEST

Task 1

Objectives covered: 93, "Apply Conditional Formats"; 94, "Perform Single and Multilevel Sorts"; 97, "Use Data Forms."

Open practice file 1701P from the enclosed CD and perform the following actions:

1. Format Column G to display in yellow fill if the number is less than 2000. Format Column K to display in a red font if the number is greater than 5000. Remove the conditional formatting from K1.

2. Sort the list first ascending by State and then sort again descending by Grand Total.

3. Perform a multilevel sort with the primary field ascending by Category, then ascending by State, and then descending by Grand Total.

4. Use the data form to find the value of 943.88 in Program 3, and edit it to 43.88. Add a new record in data form with the following values:

Month	Jan
State	CO
Category	Benefit
Program 1	525.34
Program 2	457.01
Program 3	522.01
Program 4	2654.12

Program 5   3423.01

Program 6   945.01

5. Use the data to find and delete the Jan AZ Crises record.

Check your work against the solution file 1701S.

Objectives covered: 94, "Perform Single and Multilevel Sorts"; 95, "Use Grouping and Outlines"; 96, "Use Subtotaling."

Task 2

Open practice file 1702P from the enclosed CD and perform the following actions:

1. Sort the list by Month, State, and Category (under the Sort Options, choose the month sort order).

2. Use subtotaling and create totals and averages for all the number fields by month and then by state.

3. Remove the outline.

4. Automatically re-create the outline.

5. Display Level 2 data for the columns and Level 3 data for the rows.

6. Expand Feb AL data to see the details.

Check your work against the solution file 1702S.

Objectives covered: 99, "Extract Data"; 100, "Query Databases"; 101, "Use Data Validation."

Task 3

Create a new workbook and perform the following actions:

1. Link the data from the 1703p.mdb Access file. Choose all fields except ID, Org, EduID, and Veteran. Select only dates in 1999 and sort by date. Name this worksheet Access Data.

2. Extract the data for Where PaymentType is Benefit. Move this data to another worksheet starting in A1 and name the worksheet Benefits. Format the worksheet if you want.

3. On this Benefits worksheet, add list validation in Column C (PaymentType) where the label can only be Benefit (the user is stopped from going further). For Column D (Benefit amount) add data validation to give the user a warning if the data is greater than 300 (but she can accept or reject the entry). Type appropriate warning messages.

4. Make a list for the City to include only GARY, LAKE STATION, or EAST CHICAGO (with no warning if it is not in the list). Give an input message to choose a city from the list or type a new entry.

5. To verify the data validation, do the following: Try to change the first record in PaymentType to Crises. You'll be prompted to return the value to Benefit. Change the value of Benefit to be 305 and the city to LAKE STATION.

Check your work against the solution file 1703S.

Cheat Sheet

Apply Conditional Formats

Conditional formatting enables you to change the format of a cell based on the value of what is in the cell.

Choose Format, Conditional Formatting. Identify the rules for formatting, click the Format button to open the Format Cells dialog box, and make your formatting choices.

Perform Single and Multilevel Sorts

Sorting enables you to order the data in a list.

Click [icon] Ascending to sort from 1–9, A–Z.

Click [icon] Descending to sort from Z–A, 9–1.

To sort on multiple fields, choose Data, Sort.

Use Grouping and Outlines

Outlines and grouping enable you to hide and display related rows or columns of data.

If you have sums in your worksheet, choose Data, Group and Outline, Auto Outline to create an outline.

To manually group selected rows, choose Data, Group and Outline, Group (Alt+Shift+Right).

To remove the outline, choose Data, Group and Outline, Clear Outline.

Use Subtotaling

Excel automatically adds sums or other total functions for your sorted worksheet by each field category you choose.

Choose Data, Subtotals, identify the category and function for which you want to create a calculation, and add a break in the data.

Continued

Use Data Forms

Data forms enable you to enter all information on one record in a dialog box.

To display a form, choose Data, Form.

To search for a record, click the Criteria button, type in the values you're looking for, and click Find Next or Find Prev.

Apply Data Filters

Data filters enable you to view selected rows of your data list and hide the rest.

Choose Data, Filter, AutoFilter to place arrows at the top of your data list.

Click the filter arrows and choose a value to display records with the specified value.

Extract Data

To copy records that match criteria from a data list to another part of the worksheet, use Advanced Filter.

Set up a criteria range that tells which records you want to copy and an extract range that identifies which fields you want.

Choose Data, Filter, Advanced Filter, click Copy to Another Location, and identify your data, criteria, and extract ranges.

Query Databases

You can link another database file into Excel through the Get External Menu option.

To link an Access database, choose Data, Get External Data, New Database Query, choose MS Access Database, and follow the steps of the query to choose the table, fields, criteria for records, sort order, and location for the linked data.

Use Data Validation

Data validation enables you to give a prompt for your user about the data when the active cell pointer is in a cell.

Data validation also enables you to set rules for acceptable data and give error messages if the data is not entered correctly.

Choose Data, Validation, add the rules on the Settings tab, and place prompts on the Input Message and Error Message tabs.

Using Analysis Tools

Following is a list of MOUS objectives:

- Use Goal Seek
- Use Solver
- Work with Scenarios
- Use Data Analysis and PivotTables
- Use PivotTable AutoFormat
- Create PivotChart Reports
- Create Interactive PivotTables for the Web
- Add Fields to a PivotTable Using the Web Browser

Use Goal Seek

Goal Seek enables you to specify a solution and then find the input value that produces the desired result. This is also sometimes referred to as *backsolving*. The input value could be a direct precedent to the formula or could be removed by multiple formulas. For more information on precedents, see Objective 91, "Trace Precedents."

To calculate what an input value should be when you want to change the result of a formula, do the following:

1. Set up a worksheet where an input cell is used as part of a formula (see Chapter 6, "Working with Formulas and Functions").

2. Click the Tools menu and choose Goal Seek.

3. The Goal Seek dialog box displays. In the Set Cell box, type the goal cell reference of the formula, click the goal cell, or use the Collapse Dialog button to select the goal cell.

4. In the To Value text box, type the desired solution.

5. In the By Changing Cell box, type the cell reference of the input cell, click the cell, or use the Collapse Dialog button to select the cell.

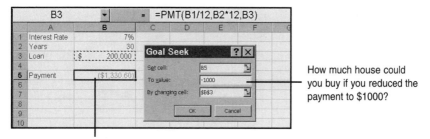

How much house could
you buy if you reduced the
payment to $1000?

The current payment of $1330 is
for a $200,000 house

6. Click the OK button.

If it's possible, Excel calculates the new input value based
on the desired result and displays it in the Goal Seek
Status dialog box.

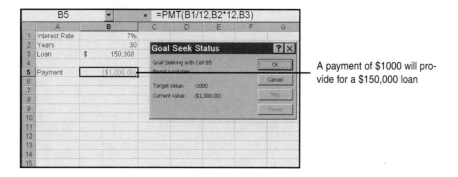

A payment of $1000 will pro-
vide for a $150,000 loan

7. If you want the worksheet to change with the suggested
solution, choose OK.

8. If you want to return to the original worksheet values,
choose Cancel. It is also possible to return the worksheet
to its original values after running Goal Seek by pressing
Ctrl+Z.

9. If the calculation takes a long time, you can click Pause to
stop the calculation and Step to see each incremental
change Excel makes.

If you want to limit the number of calculations Excel makes when looking for a goal, click the Tools menu, choose Options, click the Calculations tab, and check Iteration. Type the number in the Maximum Iterations text box Excel will calculate to reach the Maximum Change value.

103

Use Solver

Solver is similar to Goal Seek (see Objective 102, "Use Goal Seek") in that you can have Excel vary input cells to come up with a desired solution. However, with Goal Seek you can only change one input cell. With Solver you can change multiple input cells.

Solver is an add-in and must be selected before you use it. Solver will not appear on the Tools menu until you turn on the add-in. Click the Tools menu, choose Add-Ins, check Solver Add-In in the Add-Ins Available list, and choose OK.

The first step to using the solver is to set up a worksheet that has multiple input values that feed into a formula. The input cells and the formula must be on the same worksheet. If the formula is on a different worksheet, you can create a reference to the cell by typing an equal sign, clicking the sheet, moving to the cell that contains the formula, and pressing Enter (see Objective 49, "Link Worksheets and Consolidate Data Using 3D Referenes").

Create Worksheet with Formula to Evaluate

After you create the worksheet, you identify where the formula is, where the input cells are, and the possible ranges for the input cells.

Run Solver

Do the following to identify the parameters and solve the formula:

1. Click the Tools menu and choose Solver. The Solver Parameters dialog box displays.

2. In the Set Target Cell box, type the range of the formula you want to evaluate, or click the cell.

3. Choose whether you want to find the maximum value for the formula (Max), find the minimum value (Min), or set the Value of the target cell, and type a number in the text box.

4. In the By Changing Cell text box, choose which cells are a source for the formula cell. They do not have to be a direct precedent; there could be intermediate formulas that lead to the final result (see Objective 91, "Trace Precedents"). To identify these input cells, do one of the following:

   • Click the Guess button and have Excel fill in the box with the precedents to the target cell.

   • Type the cell references, range references, or range names in the text box. Separate multiple references with commas.

   • While the insertion point is in the text box, click the worksheet to fill in the By Changing Cell text box. Select non-adjacent cells or ranges by holding down the Ctrl key and dragging the mouse.

   • Click the Collapse Dialog button, select the ranges, and then click the Redisplay Dialog Box button.

5. If you try to solve at this point, you might get no solution or unreasonable numbers for the input cells. You probably need to set some constraints for the cells identified in the By Changing Cells text box.

   Click Add to open the Add Constraint dialog box. In the Cell Reference text box, type or click the input cell. In the middle drop-down list, choose an operator such as <= (less than or equal to), >= (greater than or equal to) or int (integer). If necessary, type the number or click a cell in the Constraint text box. When finished, click either Add to accept the newly created constraint and create more constraints or OK to accept the constraint and return to the Solver Parameters dialog box.

6. If you want to modify a constraint, select it and click the Change button. Repeat Step 5.

7. If you want to remove a constraint, select it and click the Delete button.

8. If you want to clear the dialog box and start over, click Reset All and choose OK to verify.

9. The Options button enables you to set the maximum time, the number of calculations Excel will attempt, and how close the value has to be.

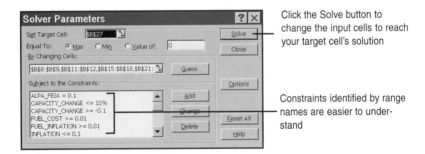

Click the Solve button to change the input cells to reach your target cell's solution

Constraints identified by range names are easier to understand

10. When you are ready to find the solution, click the Solve button.

11. If the Solver finds a solution to the problem within the constraints you specified, the Solver Results dialog box opens. You can do the following:

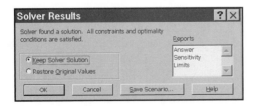

- Drag the title bar of the dialog box to see the changes to the worksheet.

- Choose Keep Solver Solution to keep changes to the worksheet. Alternatively, to return the original data to the worksheet, choose Restore Original Values.

- Choose Save Scenario, and give it a name. You can save cell values and then use this as a scenario (see Objective 104, "Work with Scenarios").

- Click the Report(s) you want to create in the Reports list box. Excel will create a new worksheet summarizing Solver's answer for each report. The Answer report will show the original and final value for the formula and all input cells. The Sensitivity report shows how a degree of change in each input cell affects the formula cell. The Limits cell shows how the upper and lower constraints of input cells affect the formula cell. To select multiple reports, hold down Ctrl and select the desired reports.

12. Click OK to return to the workbook.

104

Work with Scenarios

Scenarios enable you to show and save different results you create on the same worksheet. This enables you to see different "what-if" conditions. For example, you could be looking at three different possibilities for inflation. Instead of creating three different workbooks, you could create one workbook, change the input values (which would change the formulas), and save each possibility as a different scenario. You show the scenario to see the changes to the workbook. You can use the Report Manager to save print settings with each scenario. (See Objective 79, "Use the Report Manager.")

To create a scenario, do the following:

1. Set up the worksheet the way you want it to look with input cells and formulas.

2. Click the Tools menu and choose Scenarios.

3. On the Scenario Manager dialog box, click the Add button.

4. The Add Scenario dialog box opens. Type the name you want to use to identify the scenario in the Scenario Name box.

5. Type the reference to the changing cells or a range name, or click the Collapse Dialog button and select the cells that change as part of the scenario. To select noncontiguous cells, hold down Ctrl as you click each one.

Add Scenario

6. Check whether you want to Hide or Prevent Changes to the scenario (use this in conjunction with preventing changes to the worksheet. See Objective 111, "Apply and Remove Worksheet and Workbook Protection").

7. By default, the Comment box identifies who created the scenario and the date created or modified. Click this box and edit the note as desired.

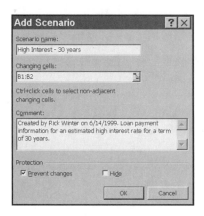

8. Choose OK.

9. Type the value for each changing cell (identified in Step 5), in the Scenario Values dialog box.

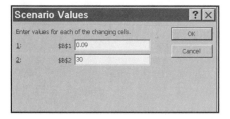

10. Click Add to add another scenario and return to the Add Scenario dialog box covered in Step 4, or click OK to return to the Scenario Manager dialog box in Step 3.

To display a selected scenario, select <u>T</u>ools and click Scenarios to display the Scenario Manager dialog box. Select the name from the list of S<u>c</u>enarios and choose <u>S</u>how. The data changes on the worksheet, and the Scenario Manager dialog box remains open.

Show Scenario

To change the values of the data in a scenario you created previously, select <u>T</u>ools and click Sc<u>e</u>narios to display the Scenario Manager dialog box. Select the name from the list of S<u>c</u>enarios and choose <u>E</u>dit. Continue with Step 4 from the preceding list.

Modify Scenario

To remove a scenario from the list, select <u>T</u>ools and click Sc<u>e</u>narios to display the Scenario Manager dialog box. Select the name from the list of S<u>c</u>enarios and choose <u>D</u>elete.

Remove Scenario

If you have scenarios on more than one workbook or worksheet for the same labels and formulas, you can combine the scenarios into one worksheet. The same input cells must be identified on the different workbooks or worksheets. Do the following:

Merge Scenarios

1. Open both workbooks that contain the desired scenarios.

2. Click the <u>T</u>ools menu and choose Sc<u>e</u>narios.

3. On the Scenario Manager dialog box, click the <u>M</u>erge button.

4. The Merge Scenarios dialog box opens.

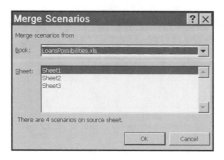

5. If the scenarios you want to merge are located in a different workbook, choose the workbook name from the <u>B</u>ook drop-down list.

6. If the scenarios are on a different worksheet, choose the worksheet name from the <u>S</u>heet list. A note appears on the bottom of the dialog box showing how many scenarios are on the selected worksheet.

7. Choose OK.

Scenario Summaries

You can create a Scenario summary or Scenario PivotTable that summarizes the scenarios of your workbook and provides a summary report. The summary report includes the changing values of the input cells and the changing results.

1. Click the <u>T</u>ools menu and choose Sc<u>e</u>narios.

2. On the Scenario Manager dialog box, click the S<u>u</u>mmary button.

3. Choose whether you want a Scenario <u>s</u>ummary (the default report type) or a Scenario <u>P</u>ivotTable.

4. In the <u>R</u>esult Cells text box, type the reference to the formulas that change when the input cells change. You can include a range name or click the Collapse Dialog button and select the cells that change as part of the scenario. To select noncontiguous cells, hold down Ctrl as you click each one.

5. Click OK. A new sheet is created with a summary of the scenario as a report or PivotTable.

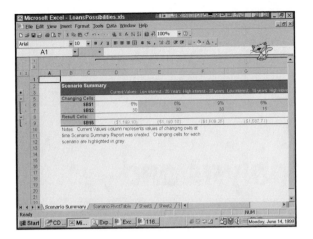

Scenario <u>S</u>ummary creates a worksheet in outline view. To work with outlines, see Objective 95, "Use Grouping and Outlines."

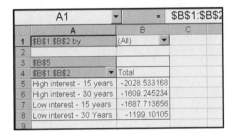

Scenario <u>P</u>ivotTable creates a PivotTable on a new worksheet. To work with PivotTables, see the following objectives, including Objective 105, "Use Data Analysis and PivotTables."

105

Use Data Analysis and PivotTables

PivotTables enable you to analyze, summarize, list, and display selected data in an interactive table format. For example, you can summarize sales data by month and salesperson. Alternatively, you can show totals for client and region. The interface for creating a PivotTable has changed and improved in Excel 2000 as well as the capability to connect to different data sources. This section highlights some of the features you'll use with PivotTables. For a more in-depth look at all the options, look in Help or Que's *Special Edition Using Microsoft Excel 2000.*

Creating a PivotTable

You can create a PivotTable from an Excel workbook, another PivotTable, a text file, another database that has an ODBC driver, an existing PivotTable or PivotChart, or an Access, FoxPro, dBase, or SQL database.

To create a PivotTable, do the following:

1. Open the workbook containing the selected data.

2. Click the Data menu and choose PivotTable and PivotChart Report.

3. The PivotTable and PivotChart Wizard dialog box opens at Step 1 of 3. Do any of the following to choose the data source:

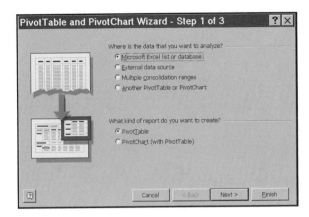

- To use the active or another Excel workbook, choose Microsoft Excel List or Database. You will use this option for Steps 4 and on.

- To use a file created in a database application, choose External Data Source. On the next step, choose Get Data; then choose from the Choose Data Source dialog box the Databases, Query, or OLAP Cubes tab, and choose from the list of data sources or choose a New Data Source. The next steps will be different, depending on the option selected. Generally, you will choose the location, file, table(s), and fields that will be used.

- To use multiple ranges on an Excel worksheet, choose Multiple Consolidation Ranges. On the next steps of the wizard, choose whether each range can be a separate set of data (page field), and select the ranges that will be part of the data source.

- If there already is a PivotTable or PivotChart on the workbook, choose Another PivotTable or PivotChart, and then choose the location in the dialog box.

OLAP (Online Analytical Processing) Cubes is a new database technology that has optimized databases for sorting, searching, and reporting data.

405

4. This procedure uses the PivotTable option. Choose Next.

See Objective 107, "Create PivotChart Reports," to use the PivotChart (with PivotTable) option.

5. If you choose an Excel list on the first step of the wizard, the second step asks where the data resides. Do any the following:

- If you started the process while the cell pointer was in the middle of data on a worksheet with data, the Range is already selected.

- Type the cell addresses of the range or a range name in the Range text box.

- Click the Collapse Dialog button, select the range, and click the Redisplay Dialog button.

- Click the Browse button, select the file that contains the data, choose OK, and type the cell reference or range name after the exclamation point.

6. Choose Next. Step 3 of 3 of the wizard displays. Choose whether to add the PivotTable to a New Worksheet or the Existing Worksheet and indicate the upper-left corner of the location in the text box.

7. Choose Finish. Excel displays the PivotTable toolbar and your workbook with a diagram for dropping fields.

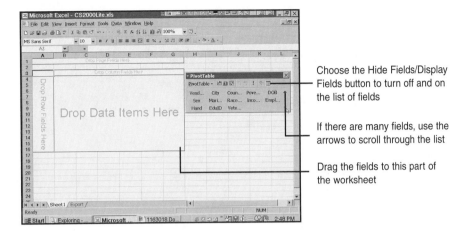

Choose the Hide Fields/Display Fields button to turn off and on the list of fields

If there are many fields, use the arrows to scroll through the list

Drag the fields to this part of the worksheet

8. Drag the fields you want to summarize to the Drop Data Items Here section of the PivotTable diagram. Usually this is a number field that you will sum or a text field that you will count.

9. If desired, drag one or more fields to the Drop Row Fields Here and Drop Column Fields Here sections. Usually these are category fields (such as region, salesrep, or state) or date fields.

10. If desired, drag one or more fields to the Drop Page Fields Here section. Page fields are also usually category fields. Page fields enable you to click a down arrow and choose which category you want to filter the data by.

As you drag the fields, Excel calculates the values. You can drag any field from one area on the PivotTable diagram to another area. To remove a field, drag it out of the PivotTable or on to the toolbar.

Page field   Column field

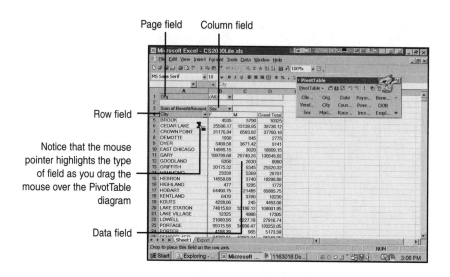

Row field

Notice that the mouse
pointer highlights the type
of field as you drag the
mouse over the PivotTable
diagram

Data field

Navigating in PivotTable

You can move fields from one section of the PivotTable to another. For example, in the preceding picture, you could drag the Sex field to the left of the City field to create a second row field.

To filter the data, click the down arrows after the attached field. Choose All if you want to see all the items.

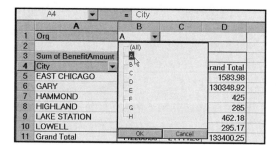

In a page field, select All or which category to show.

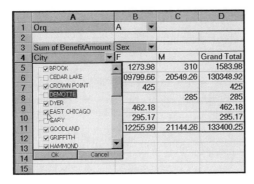

In row and column fields, check the boxes of which items you want to show.

You can do a number of things to make the table more readable or display the data in the order you want. Do any of the following:

- To combine data on a date row or column field, right-click the field, click Group and Outline, and choose Group. In the Grouping dialog box, choose the Starting at and Ending at values and the time period categories in the By list. You can click more than one category (such as Months and Years).

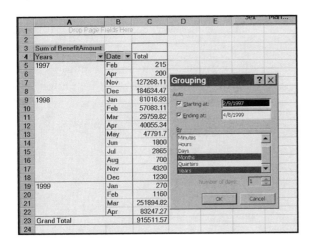

- To combine data on a numeric row or column field, in the Grouping dialog box, choose the Starting at and Ending at values and type an increment in the By text box.

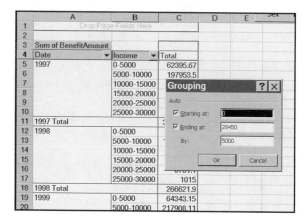

- If you have more than one row or column field, click the first field and choose ▣ Hide Detail to show only the primary field or ▣ Show Detail to show the secondary field(s). You can also get these options by right-clicking the field, clicking Group and Outline, and choosing Show Detail or Hide Detail.

- To change the summary function of the data items, double-click the field. The PivotTable Field dialog box opens. Choose a different summary function in the Summarize By list, and then click OK. Click Number to open the Format Cells dialog box to the Number tab (see Objective 24, "Apply Number Formats (Currency, Percent, Dates, and Comma)").

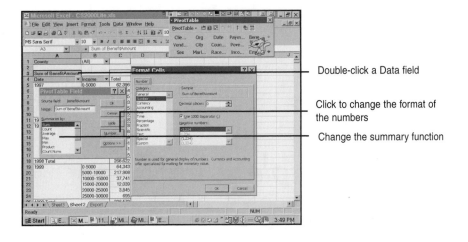

Double-click a Data field

Click to change the format of
the numbers

Change the summary function

106

Use PivotTable AutoFormat

Like a normal worksheet, you can format cells individually or use the AutoFormat feature. The built-in formats on the AutoFormat list change when your cell pointer is in a PivotTable.

To use one of these AutoFormats, do the following:

1. Position the cell pointer in a PivotTable.

2. Click the Format menu and choose AutoFormat.

3. The AutoFormat dialog box displays with formats specifically for PivotTables. Click one of the formats and choose OK.

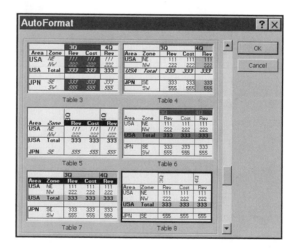

Create PivotChart Reports

Excel now combines the features of a PivotTable with charts. Just as in PivotTables, you can drag fields to place them on a chart and use the drop-down arrow associated with the field to filter the data you want to see.

To create a PivotChart report, do the following:

1. Open a workbook with your data. These steps assume that you've already created a PivotTable in this workbook.

2. Click the Data menu and choose PivotTable and PivotChart Report.

3. The PivotTable and PivotChart Wizard dialog box opens at Step 1 of 3. Do any of the following to choose the data source:

   - To use the active or another Excel workbook, choose Microsoft Excel List or Database. This option is the one that is discussed in Objective 105, "Use Data Analysis and PivotTables."

   - To use a file created in a database application, choose External Data Source. On the next step choose Get Data; then choose from the Choose Data Source dialog box the Databases, Query, or OLAP Cubes tab and choose from the list of data sources or choose a New Data Source. The next steps will be different depending on the option selected. Generally, you will choose the location, file, tables, and fields that will be used.

Create a PivotChart Report

- To use multiple ranges on an Excel worksheet, choose Multiple Consolidation Ranges. On the next steps of the wizard, choose whether each range can be a separate set of data (page field), and select the ranges that will be part of the data source.

- If there already is a PivotTable or PivotChart on the workbook, choose Another PivotTable or PivotChart. Assume this option for the following steps.

4. This procedure uses the PivotChart option. Choose Next.

   See Objective 105, "Use Data Analysis and PivotTables," to use the PivotTable option.

5. Because you chose Another PivotTable or PivotChart, the second step shows a list of PivotTables and PivotCharts in the current workbook. Select one from the list and choose Next.

6. Step 3 of 3 of the wizard displays. Choose whether to add the PivotChart to a New worksheet or the Existing worksheet, and indicate the upper-left corner of the location in the text box.

7. Choose Finish. Excel displays the PivotTable toolbar and a chart diagram for dropping fields.

Drag the fields to the chart

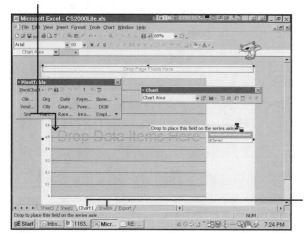

Excel creates a work-sheet with a PivotTable and a chart sheet with the PivotChart

8. Drag the fields you want to summarize to the Drop Data Items Here section of the PivotChart diagram. Usually, this is a number field that you will sum or a text field that you will count.

9. If desired, drag a field to the Drop More Category Fields Here on the bottom of the chart. These are usually grouping fields (such as region, sales rep, or state) or date fields. The values in this field will become the values on the x-axis or the different slices of a pie.

10. If desired, drag a field to the Drop More Series Fields Here section. The values of this field will become different lines or bars on your chart.

11. If desired, drag one or more fields to the Drop Page Fields Here section. These fields enable you to filter the data to see just the totals for the selected value.

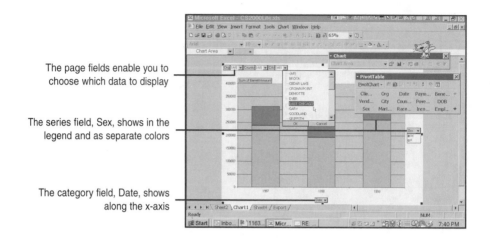

The page fields enable you to choose which data to display

The series field, Sex, shows in the legend and as separate colors

The category field, Date, shows along the x-axis

Just as with the PivotTable, you can rearrange the chart or add and remove fields by dragging them. You can also click the down arrow on any of the fields to choose which data you want to see. You can also customize the chart by choosing the chart type, axis options, colors, and backgrounds (see Chapter 7, "Using Charts and Objects").

Create Interactive PivotTables for the Web

After you create a PivotTable, you can publish it to the Web. There, using a Web browser (Internet Explorer 4.01 or later), users can interact with the data and categories they want to analyze much as they can do in Excel. To see how to add an interactive worksheet to the Web, go to Objective 18, "Save a Worksheet/Workbook as a Web Page."

To create an interactive Web PivotTable, follow these steps:

1. First create the PivotTable (see Objective 105, "Use Data Analysis and PivotTables").

2. Click the File menu and choose Save as Web Page.

3. On the Save As dialog box, type a File Name and choose a location for the Web page.

   If you have a Web server available, you can save to the server by using Web Folders ⬛ in the Places bar. Click on the Web folder to publish to the Web server. If prompted, provide a user ID and password. To set up a Web folder, click ⬛ New Folder and follow the wizard to supply the URL.

4. If you want a title to appear on the user's browser when the page is displayed, click Change Title, type the text, and choose OK.

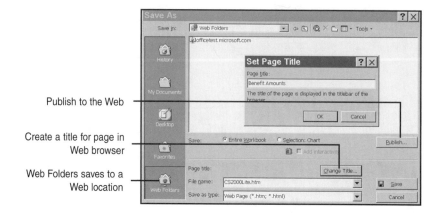

Publish to the Web

Create a title for page in
Web browser

Web Folders saves to a
Web location

5. Click Publish. The Publish as Web Page dialog box opens.

6. On the Choose drop-down list, choose the worksheet where the PivotTable resides, and select the PivotTable in the list box.

7. To enable the user to change data or the way it is displayed when viewed, check the Add Interactivity With check box. PivotTable functionality should be automatically selected in the drop-down.

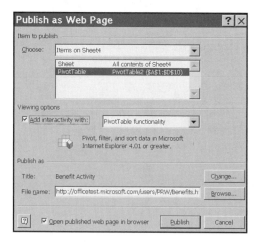

8. If you want to view your PivotTable in a Web browser after you save, check <u>O</u>pen Published Web Page in Browser.

9. Most of the other items on the dialog box are duplicated on the Save As dialog box. Make any changes as desired and choose <u>P</u>ublish.

If you chose to view the PivotTable in your browser in Step 9, Internet Explorer will launch, and you will see the PivotTable on a Web page. To continue, see Objective 109, "Add Fields to a PivotTable Using the Web Browser."

You can publish a PivotChart to the Web the same way. Before you do this procedure, select the PivotChart. In Step 7, choose <u>A</u>dd Interactivity with Chart Functionality.

To publish to a Web folder, Microsoft FrontPage Server Extensions or Office Server Extensions must be installed on the server. You also must be careful that you don't try to publish too large a file to the Web server. If you get an error message, try a smaller file. When you're practicing this objective for the MOUS test, publish to a local drive on your machine.

Add Fields to a PivotTable Using the Web Browser

After you publish a PivotTable to the Web, you might automatically be in your browser with the PivotTable open, or you can go to the file as you would any other Web file by giving the file's URL (Web address).

Field list —
Property toolbox —

Expand —
Page fields —
Column field —
Row field —

Data field —
The field list —

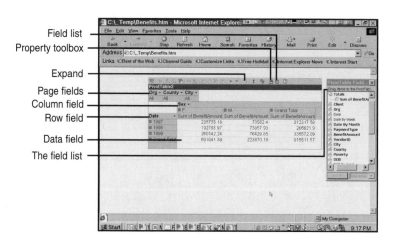

To work with the PivotTable in your browser, do any of the following:

- Click Field List to turn on the list of fields from the data source for the PivotTable. Drag a field from this list on to the PivotTable. You can drag to add a new row, column, data, or page field. Page fields are also called Filter fields. You can also drag these fields to remove them from the Pivot table.

- In the Field List, instead of dragging to the PivotTable, you can also click the field and at the bottom of the list choose whether to add the field to the Row area, Column area, Data area, Filter area, or Detail area.

- To see the detailed records, click Expand. Click the button again (the ScreenTip now says Collapse) to return to the summary view.

- Click the + (plus) next to any row or column field to expand to see the detail information for each record in that category. Click the - (minus) to return to the summary view.

- Click one of the Filter fields (also called Page fields) and select the value to view only the information for those fields.

- Click the down arrow next to the field name to choose which values you want to display.

- Click Property Toolbox to display a palette to format the worksheet.

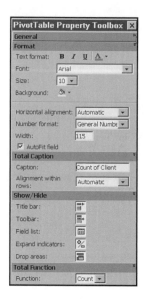

- Click Expand on the right edge of each header to see the tools associated with the section.

- To format the text with font characteristics or numbers with numeric formatting, click the field header above columns, to the left of rows, or on the filter fields. Then select the formatting options in the format section.

- To change the caption for totals, type it in the caption box.

- To display or remove the title, field list, toolbars, or drop areas, choose one of the icons in the Show/Hide section.

- To change the summary function, click the Function drop-down arrow. If the data field is a number, you can choose Sum, Count, Min, or Max. If the data field is text, you can choose Count.

TAKE THE TEST

Objectives covered: 102, "Use Goal Seek"; 103, "Use Solver"; 104, "Work with Scenarios."

Open practice file 1801P from the enclosed CD and perform the following actions:

1. Using Goal Seek on the Loan sheet, find what the loan amount would be if the payment were $1,000.

2. Using Solver on the Potential Sales sheet, find a solution where D13 will equal 500 and all items in C4:C10 must be constrained by being an integer.

3. Create an Answer report for this Solver solution.

4. Create four scenarios for the Staffing sheet. The data shown is a scenario named Low (1 Manager, 3 Concession, 1 Janitor, 1 Accounts). Create a scenario named Medium with 1 Manager, 6 Concession, 2 Janitor, 1 Accounts. Create a scenario named Moderate with 1 Manager, 9 Concession, 2 Janitor, 1 Accounts. Create a scenario named High with 2 Manager, 15 Concession, 3 Janitor, 2 Accounts.

5. Delete the Moderate scenario.

6. Create sheets with a Scenario summary and a Scenario PivotTable.

Check your work against the solution file 1801S.

Task 2

Objectives Covered: 105, "Use Data Analysis and PivotTables"; 106, "Use PivotTable AutoFormat"; 107, "Create PivotChart Reports."

Open practice file 1802P from the enclosed CD and perform the following actions:

1. Create a PivotTable that counts the number of clients (use Client field for Data Item) by City (row field) and Hand (column field). Use County as the Page field. Filter for County 2. Exclude cities Hebron and Highland from the list. Name this sheet Client Count.

2. Create a PivotTable by County and Income (row fields) and Date (column field) that totals benefit amounts (data item). Group the Date field by Year. Group the Income field by increments of 5000. Format the numbers as Currency with no decimal places. Name the sheet Income.

3. Format the Income PivotTable with Table 8 AutoFormat.

4. Create a PivotChart with Org, County, and City as Page fields. The Benefit amount should be the Data field. The Series field should be Sex. The Category field should be Date (by Year). Name this sheet Gender Chart and name the associated PivotTable Chart Data.

Check your work against the solution file 1802S.

Task 3

Objectives covered: 105, "Use Data Analysis and PivotTables"; 108, "Create Interactive PivotTables for the Web"; 109, "Add Fields to a PivotTable Using the Web Browser."

Open practice file 1803P from the enclosed CD and perform the following actions:

1. Create a PivotTable of the Sum of Benefits by City (row field).

2. Publish this PivotTable to the Web using PivotTable interactivity. Store the file on your C drive and name it Benefits.htm. When you are publishing the file, choose to display the file in your Web browser.

3. While you are in the Web browser, add the County field as a Filter field. Add the Payment type as a Column field. Change the name of SumofBenefit Amount to Benefit and format as Standard.

4. Show just County 4. Display the data for Hebron and then hide the data again.

Check your work against the solution files 1803S.xls and 1803S.htm.

Cheat Sheet

Use Goal Seek

Use Goal Seek to specify a solution and find the input value that generates the answer.

Choose Tools, Goal Seek and identify the value (Set Cell), desired solution (To Value), and the cell you want to change (By Changing Cell).

Use Solver

Solver enables you to change multiple input cells to come up with a value for a formula.

Solver is an add-in that first must be selected through Tools, Add-Ins.

Choose Tools, Solver. On the Solver dialog box, identify the formula (Set Target Cell) you want to set a value for and choose which cells will vary (By Changing Cells).

In the Solver dialog box, you can also set constraints for the changing cells to be within a certain range of integers. Click the Add button and choose the Cell Reference, an operator, and if necessary, type the Constraint.

Work with Scenarios

Scenarios enable you to name and save different "what-if" scenarios for a worksheet.

Choose Tools, Scenarios and click the Add button to identify the Scenario Name and Changing Cells. In the next dialog box, type the values of each of the changing cells.

To display a scenario, choose Tools, Scenarios, select the scenario, and choose Show.

Use Data Analysis and PivotTables

PivotTables enable you to interactively view summaries of a list of data. You can drag and drop fields to see new categories and data values.

Choose Data, PivotTable and PivotChart Report, identify the data source, and choose PivotTable. In the dialog boxes that follow, choose more information about the data source and where you want to put the PivotTable.

After you complete the wizard, a PivotTable diagram enables you to drop fields from the PivotTable toolbar to row fields, column fields, data items, and page fields.

You can rearrange the fields on the PivotTable at any time as well as click the down arrow on a field to filter the data or double-click a field to set formats and other options.

To group the data in a field, right-click the field and choose Group and Outline, Group.

Use PivotTable AutoFormat

AutoFormat enables you to apply a set of predefined text, number, and organization formats to a PivotTable.

While in the PivotTable, choose Format, AutoFormat, and select a format from the dialog box.

Create PivotChart Reports

You can also create interactive PivotCharts that enable you to drag and drop fields onto a chart.

Choose Data, PivotTable and PivotChart Report, identify the data source, and choose PivotChart. In the dialog boxes that follow, choose more information about the data source and where you want to put the PivotChart.

Drag the fields from the PivotTable toolbar to the chart diagram. Drag a field to the categories area to create x-axis divisions. Drag a field to the series area to show different data series as bars or lines. Drag the field that contains the data you want to sum or count to the center of the chart (data items). Drag fields to the page area for filtering data.

Create Interactive PivotTables for the Web

You can publish your PivotTable to the Web for viewing and modifying with Internet Explorer.

Choose File, Save as Web Page, click the Publish button, and check Add Interactivity with PivotTable Functionality.

Continued

Add Fields to a PivotTable Using the Web Browser

While you are in the Web browser, you can change the view of the PivotTable and how it is summarized.

Click Field List to display the fields from the data source. Drag the fields onto the PivotTable or from one area of the PivotTable to another area.

Click Property Toolbox to format the PivotTable.

Collaborating with Workgroups

Following is a list of MOUS objectives:

- Create, Edit, and Remove a Comment
- Apply and Remove Worksheet and Workbook Protection
- Change Workbook Properties
- Apply and Remove File Passwords
- Track Changes (Highlight, Accept, and Reject)
- Create a Shared Workbook
- Merge Workbooks

Create, Edit, and Remove a Comment

Comments are notes attached to cells in a worksheet. You can type explanations about the source of the data or a note that you need to verify the data. Use comments to keep your worksheets uncluttered. If you want to attach generic comments to the entire workbook, see Objective 112, "Change Workbook Properties."

Display Reviewing Toolbar

If you work with comments a lot, you can display the Reviewing toolbar. Right-click the menu bar and choose Reviewing. The following buttons on the Reviewing toolbar relate to comments:

- Insert a new comment.

- Move to the previous comment.

- Move to the next comment.

- Show or hide a comment in the active cell.

- Show or hide all comments.

- Delete comments in selected cells.

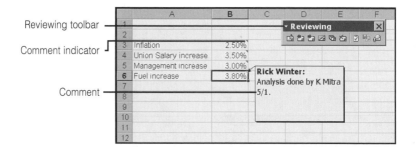

Reviewing toolbar

Comment indicator

Comment

To add a comment to a cell, follow these steps:

1. Move to the cell.

2. Do one of the following:

   - Press Shift+F2.

   - Click the Insert menu and choose Comment.

   - Click ⊞ New Comment on the Reviewing toolbar.

3. Your name appears in a yellow box. Type the comment on the next line. When you have completed entering the text, click outside the yellow comment box.

The default setting is for comments to be indicated by a small red triangle in the upper-right corner of the cell. This is called the comment indicator. You can change whether you display the comment indicator and comments in the Options dialog box.

To view comments, do the following:

- If the cell has a comment indicator, pause the mouse pointer over the cell.

- If the active cell has a comment, click ⊞ Show Comment on the Reviewing toolbar.

- Click ⊞ Show All Comments on the Reviewing toolbar.

- Right-click the cell and choose Show Comment.

- Click the Tools menu, choose Options, and click the View tab. In the Comments section, choose None to display neither the comment nor the indicator, choose Comment Indicator only, or choose Comment & Indicator to display both.

If you want to make changes to an existing comment, follow these steps:

1. Move to the comment by doing one of the following:

   - Click the cell or use the arrow keys to move to the cell.

   - Click ⊞ Previous Comment or ⊞ Next Comment on the Reviewing toolbar.

Create a Comment

Change the user name in Step 3 by clicking Tools, Options, clicking the General tab, and typing in the User name text box.

View Comments

Edit Comments

2. To move into the comment box, do one of the following:

   • Press Shift+F2.

   • Click ▦ Edit Comment on the Reviewing toolbar.

   • Click the comment if it is visible.

   • Click the Insert menu and choose Edit Comment.

   • Right-click the cell and choose Edit Comment.

3. Edit text as you would normally (position the insertion point, type text, and press Backspace or Delete to remove characters).

Remove Comments

To delete a comment, follow these steps:

1. Select the range of cells that has the comments you want to remove.

2. Do one of the following:

   • Click ▦ Delete Comment on the Reviewing toolbar.

   • Click the Edit menu, choose Clear, and click Comments.

   • Right-click the cell and choose Delete Comment.

Apply and Remove Worksheet and Workbook Protection

You can protect your workbook from unauthorized changes with worksheet and workbook protection. Use this if you just want users to see particular areas of the workbook and not make changes. If you want to hide rows and columns, see Objective 41, "Hide and Unhide Rows and Columns."

With worksheet protection, you can unprotect certain cells that might be used for inputting text. The rest of the cells (such as formulas and labels) are protected from the user.

Worksheet Protection

First unprotect any cells you want to be able to edit:

1. Select the cells you want to unprotect. Drag to select a range, or use Shift plus the arrow keys to select the first range. To select additional noncontiguous ranges, hold down Ctrl and drag the mouse pointer over the ranges.

2. Press Ctrl+1 or click the Format menu and choose Cells.

3. Click the Protection tab.

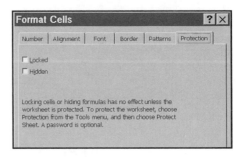

4. If you want to be able to type in the selected cells, clear the Locked check box.

5. If you want to hide the selected cells from showing the contents in the Formula Bar, check the Hidden box.

6. Choose OK.

Nothing appears to happen to the cell until you turn on worksheet protection. Do the following:

1. Click the Tools menu, choose Protection, and click Protect Sheet.

2. On the Protect Sheet dialog box, choose to protect any of the following:

- The Contents of the worksheet (except for the cells you unprotected).

- Objects, such as charts and pictures.

- Scenarios attached to this worksheet (see Objective 104, "Work with Scenarios").

3. If you want to add a password to prevent unauthorized users from removing the sheet protection, type up to 255 characters (it will be case sensitive) in the Password text box.

4. If you typed a password in Step 3, you are prompted to enter it again.

5. Choose OK.

You will be able to type only in cells that have been unlocked. You will not be able to type, edit, or delete other cells or insert, delete, or unhide rows or columns.

To remove worksheet protection, click the Tools menu, choose Protection, and click Unprotect Sheet. If you assigned a password, type the password and choose OK.

Workbook protection enables you to keep the structure of the workbook sheets. If you have a hidden sheet, the user cannot unhide the sheet. To hide a sheet, choose the Format menu, click Sheet, and choose Hide.

Workbook Protection

To protect the workbook, follow these steps:

1. Click the Tools menu, choose Protection, and click Protect Workbook.

2. In the Protect Workbook dialog box, choose to protect either of the following:

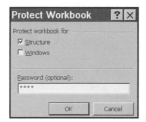

- **The Structure of the workbook**—The user won't be able to add, move, delete, hide, or unhide sheets.

- **The Windows settings**—The user won't be able to minimize, maximize, or move the workbook's window.

3. If you want to add a password to undo this feature, type up to 255 characters (it will be case sensitive) in the Password text box.

4. If you typed a password in Step 3, you are prompted to enter it again.

5. Choose OK.

To unprotect the workbook, click the Tools menu, choose Protection, and click Unprotect Workbook. If you assigned a password, type the password and choose OK.

To unhide a sheet, choose the Format menu, click Sheet, choose Unhide, select the sheets, and click OK.

If you want to protect the entire workbook from any changes or from even being opened, you can assign a password to the entire file. See Objective 113, "Apply and Remove File Passwords."

Macro Protection

In Excel 2000, you can now protect macros from being viewed or edited. To work with macros, see Chapter 15, "Using Macros."

To protect macros for the workbook, follow these steps:

1. Press Alt+F11 to open the VBA editor.

2. If the Project Explorer window is not visible, press Ctrl+R.

3. In the Project Explorer window, right-click the VBA Project (`workbook.xls`) line for your workbook and choose VBAProject Properties.

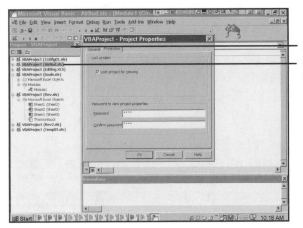

Project Explorer window

Right-click name of workbook to set the project (macro) properties

4. Click the Protection tab and check the Lock Project for Viewing box so the user won't be able to see the workbook's macros.

5. If you want to add a password to undo this feature, type it in the Password text box and the same password in the Confirm Password text box.

6. Choose OK.

7. Close the VBA Editor by clicking on the Close (×) button.

When you save and reopen the workbook, return to the VBA Editor window, and click the workbook name in the Project Explorer window, you are prompted for the password. Unless you type the password correctly, you cannot see or modify the current macros.

To undo the macro protection, right-click the workbook name in the Project Explorer window, supply the password when prompted, uncheck the Lock Project for Viewing box, and clear the password in both text boxes.

112

Change Workbook Properties

Workbook properties give you information about your file and help you find and annotate your workbook. To open a document based on its properties, see Objective 14, "Locate and Open an Existing Workbook."

To display the workbook's properties, click the File menu and choose Properties. The Properties dialog box opens with five tabs, which are described in the following sections.

You can also see a workbook's properties while you are in the Open or Save dialog box or in Windows Explorer by right-clicking on the filename and choosing Properties.

If you want the Properties dialog box to display the first time you save each file, click the Tools menu, choose Options, click the General tab, and check Prompt for Workbook Properties.

General and Statistics Tabs

The General tab shows information about the current file, including the name, location, size, dates created and modified, and file attributes such as read-only or hidden. The MS-DOS name is the eight-character name that will be used for older networks and file formats. If you want to make your file read-only, see Objective 113, "Apply and Remove File Passwords." You can also make a file read-only or hide it. Right-click it in Windows Explorer, click the General tab, and check Read Only or Hidden.

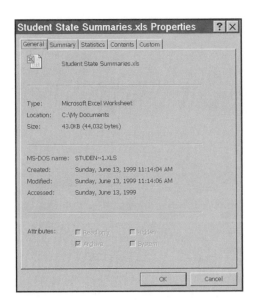

The Statistics tab contains some of the same information as the General tab, including when the file was first created, last saved, and last opened (accessed) and who last saved the workbook. Although it shows lines for editing information, this is not active for Excel.

The Summary tab provides many text boxes that you can use to identify your workbook. This will be especially useful for searching for the file if you forget the filename. The text boxes are also useful for organizing your work. The following figure shows the type of information you can store with the workbook.

Summary Tab

In addition to the first eight text boxes of searchable information, there are two additional options:

- Click the Save Preview Picture check box so you can preview the first page of the file in the Open or Save dialog box (choose the Views button and click Preview).

- Type a Hyperlink Base address, which is used as a starting point for all the hyperlinks in the file with the same base address. This can be a URL or file path. See Objective 11, "Create Hyperlinks."

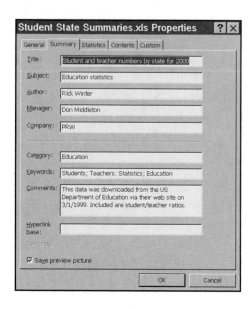

Contents Tab

The Contents tab of the Properties box shows you a list of your worksheets and chart sheets. This provides a good overview of large workbooks.

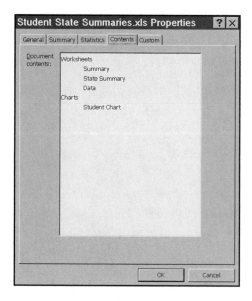

In addition to the properties provided on the Summary tab, you can create any additional properties you want. To create a property, follow these steps:

Custom Properties

1. Click the File menu and choose Properties.

2. Click the Custom tab.

3. In the Name area, type a new name for the property or select one from the list.

4. In the Type drop-down, choose what kind of information this is (Text, Date, Number, or a Yes or No value).

5. In the Value text box, type the value of the property.

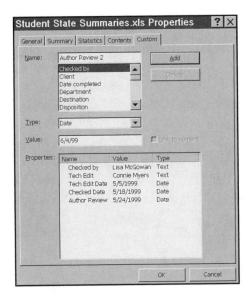

6. Click the Add button.

7. If you want to create additional properties, repeat Steps 3–6.

8. If you want to remove any properties, choose the property in the Properties list and click Delete.

9. When you finish with the Properties dialog box, choose OK.

113

Apply and Remove File Passwords

Your file might contain sensitive information that should not be altered, or you might be concerned that you might accidentally damage or change your own file. In addition to what was mentioned in Objective 111, "Apply and Remove Worksheet and Workbook Protection," you can do two things when you save your file to protect the work: You can make the file read-only, which means that you cannot over-write the filename but can create a copy; if you want to make sure only authorized people open or modify the workbook, you can add a password to the file.

To set a password and read-only options, follow these steps:

1. Press F12 or click the File menu and choose Save As. The Save As dialog box opens.

2. Click the Tools menu and choose General Options.

3. In the Save Options dialog box, do any of the following:

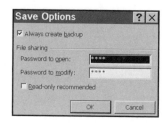

442

- If you want the program to make a backup every time you save the file after the first time, check Always Create <u>B</u>ackup. The file is named Backup of with the original filename, and it has an XLK extension.

- If you want a password required to open the file, type one in the Password to <u>O</u>pen text box. Passwords are case sensitive.

- If you want a password required if someone is going to make changes to the workbook, type one in the Password to <u>M</u>odify text box.

- If you want a prompt when the user opens the files to default to and suggest that the file be opened read-only, choose <u>R</u>ead-Only Recommended.

4. Choose OK on the Save Options dialog box.

5. If you put a password for open or modify in Step 3, you will be prompted to verify the password. Type the password again and choose OK. Always choose a password that is easy for you to remember but hard for other people to guess. If the password to open or modify is lost, you will not be able to open the file.

6. If necessary, finish filling in the Save As dialog box with the location and name of the file, and choose OK.

When you open a file with Save options, one or more of the following might happen:

If you have an open password, you are prompted for it after choosing the file in the Open dialog box. If you don't supply the correct password, you get an error message saying so.

If you have a modify password, you are prompted for it. You can either supply the correct password or click Read Only. If the file is read-only, you can make changes but not give the file the same name. When you are in the Open dialog box, you can also choose to open a file read-only even with this option if you right-click the filename and choose Open Read-Only.

If you marked Read-Only Recommended in Step 3, you get a prompt when you open a file. Choose Yes (the default) to open the workbook as read-only. Choose No to open the workbook so you can modify it.

To remove the Save Options, repeat Steps 1–2 and uncheck the options and delete the passwords.

Track Changes (Highlight, Accept, and Reject)

If you want to keep track of the changes you or others make in the workbook, use the Highlight Changes command. This enables you to see the name of the editor and the date changes were made. This feature also automatically turns on workbook sharing (see Objective 115, "Create a Shared Workbook").

Highlight Changes

You first have to turn on the Track Changes feature to record the changes. Do the following:

1. Click the Tools menu, choose Track Changes, and click Highlight Changes.

2. In the Highlight Changes dialog box, choose Track Changes While Editing. The other options on the dialog box become available. You'll use these options to display changes.

3. Choose OK. If the workbook has not previously been saved, you will be prompted to save the workbook.

Display Changes

Each change in your workbook becomes a comment (see Objective 110, "Create, Edit, and Remove a Comment"). After you edit the workbook, you might want to display various changes. Do the following:

1. If you want to see the current changes, make sure you save the workbook before you enter the Highlight Changes dialog box.

2. Click the Tools menu, choose Track Changes, and click Highlight Changes.

3. Choose one or more of the following to indicate which changes you want to display:

- **Check When**—In the drop-down box, choose to view all changes, to view those since the workbook was last saved, to view changes that have not been reviewed, or type in a date.

- **Check Who**—In the drop-down box, choose Everyone to see changes made by anybody, choose Everyone but Me, or select the name of the person who has worked on this workbook.

- **Check Where**—In the text box, type a range address or click the Collapse Dialog button, select the range where you want to see whether changes occurred, and click the Redisplay Dialog Box button.

- **Check Highlight Changes on Screen**—To display the details when the pointer rests on a changed cell and make the changes show as highlighted.

- **Check List Changes on a New Sheet**—To show the name of the person making the change, the location, and the change.

4. Choose OK.

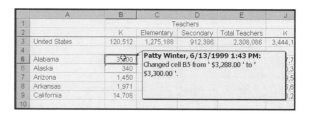

When you check Highlight Changes on Screen, the changes appear as highlighted details.

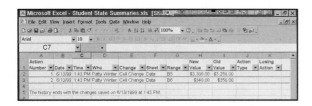

When you check <u>L</u>ist changes on a new sheet, Excel inserts a separate history worksheet and shows the old and new values, who changed the data, and when it was changed. Note that the AutoFilter feature is turned on to enable you to display selected changes (see Objective 98, "Apply Data Filters").

To turn off the recording of changes, click the <u>T</u>ools menu, choose <u>T</u>rack Changes, and click <u>H</u>ighlight Changes. Uncheck <u>T</u>rack Changes While Editing.

Accept and Reject Changes

When you or others start editing your workbook, each change is recorded. You can decide to keep each change or discard it.

To accept or reject changes, follow these steps:

1. Click the <u>T</u>ools menu, choose <u>T</u>rack Changes, and click <u>A</u>ccept or Reject Changes.

2. In the Accept or Reject Changes dialog box, choose which changes you want to see by filling in the Whe<u>n</u>, Wh<u>o</u>, and Whe<u>re</u> choices (as mentioned previously).

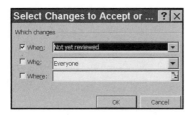

3. Choose OK.

4. Excel moves to the first change on the workbook and opens the Accept or Reject Changes dialog box. The dialog box shows a history of the changes for the cell.

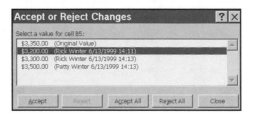

5. In the dialog box do one or more of the following for each change:

   • Select the change you want to keep and click Accept.

   • If only one change was made to a cell, click Reject to return to the original value.

   • If you want to accept all remaining changes made to the workbook (the later changes override earlier changes), choose Accept All.

   • Choose Reject All to return all remaining changes to the last reviewed state.

6. If you select one of the first two options, you can continue reviewing each change or click Close to stop the review.

After you review changes, they are no longer available for review, but you can still see the history by selecting the List Changes on a New Sheet check box on the Highlight Changes dialog box.

Create a Shared Workbook

A shared workbook enables more than one person to work on the workbook at the same time. Excel keeps track of the changes each person makes. Sharing a workbook automatically turns on Track Changes While editing on the Highlight Changes dialog box. See Objective 114, "Track Changes (Highlight, Accept, and Reject)." When you save the workbook, Excel checks to see if any other users have made changes and adds their changes to your workbook. If two people edited the same cell, you can be prompted to decide which edit to keep. You might want to protect the worksheets from certain changes when you share the workbook (see Objective 111, "Apply and Remove Worksheet and Workbook Protection").

To enable workbook sharing, follow these steps:

1. Click the Tools menu and choose Share Workbook.

2. If necessary, click the Editing tab on the Share Workbook dialog box, and check Allow Changes by More than One User at the Same Time.

3. Choose OK.

4. If you have not saved the workbook, you will be prompted for a name. If you have saved the workbook, Excel will prompt you whether it is OK to save the workbook.

Turn On Workbook Sharing

After you share the workbook and open the Share Workbook
dialog box again, you can see who else has the workbook open.
You can also disconnect a user from the workbook, meaning
that his changes cannot be saved to the shared workbook. He
can, however, save the workbook with a different name. Click
his name and choose the <u>R</u>emove User button.

Two users are editing
this workbook

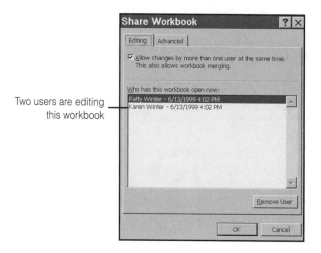

There are a number of features you cannot use when you share
a workbook, such as deleting worksheets, merging cells, defin-
ing conditional formats, setting up data validation, inserting or
deleting a range of cells (you can insert or delete rows), inserting or changing charts, assigning worksheet or workbook passwords, working with scenarios, creating PivotTables, or working
with edit macros. If you need to use one of these features, do it
before sharing the workbook.

**Handling
Conflicts**

By default, when you save a shared workbook, Excel checks
whether any other users have made changes to the workbook
and adds them to yours. If there is a conflict and you've set the
option to be prompted, Excel opens a dialog box and asks
which change you want to keep.

To handle conflicts, do the following:

1. Click the Tools menu, choose Shared Workbook, click the Advanced tab, and then check When File Is Saved (see "Advanced Options," the following section).

2. Make changes to your workbook and save.

   If another user made changes to the same cell, the Resolve Conflicts dialog box opens.

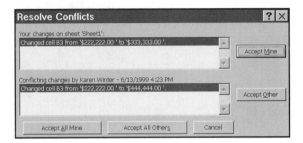

3. Do one of the following to accept or reject the changes:

   • Click Accept Mine to agree to the change you made. Excel will go to the next change, and you can repeat Step 3.

   • Click Accept Other to agree to the change the other person made. Excel will go to the next change, and you can repeat Step 3.

   • Click Accept All Mine to say that all the changes you made will override any others.

   • Click Accept All Others to say that all the changes the other person made will override your changes.

If there were no conflicts but other users made changes to the workbook, you will receive a message that other users have updated the workbook and their changes are now reflected in your file.

Advanced Options

One of the options previously mentioned is to have the workbook check for changes when the file is saved. You can set other options as well with the following steps:

1. Click the Tools menu, choose Share Workbook, click the Advanced tab, and check When File Is Saved.

2. On the Shared Workbook dialog box, make any of the following choices:

    • Determine how long you want to track each person's changes by typing in the box associated with Keep Change History for Box.

    • If you don't want to keep the changes, choose Don't Keep Change History. This turns off Track Changes.

    • Choose to make updates to the workbooks When the File Is Saved or type the number of minutes in the Automatically Every Minutes box.

    • If you choose automatic updates, you can Save My Changes and See Others' Changes or Just See Other Users' Changes.

    • When one cell has been edited by two different people, choose how you want to resolve the conflict by requesting to be prompted with Ask Me Which Changes Win or automatically letting The Changes Being Saved Win.

    • If you want to let each person have her own print settings including page breaks, print areas, and settings in the Page Setup dialog box, check Print Settings (see Chapter 4, "Page Setup and Printing").

    • If you want the choices on the Data, Filter submenu to be also saved for each person, check Filter Settings (see Objective 98, "Apply Data Filters").

3. When you finish making selections on the Share Workbook tab, choose OK.

To turn off workbook sharing, follow these steps:

1. Click the <u>T</u>ools menu and choose S<u>h</u>are Workbook.

2. Click the Editing tab.

3. Make sure you are the only person listed in the Who Has the Workbook Open Now list.

4. Clear the <u>A</u>llow Changes by More than One User at the Same Time check box.

5. Choose OK.

6. Excel will prompt you with a message that any other users logged on to the workbook will lose their changes. Choose Yes to remove the workbook from shared use.

Turn Off Workbook Sharing

115

Merge Workbooks

The preceding procedure (Objective 115, "Create a Shared Workbook") assumes that you work in a networked environment. You can also send copies (see Objective 17, "Send a Workbook via Email) of the workbook to various people and combine the changes later.

Before you send out the workbook, make sure you turn on workbook sharing by clicking Tools, choosing Share Workbook, clicking the Editing tab, and checking Allow Changes by More than One User at the Same Time.

After you get the workbooks back (they must be named differently or in different folders), do the following to merge changes:

1. Click the Tools menu and choose Merge Workbooks.

2. Excel might prompt you to save the workbook. Choose OK.

3. A Select Files dialog box opens, prompting for the files to merge. Choose the file or, if you want multiple files, hold down Ctrl as you choose each one. Choose OK.

4. One of the following things will happen:

   • If the workbook is merged, cell comments appear in the cells. If you want to review the changes and choose which changes to accept, see Objective 114, "Track Changes (Highlight, Accept, and Reject)".

- A prompt might indicate that it is not possible to merge the workbooks (because they were not made from the same copy).

- A prompt might indicate that there were no new changes in the merged workbooks.

TAKE THE TEST

Task 1

Objectives covered: 110, "Create, Edit, and Remove a Comment"; 111, "Apply and Remove Worksheet and Workbook Protection"; 112, "Change Workbook Properties"; 113, "Apply and Remove File Passwords."

Open practice file 1901P from the enclosed CD and perform the following actions:

1. Add a comment to cell B5 saying Prices good from wholesaler through Jan 30.

2. Edit the comment in B6 to say (Including wages and benefits) and remove the comment in C6.

3. Unlock cells B5:C6 and B9:C10, and protect the worksheet and workbook with the password secret.

4. Add the following file properties:

   Title: Test for MOUS collaboration objectives.

   Subject: MOUS

   Manager: Put in your name.

   Create a custom property called Objectives and add the value 110-116.

5. Create a file open password called secret when you save the workbook as Byme1 and choose Read-Only Recommended.

Check your work against the solution file 1901S. You must use the password secret when you open the file.

Objectives covered: 114, "Track Changes (Highlight, Accept, and Reject)"; 115, "Create a Shared Workbook"; 116, "Merge Workbooks."

Open practice file 1902P from the enclosed CD (the password is secret) and perform the following actions:

1. Create this file as a shared workbook, and save it as Byme2.

2. Save the file as Byme3 and change the data in B5 to 250. Change the value in B9 to 750. Save and close the file.

3. Byme2 should still be open. Merge it with Byme3.

4. Highlight changes and choose to see All Changes on a New Sheet.

5. Go to Accept and Reject Changes, reject the first change, and then click Close.

Check your work against the solution file 1902S.

Objectives covered: 110, "Create, Edit, and Remove a Comment"; 111, "Apply and Remove Worksheet and Workbook Protection"; 113, "Apply and Remove File Passwords."

Open practice file 1903P from the enclosed CD (the password is secret) and perform the following actions:

1. Remove file sharing and the file's password.

2. Remove the worksheet and workbook protection (the password is secret in both cases).

3. Remove all comments from the worksheet.

Check your work against the solution file 1903S.

Cheat Sheet

Create, Edit, and Remove a Comment

Comments are supplemental notes added to a cell on your worksheet.

Right-click the menu and choose Reviewing to display the toolbar that enables you to show, move to, and edit comments.

To create or edit a comment, choose Insert, Comment (Shift+F2).

To remove a comment, choose Edit, Clear, Comments.

Apply and Remove Worksheet and Workbook Protection

Worksheet and workbook protection help prevent unwanted changes.

To unlock cells so they can be edited when the worksheet is protected, choose Format, Cells (or press Ctrl+1), click the Protection tab, and clear the Locked check box.

To prevent all other cells in the worksheet from being changed, choose Tools, Protection, Protect Sheet and add a password if desired. To undo this protection, choose Tools, Protection, Unprotect Sheet.

To prevent changes in the organization of sheets of the workbook, choose Tools, Protection, Protect Workbook and add a password if desired. To undo this protection, choose Tools, Protection, Unprotect Workbook.

Change Workbook Properties

File properties enable you to see information about the file, such as when it was created, who has edited it, and a list of sheets. You can also add your own information to be stored with the file to help locate and describe the file.

To set file properties, choose File, Properties, and make changes on the Summary or Custom tabs.

Apply and Remove File Passwords

A file password can prevent others from opening or modifying the workbook unless they know the password.

To set file passwords from the Save As dialog box, choose Tools, General Options.

Track Changes (Highlight, Accept, and Reject)

If more than one person is working on the workbook, you can identify and see the changes each person makes.

To turn on Track Changes, choose Tools, Track Changes, Highlight Changes, and check Track Changes While Editing.

After this has been turned on, to see the changes others have made, choose Tools, Track Changes, Highlight Changes and choose which changes you want to see on the Highlight Changes dialog box and whether you want to see the changes onscreen or on a new sheet.

To decide whether to keep or remove changes, choose Tools, Track Changes, Accept or Reject Changes, choose the type of changes you want to see, and then choose whether you want to Accept or Reject individual or all changes.

Create a Shared Workbook

A shared workbook enables multiple users to work on the same workbook at the same time. Changes to the workbook are automatically tracked.

To share a workbook, choose Tools, Share Workbook, and check the Allow Changes by More than One User at the Same Time box. To remove sharing from the workbook, clear this box.

Merge Workbooks

Merging workbooks enables you to combine the changes from multiple users not connected to the same file.

First share the workbook, and then send copies to the users. When you get them back, choose Tools, Merge Workbooks, and select the files you want to merge with the current workbook.

Student Preparation Guide

Taking any test can be intimidating. Taking a test that can influence your pay or career might concern you even more. What follows is advice to make the test less formidable and to help you on your way to MOUS certification.

Before the Test

The first bit of advice is to practice. Use this book (especially the tasks at the end of each chapter) to practice, as well as to judge what your skill level is for each task. If you find one area especially challenging, try devising your own workbooks to help you understand the feature.

As a practical matter, if you have an extra $50, one strategy is not to do any studying and take the test cold. There should be no pressure, you'll get an idea of what is on the test, you'll have practice taking the test, and you'll get results on the areas you need to study.

The standard advice you receive for every potentially stressful situation applies to the MOUS exam. Get a good night's sleep before the test. If you don't know it by the night before, it's probably too late to try to pound it into your head.

During the Test

One of the most important pieces of advice concerning the tests is to read the question carefully and don't do any more or less than it asks you. Try to imagine that someone has asked you to do a task and that the person will now look at your terminal screen to see the results.

Don't change the view unless you are asked to do so. Don't obscure the view by leaving dialog boxes or toolbars floating over the slide. Don't save and close any file unless you are asked to do so.

Follow all the instructions given to you at the test site. If you have any problems with your machine at the testing center, bring it to the attention of the administrator immediately.

Be Prepared

You will have a limited amount of time to complete the test. Do not count on being able to use the Help file to find information. Try to learn more than one way to do a job. There is usually a keyboard equivalent for items on the menu bar. You will be scored on your results. In the past, some options have been grayed out, forcing the user to find alternative means. This book has been designed to help you learn alternative methods of accomplishing tasks.

The tear card inside the cover of this book also includes tables that outline the various methods for issuing a command: keyboard shortcuts, toolbar buttons, and Menu command strings. Tear out the card and use it to review the shortcuts in the last few minutes before stepping into the exam room.

After the Test

When the test is over, the administrator will give you a copy of your score. If you miss the breaking point for passing, the printout will suggest areas of study.

If you don't pass the test, don't get down on yourself. Assume that the test itself is a method to help you learn the material. Study the areas that the printout suggests as well as other areas that you don't feel comfortable with.

There is no penalty for taking the test multiple times (except your test fee). If at first you don't succeed, try again.

Exam Objectives

Excel Core Objectives

continues

Continued

continues

Continued

Excel Expert Objectives

continues

Continued

Objectives Cheat Sheet

Chapter 1, "Working with Cells"

1 "Enter Text, Dates, and Numbers"

Move cell pointer and type.

2 "Go to a Specific Cell"

Name Box or F5.

3 "Edit Cell Content"

Type over cell; double-click in cell or click in formula bar and type text or press Backspace or Delete to remove text.

4 "Use Undo and Redo"

Undo; Edit, Undo (Ctrl+Z).

Redo; Edit, Redo (Ctrl+Y).

5 "Clear Cell Content"

(Delete); Edit, Clear, Contents

6 "Insert and Delete Selected Cells"

Right-click range, Insert; Insert, Cells.

Right-click range, Delete; Edit, Delete.

7 "Cut, Copy, Paste, Paste Special and Move Selected Cells, Use the Office Clipboard"

Copy: ▣; Ctrl+C; Edit, Copy; Drag with Ctrl.

Cut: ▣; Ctrl+X; Edit, Cut.

Paste/Move: ▣; Ctrl+V; Edit, Paste; Drag (move).

8 "Clear Cell Formats"

Edit, Clear, Formats.

9 "Use Find and Replace"

Find: Ctrl+F; Edit, Find.

Paste: Ctrl+H; Edit, Replace.

10 "Work with Series (AutoFill)"

Drag fill handle (bottom-right corner of range).

11 "Create Hyperlinks"

Type URL or path; ▣ Hyperlink; Insert, Hyperlink; Ctrl+K.

Chapter 2 "Working with Files"

12 "Use Save"

▣ Save; File, Save; (Ctrl+S).

13 "Use Save As (Different Name, Location, and Format)"

File, Save As; (F12): Save as type.

14 "Locate and Open an Existing Workbook"

▣ Open; File, Open (Ctrl+O).

15 "Create a Folder"

Open dialog box: ▣; press Alt+5.

16 "Use Templates to Create a New Workbook"

File, New.

17 "Send a Workbook via Email"

File, Send To.

18 "Save a Worksheet/Workbook as a Web Page"

File, Save as Web Page: Save for HTML file; Publish for interactive.

19 "Use the Office Assistant"

☑ Excel Help; (F1).

Chapter 3 "Formatting Worksheets"

20 "Apply Font Styles (Typeface, Size, Color, and Styles)"

B Bold; (Ctrl+B).

I Italic; (Ctrl+I).

U̲ Underline; (Ctrl+U).

Font box. Font size box.

Format, Cells (Ctrl+1), Font tab.

21 "Modify Alignment of Cell Content "

☰ Left; ☰ Center; ☰ Right.

Format, Cells (Ctrl+1), Alignment tab.

22 "Merging Cells"

▦ Merge and Center

23 "Rotate Text and Change Indents"

Format, Cells (Ctrl+1), Alignment tab, Orientation section.

24 "Apply Number Formats (Currency, Percent, Dates, and Comma)

$ Currency Style; (Ctrl+Shift+$).

% Percent Style; (Ctrl+Shift+%)

, Comma Style; (Ctrl+Shift+!)

Format, Cells (Ctrl+1), Number tab.

25 "Adjust the Decimal Place"

Increase Decimal.

Decrease Decimal.

Format, Cells (Ctrl+1), Number tab, Decimal places.

26 "Apply Cell Borders and Shading"

Fill Color.

Borders.

Format, Cells (Ctrl+1) Border tab.

Format, Cells (Ctrl+1) Pattern tab.

27 "Modify Size of Rows and Columns"

Drag or double-click between headers.

28 "Use the Format Painter"

Format Painter—click or double-click to copy formats.

29 "Apply AutoFormat"

Format, AutoFormat, choose preformatted characteristics.

30 "Define, Apply, and Remove a Style"

Format, Style: Modify; OK; Delete.

Chapter 4 "Page Setup and Printing"

31 "Preview and Print Worksheets and Workbooks"

🔍 Print Preview; File, Print Preview.

🖨 Print; File, Print; (Ctrl+P).

32 "Print a Selection"

File, Print; (Ctrl+P): Selection.

33 "Set Print, and Clear a Print Area"

File, Print Area: Set Print Area; Clear Print Area.

34 "Set Page Margins and Centering"

File, Page Setup, Margins tab.

35 "Change Page Orientation and Scaling"

File, Page Setup, Page tab: Portrait; Landscape; Scaling section.

36 "Set Up Headers and Footers"

File, Page Setup, Header/Footer tab: Header, Footer; Custom Header; Custom Footer.

37 "Insert and Remove a Page Break"

Insert, Page Break; Insert, Remove Page Break.

38 "Set Print Titles and Options (Gridlines, Print Quality, and Row and Column Headings)"

File, Page Setup, Sheet tab: Gridlines; Draft quality; Rows; Columns.

39 "Use Web Page Preview"

File, Web Page Preview.

Chapter 5 "Working with Worksheets and Workbooks"

40 "Insert and Delete Rows and Columns"

Right-click column/row, Insert; Insert, Cells.

Right-click column/row, Delete; Edit, Delete.

41 "Hide and Unhide Rows and Columns"

Right click on the header, Hide.

Ctrl+A: Format, Column, Unhide; Format, Row, Unhide.

42 "Freeze and Unfreeze Rows and Columns"

Window, Freeze Panes; Window, Unfreeze Panes.

43 "Change the Zoom Setting"

`100%` Zoom; View, Zoom.

44 "Check Spelling"

Spelling; (F7); Tools, Spelling.

45 "Move Between Worksheets in a Workbook"

Tab scrolling buttons; Click sheet tab.

46 "Rename a Worksheet"

Double-click tab.

47 "Insert and Delete Worksheets"

Right-click sheet tab: Insert; Delete.

Insert, Worksheet.

48 "Move and Copy Worksheets"

Drag sheet; Ctrl+Drag to copy.

Right-click tab, Move or Copy.

49 "Link Worksheets and Consolidate Data Using 3D References"

Type = , move to cell on other sheet.Formula Palette, Collapse Dialog button, move to sheet, select range.

Chapter 6 "Working with Formulas and Functions"

50 "Enter Formulas in a Cell and Use the Formula Bar"

= cell references/numbers, {+ - * /}, cell references/numbers (for example, +B4+B5).

51 "Enter a Range Within a Formula by Dragging"

= click on cell, {+ - * /}, click on cell.
Collapse Dialog button on Formula Palette, drag range.

52 "Revise Formulas"

Double-click cell; (F2); click in the Formula Bar.

53 "Use References (Absolute and Relative)"

Absolute = reference doesn't change: F4; ($C$4).

54 "Use AutoSum"

Σ AutoSum; Alt+=.

55 "Use Paste Function to Insert a Function"

ƒ× Paste Function; Insert, Function; (Shift+F3).

56 "Enter Functions Using the Formula Palette"

Paste Function dialog box, OK, fill in arguments.

57 "Use Basic Functions (AVERAGE, SUM, COUNT, MIN, MAX)"

=FUNCTION(Range)—for example, =SUM(A5:A20).

Average—total/number; SUM—Total; COUNT—number of numeric items; MIN—lowest; MAX—highest.

58 "Use Date Functions (NOW and DATE)"

=NOW( )—current date and time.

=DATE(Year, Month, Day).

59 "Use Financial Functions (FV and PMT)"

=FV(Interest Rate, Number of Payments, Payment)—Future value of investment.

=PMT(Interest Rate, Number of Payments, Present Value or Loan Amount)—Periodic payment for a loan.

60 "Use Logical Functions (IF)"

=IF(Test condition, value if true, value if false)

Chapter 7 "Using Charts and Objects"

61 "Use Chart Wizard to Create a Chart"

Fll.

🔳 Chart Wizard; Insert, Chart: type, range, Titles/Axes/Gridlines/Legend/Data Labels/Data Table, location.

62 "Modify Charts"

🔳 Chart Wizard; Insert, Chart.

Chart or Format menus.

Click I-beam in title to edit.

63 "Insert, Move, and Delete an Object (Picture)"

Click to select; drag to move; press Delete.

64 "Create and Modify Lines and Objects"

🔳 Drawing Toolbar and drawing and formatting tools.

65 "Preview and Print Charts"

Click chart or chart tab and:

[🔍] Print Preview; File, Print Preview.

[🖨] Print; File, Print.

Chapter 8 "Importing and Exporting Data"

66 "Import Data from Text Files (Insert, Drag and Drop)"

[📂] Open; File, Open; (Ctrl+O): Files of type to Text files.

Drag from text file and choose Data, Text to Columns.

67 "Import from Other Applications"

[📂] Open; File, Open; (Ctrl+O): Files of type.

68 "Import a Table from an HTML File (Insert, Drag and Drop—Including HTML Round Tripping)"

File, Save As Web Page, Publish. Internet Explorer, click the Export to Excel button.

69 "Export to Other Applications"

File, Save As; (F12): Save as type.

Data, Convert to MS Access.

Chapter 9 "Using Templates"

70 "Create Templates"

Save As dialog: File of type, choose Template.

71 "Apply Templates"

File, New and select the template.

72 "Edit Templates"

Open; File, Open: File of type, choose Template. Edit and save the template like any other workbook.

Chapter 10 "Using Multiple Workbooks"

73 "Using a Workspace"

Window, Arrange.

File, Save Workspace.

74 "Link Workbooks"

=, move to other workbook's cell.

Workbook name in square brackets (example):

```
=AVERAGE('D:\Data\[StateSummaries.xls]Arizona'!$G$1:$G$10)
```

Chapter 11 "Formatting Numbers"

75 "Apply Number Formats (Accounting, Currency, and Number)"

Format, Cells (Ctrl+1), Number tab.

76 "Create Custom Number Formats"

Format, Cells (Ctrl+1), Number tab, Category: Custom.

Significant digits #; insignificant digits 0; thousands comma; negative numbers parentheses or dash. For example, #,##0.00.

Dates: m, mm, mmm, mmmm; d, dd, ddd, dddd; yy and yyyy. For example mmm d, yyyy

77 "Use Conditional Formatting"

Format, Conditional Formatting: conditions, Format button.

Chapter 12 "Printing Workbooks"

78 "Print and Preview Multiple Worksheets"

File, Print, Entire Workbook, OK.

Ctrl click sheets: 🖨 Print; 🔍 Preview.

79 "Use the Report Manager"

Worksheets, views, and scenarios printed.

View, Custom Views, Add.

View, Report Manager, Add.

Chapter 13 "Working with Named Ranges"

80 "Add and Delete a Named Range"

Name Box; Insert, Name: Create or Define

81 "Use a Named Range in a Formula"

Whenever a cell or range is called for in a formula, type in a range name or press F3 and choose the range name.

82 "Use Lookup Functions (HLOOKUP or VLOOKUP)"

Find values in a table—Tools, Wizards, Lookup.

Chapter 14 "Working with Toolbars"

83 "Hide and Display Toolbars"

Right-click on a toolbar, toolbar name; View, Toolbars.

84 "Customize a Toolbar"

Tools, Customize; View, Toolbars, Customize; right-click toolbar, Customize.

85 "Assign a Macro to a Command Button"

Commands tab Customize dialog box, Categories, Macros drag Custom Button to a toolbar.

Right-click Custom Button: Name; Assign Macro.

Chapter 15 "Using Macros"

86 "Record Macros"

Tools, Macro, Record New Macro.

87 "Run Macros"

Alt+F8; Tools, Macro, Macros: Double-click macro.

88 "Edit Macros"

Alt+F8; Tools, Macro, Macros; select macro, Edit.

Chapter 16 "Auditing a Worksheet"

89 "Work with the Auditing Toolbar"

Tools, Auditing, Show Auditing Toolbar.

90 "Trace Errors (Find and Fix Errors)"

Click [Trace Error] Trace Error to find references to the error in a formula.

91 "Trace Precedents (Find Cells Referred to in a Specific Formula)"

[Trace Precedents]; Tools, Auditing, Trace Precedents.

92 "Trace Dependents (Find Formulas That Refer to a Specific Cell)"

[Trace Dependents]; Tools, Auditing, Trace Dependents.

Chapter 17 "Displaying and Formatting Data"

93 "Apply Conditional Formats"

Format, Conditional Formatting and identify the rules for formatting and click on the Format button.

94 "Perform Single and Multilevel Sorts"

⬆ Ascending; ⬇ Descending.

Multiple fields sort: Data, Sort.

95 "Use Grouping and Outlines"

With SUMS in worksheet—Data, Group and Outline, Auto Outline.

Manually group selected rows—Data, Group and Outline, Group; (Alt+Shift+Right).

Data, Group and Outline, Clear Outline.

96 "Use Subtotaling"

Choose Data, Subtotals and identify the category and function.

97 "Use Data Forms"

Data, Form.

Search for a record: Criteria button, Find Next or Find Prev.

98 "Apply Data Filters"

Data, Filter, AutoFilter to place filter arrows at the top of your data list.

99 "Extract Data"

Data, Filter, Advanced Filter, Copy to another location and identify your data, criteria, and extract ranges.

100 "Query Databases"

Link Access database—<u>D</u>ata, Get External <u>D</u>ata, <u>N</u>ew Database Query, MS Access Database.

101 "Use Data Validation"

<u>D</u>ata, <u>V</u>alidation, add the rules on the Settings tab, place prompts on the Input Message and Error Alert tabs.

Chapter 18 "Using Analysis Tools"

102 "Use Goal Seek"

Change the value of one input cell in order to come up with a value for a formula—<u>T</u>ools, <u>G</u>oal Seek.

103 "Use Solver"

Change multiple input cells in order to come up with a value for a formula—<u>T</u>ools, Sol<u>v</u>er.

104 "Work with Scenarios"

Save different inputs—<u>T</u>ools, Sc<u>e</u>narios.

105 "Use Data Analysis and PivotTables"

Interactively view summaries of a list of data—<u>D</u>ata, <u>P</u>ivotTable and PivotChart Report.

106 "Use PivotTable AutoFormat"

In PivotTable: F<u>o</u>rmat, <u>A</u>utoFormat.

107 "Create PivotChart Reports"

Interactive PivotCharts drag-and-drop fields—<u>D</u>ata, <u>P</u>ivotTable and PivotChart Report.

108 "Create Interactive PivotTables for the Web"

File, Save As Web Page, Publish, Add interactivity with PivotTable functionality.

109 "Add Fields to a PivotTable Using the Web Browser"

Field List. Drag the fields on to the PivotTable or from one area of the PivotTable to another area.

🖼 Property Toolbox to format the PivotTable.

Chapter 19 "Collaborating with Workgroups"

110 "Create, Edit, and Remove a Comment"

🖼; Insert, Comment; (Shift+F2).

🖼; Edit, Clear, Comments.

111 "Apply and Remove Worksheet and Workbook Protection"

Unlock cells—Format, Cells (or press Ctrl+1), Protection tab, clear the Locked check box.

Tools, Protection: Protect Sheet; Unprotect Sheet.

Tools, Protection: Protect Workbook; Unprotect Workbook.

112 "Change Workbook Properties"

File, Properties: Summary tab; Custom tab.

113 "Apply and Remove File Passwords"

Save As dialog box: Tools, General Options.

114 "Track Changes (Highlight, Accept, and Reject)"

Identify and see the changes each person makes—Tools, Track Changes, Highlight Changes, Track changes while editing.

Tools, Track Changes, Accept or Reject Changes.

115 "Create a Shared Workbook"

Multiple users work on the same workbook—Tools, Share Workbook, Allow changes by more than one user at the same time.

116 "Merge Workbooks"

Combine the changes from multiple users—Tools, Merge Workbooks.

Index

Get External Data,
  Import Text File, 233
Group, 360
PivotTable, 404
Sort, 358
Subtotals, 363
Text to Columns, 235
Validation, 380
Data Range, 206
Data Table button, 213
Data Table tab, 210
Data Validation dialog
  box, 380
databases
  importing data,
    236-237, 247-248
  queries, 375-378, 388
    editing, 378
    practice elements,
      385-386
Databases tab, 375
date functions
  DATE, 191, 201
  now, 190, 201
  practice elements,
    198-199
  today, 190, 201
dates
  changing control panel
    settings, 5
  entering into a cell,
    5-6, 40
decimal places, 98,
  112-113
Decrease Decimal
  button, 271
Decrease Indent button,
  90
Define Name dialog
  box, 301
Degrees text box, 90
Delete command
  (Edit menu), 14, 143

Delete Sheet command
  (Edit menu), 156
deleting. See also clearing
  cells, 15-16, 41
  columns, 142-143,
    163, 166
  comments, 432,
    456-458
  constraints, 397
  formatting styles, 110
  named ranges, 302,
    313
  objects, 218, 224-226
  outlines, 362
  page breaks, 131-132,
    137-140
  pictures, 218, 224-225
  rows, 142-143, 163
  scenarios, 401
  subtotals, 364, 385
  tracer arrows, 346, 348
  worksheets, 155-156,
    164, 167
delimited text files, 232
dependent cells
  selection of, 348-349
  tracing, 347-348,
    350-351
dialog boxes
  Accept or Reject
    Changes, 447
  Add Constraint, 396
  Add Report, 292
  Add Scenario, 399
  Advanced Text Import
    Settings, 233
  Apply Names, 303
  Arrange Window, 262
  Assign Macro, 322
  AutoFormat, 106, 412
  Choose Data Source,
    375, 413
  Clip Art, 217

Conditional
  Formatting, 281, 354
Confirm Password, 54
Convert to MS Access,
  242
Create names, 302
Criteria Range, 373
Custom AutoFilter,
  371
Custom Views, 292
Customize, 318-319
Data Validation, 380
Define Name, 301
Edit Hyperlink, 35
Edit Links, 266
Find, 24, 57
Font, 130
Format Cells, 82-88
Go To, 8, 218, 345
Goal Seek, 392
Goal Seek Status, 393
Grouping, 409
Highlight Changes,
  445
Hyperlink, 31
Import Data, 234
Insert, 14, 155
Insert Hyperlink, 31
Lookup Wizard, 306
Macro, 331
Macro Options, 334
Merge Scenarios, 401
Move or Copy,
  158-159
New, 60
New Folder, 59
Open, 55, 230, 263
Page Setup, 119, 130
Paste Function, 161,
  182
Paste Name, 304
Paste Special, 266

494

G

H

I

X-Y

Z

CD-ROM Installation

Windows 95 Installation Instructions

1. Insert the CD-ROM disc into your CD-ROM drive.

2. From the Windows 95 desktop, double-click the My Computer icon.

3. Double-click the icon representing your CD-ROM drive.

4. Double-click the icon titled START.EXE to run the CD-ROM interface.

Windows NT Installation Instructions

1. Insert the CD-ROM disc into your CD-ROM drive.

2. From File Manager or Program Manager, choose Run from the File menu.

3. Type *<drive>*\START.EXE and press Enter, where *<drive>* corresponds to the drive letter of your CD-ROM. For example, if your CD-ROM is drive D:, type D:\START.EXE and press Enter. This will run the CD-ROM interface.

If Windows 95 is installed on your computer and you have the AutoPlay feature enabled, the START.EXE program starts automatically whenever you insert the disc into your CD-ROM drive.